WEIRD
PENNSYLVANIA

STERLING
New York / London
www.sterlingpublishing.com

WEiRD PENNSYLVANiA

Your Travel Guide to Pennsylvania's Local Legends and Best Kept Secrets

BY MATT LAKE

Mark Sceurman and Mark Moran, Executive Editors

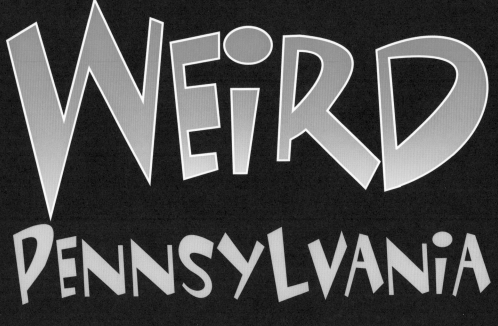

WEiRD PeNNSYLVANiA

Published by Sterling Publishing Co., Inc.
387 Park Avenue South, New York, NY 10016

© 2007 Mark Sceurman and Mark Moran

Distributed in Canada by Sterling Publishing
c/o Canadian Manda Group, 165 Dufferin Street,
Toronto, Ontario, Canada M6K 3H6

Distributed in the United Kingdom by GMC Distribution Services,
Castle Place, 166 High Street, Lewes, East Sussex, England BN7 1XU

Distributed in Australia by Capricorn Link (Australia) Pty. Ltd.
P.O. Box 704, Windsor, NSW 2756, Australia

ISBN 13: 978-1-4027-3279-9
ISBN 10: 1-4027-3279-1

4 6 8 10 9 7 5

For information about custom editions, special sales, premium and
corporate purchases, please contact Sterling Special Sales
Department at 800-805-5489 or specialsales@sterlingpub.com.

Design: Richard J. Berenson
   Berenson Design & Books, LLC, New York, NY

CONTENTS

DEDICATION

None of this would have come to any good without decades of careful grooming, guidance, and preparation provided by a cast of strange characters, beginning with Iris and John Lake (who seem normal at first glance but have hidden depths), moving on to Andy, Nick, and Rich, and eventually expanding to include Emma and Eleanor, and ending with the stars of the show, Caroline, Christopher and Julia. You're all strange in the best possible ways. Long may it continue.

Foreword: A Note from the Marks

Our weird journey began a long, long time ago in a far-off land called New Jersey. Once a year or so we'd compile a homespun newsletter called *Weird N.J.*, then pass it on to our friends. The pamphlet was a collection of odd news clippings, bizarre facts, little-known historical anecdotes, and anomalous encounters from our home state. The newsletter also included the kinds of localized legends that were often whispered around a particular town but seldom heard outside the boundaries of the community where they originated.

We had started *Weird N.J.* with the simple theory that every town in the state had at least one good tale to tell. The publication soon become a full-fledged magazine, and we made the decision to actually do all of our own investigating to see if we could track down where all of these seemingly unbelievable stories were coming from. Was there, we wondered, any factual basis for the fantastical local legends people were telling us about? Armed with not much more than a camera and a notepad, we set off on a mystical journey of discovery. Much to our surprise and amazement, a lot of what we had initially presumed to be nothing more than urban legend turned out to be real—or at least to contain a grain of truth, which had sparked the lore to begin with.

After a dozen years of documenting the bizarre, we were asked to write a book about our adventures, and so *Weird N.J.: Your Travel Guide to New Jersey's Local Legends and Best Kept Secrets* was published in 2003. Soon people from all over the country began writing to us, telling us strange tales from their home state. As it turned out, what we had perceived to be something of very local interest was actually just a small part of a larger and more universal phenomenon.

When Barnes & Noble, the publisher of the book, asked us what we wanted to do next, the answer was simple: "We'd like to do a book called *Weird U.S.*, in which we could document the local legends and strangest stories from all over the country." So for the next twelve months we set out in search of weirdness wherever it might be found in the fifty states. And indeed, we found plenty of it!

After *Weird U.S.* was published, we came to the conclusion that this country had more great tales than could be contained in just one book. Everywhere we looked, we found unwritten folklore, creepy cemeteries, cursed locations, and outlandish roadside oddities. With this in mind, we told our publisher that we wanted to document it ALL and to do it in a series of books, each focusing on the peculiarities of a particular state.

But where would we begin this state-by-state excursion into the weirdest territory ever explored? Our first inclination was to go to the state we had already collected the greatest volume of material about: Pennsylvania. For several years, we had been writing about New Jersey's neighbor to the west in our magazine's "Fringe" section. Letters were always pouring in from Pennsylvanians who were eager to fill us in on the many strange sites, unusual histories, and local legends to be found in their home state.

When it came time to decide on a Pennsylvania author, we were fortunate to have a ready cohort. Matt Lake was introduced to us by our publishers a couple years before when he was brought on board to edit

Weird N.J. Not only did he manage to boil down the vast volumes of material we gave him into a concise and entertaining document, he somehow did it without changing the peculiar voice of the narrative. Because of this, we realized that Matt "got it." From that day forward, straight through our collaboration with him again on *Weird U.S.*, Matt was like a kindred spirit in weirdness. Though we hadn't yet met him in person, it was clear to us that he had what we refer to as the "Weird Eye."

The Weird Eye is what is needed to search out the sort of stories we were looking for. It requires one to see the world a different way, with a renewed sense of wonder. All of a sudden, you begin to reexamine your own environs, noticing your everyday surroundings as if for the first time. And you begin to ask yourself questions like, "What the heck is that thing all about, anyway?"

and "Doesn't anybody else think that's kind of weird?"

The only reservation we had about asking Matt to spearhead the *Weird Pennsylvania* project was this: Was it right to ask an Englishman to write a book about Pennsylvania? (It is, after all, the very state that gave England its walking papers, back in 1776.) In the end, though, we felt there was no one better suited to point out the eccentricities of the state than someone who had come from someplace else and had CHOSEN to make this weird state his home.

So come with us now, and let Matt take you on a tour of the state that has become his adopted home (we promise he'll drive on the right side of the road—most of the time). With all of its cultural quirks, strange sites, and oddball characters, it is a state of mind that we like to call *Weird Pennsylvania*.

—Mark Sceurman and Mark Moran

Introduction

It all started in a deserted parking lot on an empty road next to an old, abandoned factory. Inside the building, pools of greenish-blue liquid dripped into puddles on the floor. It was quiet, and I sat in the driver's seat, utterly alone, with a sheet of instructions on my lap. I cut off the engine, put the car in neutral, honked the horn three times, and waited.

A strange vision appeared before my eyes: A man with a beard was walking toward my car. Another man followed. They both wore hats, and dark glasses hid their eyes. As I looked up, I could see only my own face reflected in their impenetrable black lenses.

"We're Mark and Mark," they said, "You must be Matt. We want you to write *Weird Pennsylvania*."

Some native Pennsylvanians bristle when you describe their state as weird. To them, there's nothing strange about the state that introduced the world to Girl Scout cookies, *Mr. Rogers' Neighborhood*, and Legionnaire's disease. To many Pennsylvanians, it's normal for farmers to speak an eighteenth-century German dialect and drive only horse-drawn vehicles. What's strange, they ask, about a place where you can't buy beer and wine in the same store? It's all perfectly normal. At least, it is in this neck of the woods.

But although Pennsylvania does have its ordinary, everyday side, it is an extraordinary place. A huge amount of innovation has taken place in this state for centuries, so it's perfectly normal for some strangeness to float to the surface. That's exactly what you'll find here. Next to a perfectly trimmed and manicured suburban house, you'll find a tree carved in the shape of a monkey demon, baring its teeth at passing traffic. Annexed to a hospital, you'll find a museum proudly displaying a collection of pitted and deformed skulls. And in pleasant, family-friendly parks, you'll find a mysterious abandoned path or a centuries-old stone dwelling with ominous legends attached to it.

Pennsylvania is big enough to welcome all of these elements into one strange and wonderful state. And we have the man who gave his name to the place, William Penn, to thank for that. When he invited the persecuted religious oddballs of Europe to a land that would tolerate them, his goal was not to create a melting pot where everything would blend together into bland uniformity. His

other stories they hadn't heard yet. And they asked me to pull it all together. It was a leap of faith on their part, as anyone who's ever heard me say the word *water* will know. Unlike all of my neighbors, I don't say *wooder*. I don't even say *wahdr*. Every time I open my mouth, people know I wasn't raised in these parts. "You know, I'm not actually from Pennsylvania," I told the Marks in a distinctly English accent. The reply was succinct enough. "Neither was Benjamin Franklin. What difference does that make?"

It's true. Like Franklin, I found a home away from home in Pennsylvania. From the time I first set foot in Pittsburgh, some time last century, I've forayed through the state, found somewhere to live, and dug myself in pretty deep. From my home base, I've clocked thousands upon thousands of miles traveling across the commonwealth, meeting strange and interesting people, seeing ancient and mysterious relics, and passing many a house built in the shape of a shoe or a boat or adorned with broken plates or machinery. It continues to be a wild ride.

experiment was more like a stew pot, in which everything simmers together, subtly changing the flavor of everything around it without destroying the unique qualities of each ingredient. And that's exactly what he achieved.

Fast-forward a few centuries from young William and his Holy Experiment, and you'll find two guys from New Jersey approaching a resident of greater Philadelphia with their own wild plan. Mark Moran and Mark Sceurman of *Weird N.J.* wanted some of the stories they'd been hearing about the Keystone State collected in book form, along with a couple hundred

Pennsylvanians are rightly proud of the place where they live, and they're very willing to share it with strangers who appreciate it the way they do. I'm grateful to the many people who spoke to me during my travels or wrote to me when they got wind of this project. You know who you are. And if you don't, you'll probably find your names on the pages ahead. But even with the collected research power of the state, I'm sure there are many compelling stories out there waiting to be told. If you know of any, write in and tell all. The world deserves to hear about more of Pennsylvania's particular weirdness.

Local Legends and Lore

Deep within the human mind, yours and mine, lurks a desire to be scared senseless. It's this desire that has given rise to countless tales of skulking terror in books and movies. But this love of fear is more than just a way for writers and filmmakers to make money. It's good for us! For some reason, we need to be frightened. If our lives are too calm and structured, we'll scare ourselves silly at night in our dreams.

Sadly, the tide of commercial fiction has swept away many of the old folk tales of mystery and horror that once entertained our ancestors around the fireplace at night. Most of the stories that remain are mere tall tales and generic yarns of travelers waking up in hotel bathtubs with their vital organs removed. But fortunately, some stories based on real places and real people do survive. Strange spirits lurk in dark places throughout the commonwealth. So fill up your gas tanks and wait for night to fall. You're about to embark on a strange journey into the wilder and weirder parts of Pennsylvania, the things that the tourism machine tries to sweep under the rug.

Devil's Road and the Cult House

There are woods in southeastern Pennsylvania, right on the Delaware border, whose twisted appearance has made it the star of a blockbuster movie. True, the film in question, *The Village,* was written and directed by a local boy, M. Night Shyamalan, but when an A-list Hollywood director brings a woods full of misshapen trees into the Cineplex, you know the legend has legs.

Devil's Road winds its way a couple of miles through woods in Chadds Ford, just north of the Delaware border. Map readers will recognize it as Cossart Road, and it has been known for its general aura of evil for decades. The exact location of the weird part of the stretch is often misreported as being somewhere in northern Delaware, but all the stories agree on one point: The trees that line this narrow, winding lane rear back from the road as if recoiling from something unspeakable.

Farther into the woods, they say, up a densely wooded hillside, stands a massive stone mansion known as the Cult House, which Delaware residents claim was once owned by a member of the DuPont family. The Cult House, naturally, housed a cult of some kind, but the nature of its ceremonies remains a bit vague. Fans of plutocratic conspiracy theories spin wild stories of DuPont family members marrying their cousins in the house so that the family's wealth would stay within the fold, and then using the place to hide whatever inbred spawn these unnatural unions produced. The less fanciful rumors fall back on the old favorites: Satanists and the Ku Klux Klan. The house's windows are said to be in the shape of a cross or, among the Satanist believers, in the shape of an inverted cross.

But it's getting harder and harder to explore Devil's Road. For one thing, the street signs have been removed from Kennett Pike, so it's easy to miss the Cossart Road turn. (Don't mistakenly turn into a private road called Cossart Manor Drive a few miles up the pike.) Even if you find the road, you'll see that it's liberally posted with NO STOPPING and NO TRESPASSING signs. Too many noisy explorers have imbibed there by night, disturbing the residents, spray-painting everything in sight, and committing various acts of vandalism. The police and private security guards regularly patrol the lane, which probably accounts for the many tales of visitors being chased down the road.

So we'd advise people to proceed with caution when they think about treading down the darkness of Devil's Road. Don't pull over on this dark and winding strip, unless you want to get ticketed for parking in a no-stopping zone. And certainly don't start tramping through private property if your fear of being arrested is greater than your curiosity about mysterious places. After all, you can always get a good look at the woods in the film *The Village* instead.

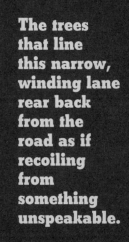

The trees
that line
this narrow,
winding lane
rear back
from the
road as if
recoiling
from
something
unspeakable.

Devil Worship and Dead Animals

Driving down the road toward the mansion, we noticed a pile of dead animals, mostly raccoons, slit from throat to genitals and completely gutted. It was like there was just a frame of the animal left. When we finally approached the mansion, I was even more disgusted. Hanging from the black iron gate were more carcasses like the ones we'd just seen. It's also said that if you go at night, you can hear the Satanic worshipping that goes on inside, word for word. Fortunately, we were there during the day.
−*Brooke Meadows*

Checking Out the Cult House

When I was in high school, there was one particularly prevalent story about a mansion located in the woods of the Brandywine Valley. Everyone called it Cult House. There is a "guardhouse" on the grounds that houses a fleet of red pickup trucks. If you drive past the house too often, one or several of the trucks will come out of the house and chase you away. No matter how close it gets, you will never be able to catch a glimpse of the driver's face. According to the legend, a human sacrifice is performed on the grounds every Halloween.

Well, that's the rumor. Here is my personal experience with the Cult House. (I have been occasionally driving by the place with friends and researching its history for about 7 years now.) The trees do grow at an extreme angle away from the house. I've never seen trees grow so off-kilter before. This phenomenon stops once you get about 1/4 mile past the house. Red trucks from a guardhouse actually followed me on two occasions. The first was at night, and the truck's lights were off. This is amazing, because there are no streetlights, and the trees allow in no moonlight. I couldn't understand how the driver was able to even stay on the road! I was behind it at first. The truck pulled over and waited for me to pass. It then pulled out and followed me until I was several miles from the house. I had one passenger in the car, and you can imagine the state we were in. We were scared to death, but REALLY excited!

The next time was also at night, this time with a different friend. After we had driven past the guardhouse several times, we noticed that we were being followed by a red truck. We hadn't seen it even come onto the road. We never saw the driver's face. Again, we were followed until we were several miles from the house; then the truck just pulled over to the side of the road. Again the headlights were off.

I have been able to find absolutely no evidence of sacrificial rites being performed during Halloween or at other times. I have also, up to this point, been unsuccessful in trying to dig up deeds or any type of records of transfers for the property.−*Deena Haiber*

On Bended Tree

There is a legend about a road nicknamed Devil's Road, located off of Route 202 near Concord Pike. As rumor has it, there is a house or church that used to perform Satanic rituals. At the beginning of the road, there are two arrow-shaped pickets known to many as the Gates of Hell. On this road, the trees are bent away from the church, and there are many trees spray-painted with the number 666, and many other disturbing words and images. There is a gate to the side of the road, and off that road behind the gate is the church. I have been on this road many times, and the only strange thing I saw was on Mischief Night (the night before Halloween), when I and my friends saw shadowy orange lights lighting up the house. I am pretty sure that it was candlelight, but we did not want to make any assumptions.−*CiCi*

Chased by Satan on His Very Own Road

The entryway to Satan Road, as it is affectionately called, is so overgrown with trees and vines that it resembles a tunnel. Once you start down the road, there is no turning back. It is very windy and, despite being a two-lane road, is uncomfortably narrow for even a single car. About halfway down the road, you come around one of the bends, and you see it plain as day and indisputable: the Cult House. All the trees near it grow up a few feet; then they all turn at an angle so sharp that they are almost parallel to the ground, always away from the house. It's not just two or three trees; it's every tree for several hundred feet.

The Satan worshippers wait for your arrival at the entrance to the road in a black SUV. As soon as you start to slow down and turn, they turn on their headlights, pop out from hiding, and chase you out to a bridge on Route 100. I myself have been chased once by the SUV and have seen some sort of eerie bright blue flash when we were about to enter the road; that scared us enough to not even bother with the road that night. —*Greg H.*

Run When You See the Whites of Their Eyes!

I hail from the great town of Broomall, in Delaware County. If anyone has written from my area, it's probably been about Satanville, located off Route 1 just before the Brandywine Civil War Museum. All my life I've heard the stories about the place. Sometimes called Hells House, it is actually an old church in the middle of a field. You go down this road where the trees bend completely away from the road. Legend has it that the devil, in a fit of rage, let out an ear-piercing scream down the road one night, and from that point on, the trees have grown away from it.

Now comes the tricky part—finding the church. We followed the road for at least 2 hours, until we found the gate leading back to the church. Of course, the road is completely littered with KKK and devil worshipper graffiti. The gate was secured with a fresh padlock, and the path leading back to the church was extremely overgrown; thus my Bronco would not have fit. You definitely need a Jeep or just to go on foot. Just around the time of finding the gate, a car passed us. The drivers' faces were completely white, with dark hair, sporting the gothic look. Their eyes were also white. Like perhaps they were rolled up all the way. Needless to say, we were outta there like a bat out of hell.

Numerous people, including close friends, have been there. Usually you get chased away by black pickup trucks or black Broncos that chase you to the exit before veering off.—*Steve*

Chased Off Devil's Road

I have been on Devil's Road numerous times, at least a hundred. I have been up to the Devil's House. The roof is lined with metal crows all facing in the same direction, and there is a white cement bench in the front yard with a demon's face perfectly carved on it. People really do chase you out of there. I remember one time around 2 PM, I was driving with one of my friends on Devil's Road, and a black SUV sped up behind us, then turned into the woods. There was no dirt road or anything; it just turned right into the woods. Then the next thing I knew, he was coming full speed right towards us. One time when there was a full moon, I could see a fire and the outlines of about 12–15 people standing in a circle around it. Then I got chased off by two Bronco SUVs.—*Stephanie*

Beware the Tree

There are so many trees in Pennsylvania that the entire state was named after them. ("Sylvania" means "forestland.") So it's hardly surprising that the state also has its fair share of creepy tree stories.

Skull Tree

Probably the most famous tree in the state is Skull Tree on Devil's Road, one and the same road we were just talking about. It's a misshapen growth on an embankment along one of the road's more treacherous curves. Erosion has exposed the roots, which look like an enormous human skull or the skeletal fingers of a hand clawing at the earth. Its grotesque trunk has earned the tree many names, including Skull Tree, Devil's Tree, and Baby's Cradle. And it has attracted many tales as well, including one about an infant sacrifice left among the roots. In a gruesome nod to this tale, you can sometimes find decapitated baby dolls cradled within the tree's bony fingers.

Baby in the Tree

There's a tree with a hole in it along the road, and a mother put her baby in it and left it for dead. If you stop your car, kill the engine, and turn the lights off, they say that you can hear the baby crying still. Every night I got close to the place, I'd have horrible dreams that seemed all too realistic.—*Dan A.*

The Skull Tree Awes Me

My friend pointed out a tree growing at the roadside behind us. Half of its roots were exposed by erosion, and when he put the car in reverse, the lights created quite a display in the shadows of the roots. The roots took the form of a five-foot-high skull. I had more of a sense of awe than fear looking at it.—*Matt*

Girl in the Tree

There is a tree near Jerseytown, where a girl supposedly hung herself. When people go there, they say they have been followed (chased away) by a black Jeep.

Once, I went there, and there seemed to be a car following me on the road, which had a lot of intersections. So I slowed down, and it slowed down too. I stopped and got out. I went over to the truck, and there was an old guy inside. He asked me what I was doing there and told me not to make any trouble. He asked me a couple of times if I was a ghost.—*Hal Smith*

Skull Tree Filled with Concrete

The stories I've heard go as far back as my father's teen years. I have had some weird experiences down there back in my high school days as well. I was stopped by the security patrols when I had to pull over for a flat. They didn't believe my story of being lost, which I used to get myself out of trouble. The security did go to great lengths to make me understand that the Cult House is a myth. I personally don't believe them. The tree that people refer to with the exposed roots has been filled in with concrete as of late June 2004.—*Lou Marziotti*

The E(e)rie Death Stump of Millcreek

It's been a while since I moved from Erie, but I remember one story from my days there. In Millcreek, there was a place in the woods where you could see the foundation of an old small house and a rock pathway that led to a small creek nearby. In the creek, there's a tree stump. The story goes that a man found out his wife was unfaithful to him. He chased her down to the creek with an ax and cut her head off on the stump. Then he killed himself by lighting the house on fire. His ghost is said to haunt the area. A friend showed me the site. The foundation, stump, and walkway were there. I have no proof of the story, but this was a big local legend in the Erie area. –*Steven E. Johnson*

Big H Tree

Lansdale in Montgomery County has the most exclusive tree tale of them all. The evil H-shaped tree that used to stand on the top of a rock there was removed to make way for a new housing development. In its day, though, it was one of only three trees in the world shaped that way. Anyone care to guess what the H stood for?

H Tree Marks the Spot

There is a story in Lansdale of two side-by-side trees in the shape of an H. The story goes that there are three H trees in the world and they all mark the gateway to hell. The tree stood on top of a 12-foot-tall cliff, and the story goes that if you walked under the middle of the trees and around the trunk of one of the trees six times and jumped off the cliff, the ground would open up and take you to hell. The tree was knocked down during construction, and homes were put up. I certainly wouldn't want to be the family who lives in the house that was built over the tree! –*Jeff in Lansdale*

For a colony founded on principles of religious freedom, Pennsylvania seems to be overly endowed with routes to Hades. Perhaps it's true that the road there is paved with good intentions, but in any event, the H-shaped tree in Lansdale is only one of the supposed gateways to the underworld. As a travel destination, hell is hardly as popular among the locals as, say, the Outer Banks or the Jersey Shore, which is perhaps why the gates are not on heavily traveled roads. However, if you look hard enough, you may find the way.

Downingtown Gates of Hell

Near the twin tunnels on Valley Creek Road in Downingtown is Chester County's entrance to the netherworld. Old tales of the area talk of a pair of red cast-iron gates in the vicinity of Saw Mill Road, leading to a long-abandoned mansion. This place was the scene of a grisly murder, the story goes, in which a father killed his entire family. The house lay empty afterward, left exactly as it had been, right down to the bullet holes in the walls and doors. All the bodies had been buried on the grounds. Rumors have circulated constantly for the past fifty years about the activities of cults, Satanists, and mafiosi in the mansion and on its grounds. Other stories are more supernatural and talk of a portal for angels to descend to the underworld. Thankfully, there has been no talk of a revolving door allowing otherworldly residents to visit the earth.

But most visitors who explore the area nowadays can find no signs of any gate. Chain-link fences surround the likeliest old properties in the area, and the yards look untended. As you follow the gravel track into the woods and make your way through the trails, no iron gates are to be found. There are stone ruins of various dwellings, the odd piece of litter, and lots of NO TRESPASSING signs. But no gates.

Some of the people who boost themselves over a chain-link fence into a yard where they assume the original iron gate once stood have come back with tales of lanterns glowing in the abandoned building, illuminating furniture covered with dustcovers. Others claim they were chased off by large and very real-looking dogs. Not mythical hellhounds—just plain Dobermans.

So are there iron gates guarding some dark place in Chester County? (And are we better off not finding it?) Or is this one of those legends that spring from the wildness of the area? At this point, the truth is hidden in a tangle of contradictory stories. But Downingtown thrill seekers still tramp the woods in their quest for the supernatural portal. If any of them have found it, they've not returned to tell us about it.

Seven Gates of Hell

For a nice little place in southern Pennsylvania, York County seems to be unusually blessed with portals to the underworld. One local legend speaks of the Seven Gates of Hell in a woods on the outskirts of a town that some signs call Hallam and others call Hellam. (We're not making this up.) If you proceed through these seven gates, you will go straight to hell, they say, but they insist that nobody has ever made it past the fifth gate.

The gates begin in the woods off Trout Run Road, which was once the scene of a tragic insane-asylum fire. But if, as it is said, the road to hell is wide and well traveled, *Weird Pennsylvania* has some doubts about this York County portal. The first gate is hard enough to see, standing as it does half hidden by the undergrowth at a bend in the road. To further confuse things, there are two other gates right beside it. But it's the middle one, a buckled iron-pipe affair with a loose, rotten frame, that they call the first gate. The other two are merely distractions.

And the remaining six gates? Well, here's the catch: Gates two through seven are invisible during the day. But by the half-light of night, you're supposed to be able to find them by squeezing past the first gate and tramping through the undergrowth of the forest behind it. Of course, in the dark, it's hard to see the NO TRESPASSING signs liberally posted on trees, so the gates will be an even more obscure goal. To your left, you find a large circular clearing that at least one coven of Wiccans uses for their meetings and ceremonies. The gates, they say, stand deeper in the woods.

During our research trek—a daytime excursion, it's true—we found no gates past the first one, but plenty of felled trees that would look like gates by night: bent boughs that even a skeptic could see as barricades to another world. Despite our doubts, we stopped after passing five of these broken-down trees and decided to return to the car. After all, there's no sense in being reckless.

Hell Gates and Toad Road Asylum

There is a mysterious history and a dark underside to the city of York. It is a story of death and despair. It is the story of Trout Run Road, and it is so heinous that its name has been changed to Toad Road. In the 1800s, a colossal mental asylum stood in the woods on Toad Road. Because of its remote locale, firefighters were unable to get there when a fire broke out in the asylum. Many patients burned to death in the upper floors of the building, and hundreds of others fled into the surrounding woods. Frightened by the reputations of the asylum's inmates, the search party was extraordinarily aggressive, beating some victims they found into submission and killing others. The psychic impact of these horrible events forever cursed Toad Road.

People nowadays say that the area is in fact so cursed that it is the location of seven gateways to hell. York officials had constructed seven barriers along the paths to the former site of the asylum. Most local adventure seekers never even locate the first one. For those who manage to find the path, it is said that the sense of evil and overpowering feelings of death will turn even the bravest explorer back by the fifth gate. Apparitions are often seen along these paths. Strange noises and menacing screams are heard frequently.

Legends say that if one did manage to get past all seven gates, they would be standing upon the burnt remains of the mental hospital, a bona fide passageway to hell itself.–*Marcus Malvern Jr.*

Fire and Brimstone in Hellam

The town of Hallam near York shouldn't really be called Hallam at all. It began life as Hellam (Hell Town) on May 7, 1739, when Hellam Township was created. Why the Hell? There's a sulfur pit on the outskirts of town, near an old coaching house, and to the original settlers in the area, boiling brimstone coming out of the ground could mean only one thing. It's small wonder that the legendary Seven Gates of Hell are located within the township's borders. It wasn't until nearly two hundred years later that a stroke of post-Victorian Puritanism (or poor copying skills) took the Hell out of the area: The borough of Hallam was incorporated almost 170 years later, in 1902. Nowadays, the place lives a schizophrenic life: You'll see signs for the town of Hallam and Hellam Township all around the area.–*Donna C.*

Witchcraft and Murder in Hex Hollow

If you walk the roads in Hex Hollow in the right sequence on Halloween night, you will pass through the gates of hell. You'll know the place because the trees will grow thick above your head and the woods are dark even at the brightest time of day. It is said that there are places here where the sun has never touched the ground.

Hex Hollow, also known as Spring Valley Park and Rehmeyer's Hollow, is in southern York County. It is a maze of trails and dirt roads twisting in and out of each other, paths cut randomly through the vegetation. As a boy, I would spend an entire day hiking, climbing, crossing streams, trying to learn the trails just as I'd first learned the stories of this haunted place.

There is a lonely grave in Hex Hollow, marked with a pentagram, where Nelson Rehmeyer, a black magician, is buried. Men were murdered in his house. On some nights, the moon casts light upon Rehmeyer's specter, wandering his lands.

But most people, I have found, do not like to speak of Hex Hollow's legend—or truth. When asked about it, they give short answers or none at all.

Most of the area is a county park now, but it's not well used, partly because it's off the beaten path, but mostly because it is Hex Hollow. It's not easy to find, but you know it when you're there. The world becomes a little darker. How much darker it must have been in 1928, when the hollow's one resident was Nelson D. Rehmeyer—a loner well over six feet tall, with deep-set eyes and a powerful presence. Rehmeyer was married, but his wife lived outside the hollow because he was, in her words, "too damn peculiar."

Rehmeyer was what is commonly called in this area a powwow doctor. They are also called Brauchers or, in a more negative light, Hexenmeisters, or just Hexers. A strong tradition of faith healing and folk magic continues even to this day among the Pennsylvania Germans.

With some searching, and no maps, my wife, Alison, and I found the Rehmeyer house. There's not much peculiar about the place itself, but there is certainly something about the old farm that people pick up on. Perhaps it is the uninviting angle at which the house sits or the neglected outbuildings that surround it. There is no witch's grave here, no pentagrams, and few hex signs (which are a common sight in these parts). The only outwardly "witchy" feature of the house is the red 13 painted on one of the barns. Yet Hex Hollow has a feeling that Alison likens to a graveyard: peaceful and quiet but with an undercurrent of foreboding.

In Rehmeyer's time, there were hundreds of informal powwow practitioners throughout this area. One was named John Blymire, a sickly and sad man from a family of Brauchers who traced their spiritual lineage back to Pennsylvania's most famous witch, Mountain Mary. But John Blymire could keep none of his powwow patients. He was reduced to working in a York cigar factory. He could figure out no explanation for his hardship, save perhaps the answer obvious to someone of his background: He must have been hexed.

Blymire visited every powwow doctor, witch, and faith healer in the area, trying to get his hex broken. He had no luck until he found Nellie Noll, a.k.a. the River Witch. After many visits—and payments—to Noll, she revealed the source of Blymire's curse: Nelson D. Rehmeyer of Rehmeyer's Hollow.

Noll told Blymire that the only way he could break the curse was to get a lock of Rehmeyer's hair, or his hex book, or both, and bury them six feet down. Finally Blymire had a reason for his plight. He quickly enlisted two teenage boys, John Curry and Wilbert Hess, to help rectify it. Both boys came from families who had fallen on

If you walk the roads in Hex Hollow in the right sequence on Halloween night, you will pass through the gates of hell.

hard times, and it didn't take much for Blymire to convince them that they too were cursed and that Nelson D. Rehmeyer was the source.

On a dark and rainy November night in 1928, the three went to confront Rehmeyer. The old man invited them in, and the men stayed up late, talking of many things. Rehmeyer asked them to stay the night, then went upstairs to sleep while his three guests slept downstairs. In the early morning, Blymire tried to convince Curry and Hess to go to the basement to find Rehmeyer's hex book. But no way were the boys going into a dark basement for a book of devil's curses. After Rehmeyer fed them breakfast, the trio left.

But they returned the following night, and this time Blymire was determined to get the hex book. It took all three of them — Blymire, Curry, and Hess — to wrestle the powerful Rehmeyer to the ground. When he failed to give up the book, they tied

a rope around his neck and beat him to death. Upon hearing his death rattle, Blymire exclaimed, "Thank God, the witch is dead!"

Even with Rehmeyer dead, the trio could not muster the courage to descend into his basement to look for his hex book. Instead, they decided to burn the body and the house. They poured lamp oil over the corpse and the floor, set them ablaze, and left. Rehmeyer's nearest neighbor found his body two days later, on Thanksgiving.

Hex Hollow still feels lonesome and cold. Places seem to take on elements of their reputation. Most people don't know the real story of the place, but they know to stay away from it, especially at night. They know it is associated with witchcraft and murder. I still spend a lot of time there. Now I know all of the paths. I know there's no black magician, but I'm still searching. After all, there are tales of Rehmeyer's wandering ghost to explore.

—*Timothy Renner*

There's an empty church on Buckingham Mountain where the youth of Bucks County engage in the ultimate test of stamina, speed, and bravery—a footrace against the devil himself. The race ends in the graveyard of Mount Gilead Church, an African American church that once housed escaped slaves on the Underground Railroad. Except for occasional graveyard visits and infrequent services, the only activity the church sees these days is the contest with the Prince of Darkness. And if he wins, his challengers face dire consequences.

The rules of the race vary, depending on who's telling the story. You never see your demonic opponent, but you can tell by the wind who won the race. If you feel a gust of wind before the end of the race, it's the devil going past, and he wins. If you feel the wind after the race, he's coming in behind you. And if there's no wind at all, he was ahead the whole time.

What are the consequences? Some say winning brings a year of good luck and losing gives the same span of misfortune. Others say that losing brings death, and they cite a true tale of death by misadventure to make their point.

Some years back, a local student died at a party from internal burn injuries. He and some of the students at the party were breathing fire—a trick using lighter gas that creates a large fireball unless you breathe in by mistake, in which case, the fire descends into your lungs—and he had the misfortune of inhaling the stuff. Some locals insist that this happened the day after he had tripped and lost a race with the devil at Mount Gilead Church.

The legend could have many origins. A celebrated hermit named Albert Large lived near the area between the 1830s and 1850s, and hermits are always good for inspiring tall tales among the townsfolk. And there has been a lot of talk of black magic being performed in the church and its vicinity. Whatever the origin of the story, though, the area attracts many nocturnal sprinters for the high-stakes footrace in the moonlight. We wish them all a long and fleet-footed life.

Haunted Moonshine Church and the Blue-eyed Six

There are not one but two sets of apparitions associated with the little village of Indiantown Gap in Lebanon County. One involves the army base at Fort Indiantown Gap, which houses a green-and-white church called Moonshine Church, named after Henry Moonshine (1760–1836), who had donated the land for it. Moonshine had designated the acreage as free burial land in memory of his son, who died at the young age of fourteen.

The original log church burned down in the 1960s and was replaced by the one that stands on the grounds today. It's not a smart idea to stroll into military camps, but those who have peeked into the church say they see dead people walking around inside. Given the sad history of the place, nobody's sure whether it's supposed to be Moonshine or his relatives wandering around there, but some say it may be a murder victim named Joseph Raber. And that's the man who features in Indiantown Gap's other set of apparitions.

After Raber's untimely death in December 1876, a sordid tale of greed and betrayal was revealed, involving six men: Israel Brandt, Josiah Hummel, Charles Drews, Franklin Stichler, Henry F. Wise, and George Zechman, who were arrested and tried for Raber's murder. During their trial, a reporter noted that all the defendants had blue eyes, and so history remembers them as the Blue-eyed Six. They apparently had taken out a life-insurance policy on Joseph Raber, a local laborer in his late fifties. Raber, who lived in a one-room shack with his common-law wife, was not related to the six — but the so-called graveyard policy they took out didn't require him to be. Simply stated, if the six kept up the premiums, they would walk away with either $8,000 or $10,000 (sources disagree) when Raber died. Although this plot was ghoulish, graveyard policies were perfectly legal then and are still, in fact, to this day.

What wasn't legal was the plot this unsavory crew hatched to hasten payday by doing Raber in. In barroom meetings, the six discussed how they would do the deed (rather too loudly, as it turned out), and they settled on drowning Raber in Indiantown Gap Creek. After knocking him into the water, at least two of them held him under until he expired. Unfortunately, murder plots have a way of coming unraveled, and all but one of the six ended up being hanged. Only Zechman was not convicted, but he died a year later anyway.

Although the Blue-eyed Six were not allowed to be buried in the Moonshine graveyard, where their victim had been buried, the story goes that if you drive to the graveyard at night, you can see floating blue lights along the road and in the graveyard. Blue for their eyes? Or for the sad end they had met?

Eyes Still Have It at the Haunted Moonshine Church

There is a tale around Elizabethtown about Fort Indian Town Gap. It's an army base that stores tanks and ATVs. Inside the base is a church called Moonshine Church. It looks in bad shape but is still in use. Across the road from it is a graveyard where the notorious Blue-Eyed Six are buried.

I have heard many tales about the church and the six. One is that the church used to be a murder house, where many people were killed. People have told me that if you wander around in the woods out back around midnight, you cannot find the church again, and if/when you do, a pentagram is visible on the back door. If you look inside the windows, you can see ghosts and soldiers walking around.

In the graveyard are the Blue-Eyed Six, who were put on trial and hung for drowning a man in St. Joseph's Spring. The Six killed the man for his life insurance, which was worth 1,000 dollars. They were caught, hung, and buried in the church's graveyard. Sometimes you can see their eyes roaming in the graveyard or alongside the road. This only really occurs around midnight. Other times, if you are speeding, your car will stall for no reason. This has happened to a few of my friends. A warning, though—never turn your car off if you arrive there; it may not start up again!—*James*

Lights Still Burn in the Funk Mill Burned House

I have an eerie personal story about the southeastern part of PA, alongside Funk Mill Road, a short drive from Hellertown. A feeling of oppression comes over me every time I visit the charred remains of a farmhouse about half a mile down this desolate stretch of road. Its three remaining white walls rise out of the sumac and vines. The roof and flooring have completely collapsed.

I was told that the house caught fire in the dead of winter sometime in the early 1980s, with a mother and child at home. The man of the house was at a bar in Hellertown when he heard the news, and knowing that his wife and child might be in danger, he sped home. He hit ice rounding the turn onto Funk Mill, hit an embankment, and was killed.

It is said that in the winter, his car speeds down the road leading to Funk Mill but crashes as it turns the corner onto the road. I have on numerous occasions seen lights on and window fans working in the upper windows of the home. There is no floor in this house, let alone electricity!

To best see the house, follow Funk Mill Road until you see the BRIDGE OUT sign on the left, turn around there, and make a second pass. The vegetation isn't nearly as thick there. A few words to all: A forest ranger lives along the road; the neighbors have big dogs. They don't like late-night company, and I can't count the times the ranger has yelled at us, thinking we were there to party. *–Shadowynn*

Midnight Recess for Valley Forge Kids

In Valley Forge Park, right before Route 252 hits Route 23, it winds around a stream that passes under the historic covered bridge. As teenagers, we would often drive down that road through the park in the dark, and on occasion, I would see what seemed to be children or little people just as I turned around bends of the road. One night while speeding around a turn, I saw a child in the road and slammed on the brakes. By the time I came to a stop, the child was gone. The people in the car with me thought I was crazy.

When my husband was a teenager, he lived in this area. One evening around 2:30 a.m., some friends of his were coming down Yellow Springs Road, just up the road near the bridge, when they saw a child run in the road in front of their car. They thought this was strange for so late at night. Here's the interesting part: Just up the street from where we saw the children, at the corner of Yellow Springs and Diamond Rock roads, stands a very old octagonal schoolhouse. This Mennonite schoolhouse dates back to the early 1800s and was abandoned in 1865. This could explain all the children running around in the area.*–Rachel Cooper*

Pittsburgh's Green Man

The legend of the Green Man has been a favorite in the Pittsburgh area for decades. Somewhere in Greater Pittsburgh, as the story goes, a man suffered a massive jolt of electricity. He was a West Mifflin or Dravosburg man working for the power company, and he was struck by lightning or shocked by a downed power line during a storm. Whatever the cause, all agree that the unfortunate man suffered terribly as a result. His skin turned green, and his face was horribly disfigured, with the features melted together. Some say the sparks put a hole through one of his cheeks.

Depending on who's telling the tale, the Green Man either died immediately (so all subsequent sightings were of his ghost) or survived and hid out in a boarded-up house. Either way, he comes out only at night, when there's little danger of his being seen. Those that do see him, however, are morbidly fascinated by his disfigurement and by his habit of smoking cigarettes through the hole in his cheek.

A variant of the story gives late-night thrill seekers a place to look for the green glow of their hero's skin. The accident took place near one of the many abandoned railroad tunnels in Greater Pittsburgh, and that's where the man ran to after his accident. They say that if you drive to the tunnel late at night, turn off your car headlights, and call him, he will appear and touch your car. The trouble with this is that the electricity he still carries with him will mess up the electrical system in your car and you won't be able to restart it.

Many different locations are touted as the site of the Green Man's tunnel, but the most popular is in South Park township, just off Snowden Road. The tunnel is officially called Piney Fork Tunnel, on the abandoned Peters Creek Branch of the Pennsylvania Railroad. Though it is currently used by the township for storing rock salt for snowy days, it is slated to be part of the Rails-to-Trails bike trail network. Let's hope bike lamps won't suffer the same fate as your car's electrical system after the Green Man's touch.

Green Man Lives!

There is much myth to the story of the Green Man, but most people don't know that he actually existed. The story was told to us at the Pittsburgh Historical Society. Supposedly his name was Ray Robinson, and he lived just outside the small town of Koppel in Beaver County. He roamed the night because he was disfigured and was afraid to walk around in public during the day. Some say he was flying a kite that got caught in the power lines, and others say he was climbing a telephone pole to retrieve his kite, but all agree that he was electrocuted, disfiguring his face and arm. The green in the Green Man apparently came from the types of shirts he wore, which would reflect green in the headlights of the adventurous. I've heard some people eventually started to stop while passing him by and actually got out to meet him. They would take their picture with him and even buy him beer and cigarettes!
—Joel Rickenbach, Eeriepa.net

Dark Tunnels of Downingtown

There's something about the Downingtown area that attracts weirdness. Not only is the area a supposed portal to hell, but the twin tunnels on Downingtown's Valley Creek Road are also a source of strangeness. Within the tunnels, vertical shafts ascend to the top of the hill, allowing in air and light. It's these shafts that people tell tales about.

Many of them involve hangings. One story goes that in the late 1800s or early 1900s, a young woman was run out of town after giving birth out of wedlock. Ashamed and desperate, she went to the top of the hill and, holding her baby, hanged herself. The child slipped from her fingers and fell to its death in the tunnel below. They say that if you walk into the tunnel at night, you can sometimes hear the baby crying or even see its ghostly apparition. Another story tells of a man who hanged himself in the shaft and whose death rattle can be heard in the tunnels at night.

Wired for Sound

A wire runs between the two tunnels in Downingtown, and supposedly, a man hanged himself from it. The local legend goes that if you drive into one of the tunnels, turn off your lights, and roll down your windows, you can hear footsteps of someone splashing through the puddles in the tunnel, followed by the snap of a wire suddenly going taut.–*Morgan Frew*

Case of the Two Tunnels

The tunnels in Downingtown were supposed to be the site of a particularly brutal murder. A biker gang apparently murdered a woman and chopped her up. They put the parts into a suitcase, which they left in the tunnel. You can see a sick picture spray-painted on the wall of the tunnel, showing a suitcase with an arm coming out of it and a speech bubble saying, "Help me!" on it.–*Bill Fields*

Nighttime Police Line

When we were in high school, we used to make trips to the tunnels every weekend. They were definitely creepy—pitch black and deathly quiet except for the sound of dripping water. We would all link arms and walk to the middle of the tunnel where the girl hung herself.
–*Nick Lombardo*

Headless Horrors at Allison's Grave

About eighty miles north of the state capital of Harrisburg, up in Lycoming County, just south of the Susquehanna River, lies a pleasant biking and hiking trail in the Williamsport Municipal Water Authority's watershed area. On the outskirts of Duboistown and South Williamsport is something a lot less pleasant—the cursed grave of a headless heroine named Allison.

The legend has it that Allison was a nurse or driver during World War I. When her tour of duty on the Continent was over, she boarded an airplane for England, from where she was to take a ship home. However, her plane was shot down by enemy fire before it left the war zone. In the search for survivors, her disfigured body was recovered, but her head was never found. The U.S. government transported home what was left of her, where she was buried in the family plot on Mosquito Valley Road.

Precisely what curse the grave carries is open to dispute. Perhaps Allison, whose life was cut short on the brink of her return to her loved ones, simply cannot rest. Or maybe she just misses her head. Some believe that if you visit the graveyard at midnight on Halloween, her truncated body can be seen rising up and moving about. Others say that if you visit the graveyard after dark on any night of the year and see a shadow running through the woods, some great evil will befall you before you cross the stone bridge leading away from the cemetery. Whichever tale you choose, it's a place that locals like to drive to for a special late-night thrill.

Even the Church Is Scared

Everyone around here believes in the story of Allison's Grave. If you see a shadow moving through the graveyard at night, you'll have an accident of some kind. The lucky ones have a minor scrape in their car right away. The unlucky ones have to wait, and wait, and wait . . . until misfortune strikes. A while back, a group of people went there in a couple of cars—including a pastor of a local church. Sure enough, they saw the shadow. It scared them a lot, so they got out of there in a hurry. The first car made it across the Stone Bridge fine, but the second had a mysterious blowout. They had to get out in the dark and put on the spare. It scared the bejabbers out of everyone. –*Nedstal*

Hexenkopf: The Witch's Head

In Bucks County stands a hill called Hexenkopf, the German word for "witch's head." A whole slew of local legends revolve around this place, including tales of cults and witches. Some speak of a witch who lived on the forested hill and cursed her nosy neighbors for interfering in her affairs. When people started falling sick, the nearby farmers and villagers decided to take justice into their hands and hanged the witch. She was later seen wandering the hill looking for a chance for vengeance.

A neat little tale but probably not true. What is true is even stranger and more worthy of notice. Apparently, Hexenkopf Hill was a ritual focus for the local Indian tribes. The shamans would perform ceremonies to draw the evil spirits out of those sick or afflicted. These evil spirits would then be imprisoned in the mountain. It is said that the hill used to glow at night from all the evil trapped inside. Early settlers in the area were quick to note it as well. They were so impressed with the shamans' results that they began to learn how to do it. For the next century or so, long after the Indians were gone, local witch doctors performed powwows, as they called it, to drive the evil spirits from sick people.

While working for the local daily paper, the *Express-Times,* I discovered the daughter of one of the last powwowers of Hexenkopf. This elderly lady told me her father was a skilled powwower and had worked its rituals well into the early 20th century. She remembered specifically an incident that happened when she was a child. Her older sister had just given birth, and the baby was sick with a fever. Her father, in her words, "took the fever out of her and put it in the rock." She told me that the spirits dance on the rock on Allhallows Eve and that she was planning on going up and joining them. I never did find out if she did.

The hill itself has long lost its eerie night glow. Skeptics speculate that the glow had been caused by a coating of a specific mineral that has since eroded away due to deforestation in the 19th century. But some say it's because the spirits aren't in the rock anymore; they're out in the woods, roaming free and looking for a new host.

All I know is that I have been up there at night and it is definitely something that makes your flesh crawl. Strange lights and shadows are all I can report having encountered (besides the weirdo with the machete who was sitting alone on the rock in the dark. He was friendly to us but still . . .). Others have reported seeing people walking alongside them in the night woods.

Hexenkopf is easy to find. Just take Route 78 to the Easton exit. Turn left at the exit stop and head up Morganhill Road into Williams Township. About five miles down this road is Hexenkopf Road on the right. While driving down Hexenkopf Road, the hill will be on your left.–*Rick Cornejo*

Train Does the Witching Thing

Something weird happened to me and some of my friends a year or two back. Outside of a town called Easton, there's supposed to be this witch's rock where witches do all of their witching stuff. (I'm not too into the technical terms here.) We would spend hours looking for this stupid rock and never found it, but driving home one night along a deserted open road, we saw a train off to the right, down an embankment. We could see this train clearly for at least a mile. We turned around for about 15 seconds, and when we came back, the train was nowhere in sight. None of us had any clue how to explain it, because all five of us saw the train, saw that it went on for at least a mile or so, and yet it just totally disappeared.–*Sleepykitten8*

Ancient Mysteries

When the past speaks to us, its messages are often written in stone, in strange languages perhaps created by unknown people in unknown times. Bizarre rock carvings and formations litter Pennsylvania, sometimes buried a few feet beneath the ground, sometimes hidden in woods, sometimes perched high up on mountains. What do they mean? Some believe the curious rock markings and formations are messages from lost cultures. Archaeologists might say they are the result of some geological anomaly or the work of hoaxers. (The archaeological world has been bitten too often by pranksters to be very trusting.) So when we stumble across some mysterious markings on a piece of rock, or find odd groupings of rocks and boulders, we might have to guess for ourselves their significance. Most of the cryptic engravings will forever be shrouded in mystery, protected by the misty veils of time. But it's certainly fun to check them out and try to pierce that veil.

The Allegheny River's Indian God

About five miles south of Franklin in Venango County, on the left bank of the Allegheny River, stands a large rock that's been famous for hundreds of years. It's covered with graffiti dating back to 1749, when French explorers discovered it on an expedition to the Ohio Valley. But etched into the side of the rock facing the river are more ancient carvings, and it's these pictures that have earned the rock a dramatic name—Indian God.

This huge sloping rock stands twenty-two feet high. On its flat surface are hundreds of ancient petroglyphs, as well as thousands of more recent sightseers' initials and other carvings. The sheer size and distinctive nature of the rock have made it an instantly recognizable landmark for almost three hundred years. Explorer Bienville de Celeron buried one of his territorial markers next to the rock to claim the surrounding land for France on August 3, 1749. In his diary that day he wrote, "Buried a lead plate on the south bank of the Ohio River, four leagues below the Riviere Aux Boeufs, opposite a bald mountain and near a large stone on which are many figures crudely engraved."

The fame of these crudely engraved figures has long outlived the French claim to the land. And so has their mystery. It's hard to tell what these carvings portray, especially since some 260 more years of hard weather have eroded the face of the rock. Certainly, it's possible to distinguish people, hands, arrows, and specific animals, like birds, snakes, and turtles, but other glyphs are more elusive. One looks like a bizarre two-legged chrysalis— maybe a symbol of one of the famous seventeen-year cicada infestations that plague much of the U.S. East Coast. Some look like X-ray images of human figures, while others are pared-down geometric shapes resembling the Greek letters phi, chi, and gamma.

But the question lingers, what do all the carvings mean?

People have long believed that the rock told tales of daring feats and exploits. A typical amateur analysis appeared in an anonymous article in the *Democratic Archives* of 1842: "This rock undoubtedly records the history of many hundred years. Among the figures you can distinguish a turtle, a snake, an eye, an arrow, a sun. These are symbols or hieroglyphics. They record the exploits and illustrious actions of departed and forgotten nations and their battles. Who shall decipher these wondrous characters?"

Who indeed? It's hard enough to figure out who created them. Some experts believe that the pictographs are of Native American origin, created either by the Algonquian or by ancestors of the Shawnee, probably carved sometime between 900 and 1650. But that's a broad range of time and a pretty vague guess of the people responsible.

Another theory is that the markings had their origins in the Old World. According to an article by R. W. Criswell in the newspaper *Oil City Derrick* in 1889, the carvings could have been the work of Norse explorers from about the year 1000. Criswell's article cites similarities between the glyphs on Indian God Rock and those on a Massachusetts pictographic stone called the Dighton Rock. Two antiquarian professors—Rafu and Anderson of the University of Wisconsin—analyzed the runelike characters of the Dighton Rock and concluded that they were the work of one Thorfinn Karlseine, who came to North America in 1007. So perhaps Indian God Rock belonged in Valhalla instead of the happy hunting grounds.

While the Norse explanation is possible, it seems less likely than a Native American one. The nineteenth-century scholar-adventurer Henry Schoolcraft, who spent thirty years among the tribes of the Great Lakes region, had no qualms about ascribing the ancient carvings to native tribes. He made a thorough analysis of the markings before too much graffiti had encroached on them. (Because of the centuries-old tradition of carving your own mark on Indian God Rock, which is now strictly prohibited at historic places like this, it's harder these days to know where the ancient markings end and the ones from the eighteenth century and later begin.) Schoolcraft had the benefit of a less vandalized rock and a greater knowledge of Native American cultures to work with when he recorded his findings about Indian God Rock:

The inscription itself appears distinctly to record in symbols the triumphs of hunting and war; the bent bow and arrow are twice distinctly repeated, the arrow by itself is repeated several times, which denotes a date before the introduction of fire arms. The animals captured . . . are not deer or common game, but objects of higher triumph. There are two large panthers or cougars, variously depicted. . . . The figure of a female denotes without a doubt a captive, and various circles representing human heads denote deaths. One of the subordinate figures depicts by his gorgets a chief. The symbolic sign of a raised hand drawn before a person represented by a bird's head denotes apparently the name of an individual or tribe.

The rock was put on the National Register of Historic Places in 1984 and can be seen free of charge from a handicapped-accessible viewing platform—much better than slip-sliding down the bank and wading into the water, as earlier visitors used to do. You can get to the site along the Allegheny River Trail, either cycling south from Franklin for about eight miles along the winding river or hiking a couple of miles up from the river's edge at Brandon. Do it soon before the older glyphs are washed away.

Safe Harbor Petroglyphs

Ancient rock carvings were once so common along the southern stretch of the Susquehanna River that early European settlers would break them off and use them as garden ornaments. But when more people settled there and began damming rivers to create reservoirs, many ancient relics were submerged permanently as a result of the new high water levels. One remaining example is located south of the Safe Harbor Dam in Lancaster County, where hundreds of petroglyphs are still visible— if you have a kayak, that is.

There are two main sites, called Little Indian Rock and Big Indian Rock, and five smaller ones, where carvings cover the surface of the rocks. Some of the etchings are symbols; some show human figures.

In the early 1930s, state archaeologist Donald Cadzow spent two years making casts of the designs and removing rocks that would be submerged when the dam became operational. Some of the rocks are on display in the State Museum of Pennsylvania in Harrisburg, but the casts have somehow gone missing.

A group called Friends of the Safe Harbor Petroglyphs is currently documenting and mapping the carvings that are still visible and interpreting their meaning. One member of the group, Paul Nevin, believes that some of the carvings are linked to solar calendar events. In 2000 and 2001, he made two significant observations. In one carving, parallel serpentine designs were almost perfectly in line with the east–west axis of the compass, and on the spring equinox he observed that the sun rose exactly in line with the parallel designs. In another carving, a human figure faced east, pointing with one arm toward the horizon. At sunrise on the summer solstice, Nevin observed that the pointing hand aligned directly with the sun.

But with more than three hundred visible carvings, these few observations only scratch the surface of possible creators and meanings. Nobody knows who made these markings or even how many different cultures were involved.

All we can do is paddle along in our boats, marvel at these messages from the past, and wonder what they're all about.

The Stone of the Rising Sun

Pleasant Mount in Wayne County is an outdoors-man's dream, with hills that provide rugged hiking, capped off with some stellar views. It's also the place where in 1974 a high school student discovered a large stone that ignited a firestorm of controversy. Jim Knapp was near an outcropping of rocks along the west branch of the Lackawaxen River when he found a foot-long chunk of sandstone with a carving of tree-covered hills capped with a large shining sun. Along the top were some mysterious-looking symbols that looked like alien letters. Like any student would, Knapp took the curious piece home and kept it as decoration. If he hadn't read an article about mysterious stones and their archaeological significance, nobody would have heard more about it.

But he did, and he told a local newspaper, the *Wayne Independent,* about his find. Once the information was in print, it was only a matter of time before someone came knocking on his door.

During the late 1970s, a new breed of archaeologist emerged—highly educated mavericks who explored obscure finds like Knapp's stone and used their findings to support radical theories of history. With their Indiana Jones appeal, they attracted avid research assistants, who scoured newspapers for interesting items to investigate. Sure enough, a research assistant told the most Indiana Jones of them all, Salvatore Michael Trento, about Knapp's find, and Trento paid him a call.

One of Trento's colleagues was a brilliant linguist named Dr. H. Barraclough Fell—Barry to his friends. Fell brought to his work a knowledge of ancient languages such as the Latin, Greek, Sanskrit, and Gaelic languages and Egyptian hieroglyphics, as well as of numerous modern languages, including French, German, Danish, and Russian. He also had done years of research in a bewildering range of subjects. He checked out the lettering on Knapp's stone and concluded that the inscription had Iberian and Portuguese roots and was written in a style dating back to between 300 and 200 B.C. Fell's interpretation of the script reads, "On the appointed day, the sun sets in the notch opposite the House of Worship."

In Trento's 1978 book, *The Search for Lost America,* he describes finding the site depicted on the stone using the position of the sun at the winter solstice. The ruins of what may once have been a chamber are nearby. The stone, then, appears to be some kind of marker for European travelers—something like an advertising flyer for the house of worship.

The traditional academic community dismissed this interpretation and described Fell and Trento as "trait chasers"—people who use too little evidence to support their hypotheses. The jury is still out regarding Knapp's stone, with strong supporters on one side and strong detractors on the other. There are no absolute truths to fall back on here. Pick a side . . . any side. Your choice is as good as anybody else's.

Piles of Rock

All across Europe and in odd places around the United States, people at one time used to pile up rocks into structures called cairns. These careful arrangements of stone sometimes look like truncated cones or pyramids; sometimes like rounded beehives. But no matter what their shape, they have withstood the driving wind, ice, and rain of the centuries. Who made them, and what did they make them for? That remains a mystery. It's not even known whether American cairns were made by European settlers or by Native Americans. But northern Pennsylvania has a huge number of these formations, mostly on private land. We have explored some of them but still have precious few answers.

Tripp Lake Rock Piles

In Liberty Township in Susquehanna County, just this side of the New York State border, there's a water-filled glacier depression called Tripp Lake. It's not a huge lake, but the water is deep — sixty-five feet. The lake is well known to the many summer campers who visit the area. Slightly less well known, however, are the sixty rock piles in the woods. Naturally, campers and camp counselors have their own stories about these stones, but these stories are about as credible as the tales of the Tripp Lake monster that are used to frighten rookies around the campfire. These days, visitors to the cairns have left little "enhancements" made of sticks on top of the cairns. But beneath these frivolous additions, the rock piles clearly are pretty old structures. Naysayers try to dismiss the theory that they were built according to a purposeful design, but it's there if you examine the structures carefully: There's always one side that looks even and more deliberately tidy than the other sides — and that side almost always faces east.

Like most cairns in this part of the world, the Tripp Lake ones are in what are called second-growth woods. This means they were most likely constructed out in the open on land that had been cleared for agriculture. Many people assume that this means that they were colonial in origin, but there's strong evidence to suggest that the Susquehannock tribe that had once lived there may have cleared the land for agricultural purposes.

Be that as it may, there are few clues and almost no serious archaeological studies to indicate when these rock piles originated, who made them, or what their purpose was. Some believe that they are part of the foundations of old houses, constructed either just before or just after the colonial period. They don't look much like foundations, but anything's possible. Then there's the theory that they may have been built by Celtic or Phoenician explorers as early as 800 B.C. Pondering these theories will give you something to think about as you pause for breath during a long hike through the woods.

Exploring the Cairns of Susquehanna County

Somewhere deep in the woods of Susquehanna County, up a hill and along a ridge, is the most extensive ancient rock-pile site in the state. Not many people know it's there, and the prospect of seeing it had drawn together a motley group to investigate. Dee Dee, Mimi, and Carol are naturalists and hikers, and Norman is a Princeton professor who has been studying ancient rock piles for years. Two members of the *Weird Pennsylvania* research team were along for the ride, and frankly, we were lagging behind a bit. There was no trail, the weather was sticky even for early summer in Pennsylvania, and if that wasn't bad enough, one of our fellow hikers began talking about this year's victims of rattlesnake bites.

"We'll be all right as long as we keep the stream to our right. It's not far now," said Dee Dee. It wasn't the first time she'd said this, and we were beginning to doubt her sense of direction. But we were prepared to give her the benefit of the doubt.

"Here we are," said Dee Dee, fifty feet ahead of us and obscured by trees and undergrowth. A few steps later, there we were indeed. In front of us was a cluster of three cairns—piles of small rocks atop a larger foundation stone. They were conical, with flat tops, and seemed to be arranged in a triangle. Beyond them was another cluster of rock piles, also in a triangular formation. Beyond them stood yet more. And beyond them, obscured by trees, who knew how many more there were.

We tried to count all we could see from where we stood, and gave up after forty. New ones kept popping up as we stepped to one side of a tree or another. Over the next few hours, as we crossed little ridges and scaled the steeper parts of the hill, more appeared. It became clear that we wouldn't get a definitive count, but there were certainly more than two hundred. This wasn't just a few cairns in the woods; this was the mother lode.

Tens of thousands of irregular-sized rocks, many of them too large for a single person to carry, were piled carefully on top of foundations. Some of the cairns were flat-topped, others were shaped like beehives. Some had caught fallen leaves and seeds in their crevices and now sprouted saplings. A number of trees were surrounded by rings of rock that were probably once cairns but were gradually torn apart by the growing trees.

Nobody knows for sure who piled these rocks on the hillside or why. The obvious answer is that farmers needed to clear land for agriculture, so they had dug up the rocks and piled them there. That doesn't wash, because it is clear that they were painstakingly piled together and have maintained their shape for hundreds of years. If you're clearing land, you usually simply sling rocks every which way in a heap. So what rationale could there be for the strenuous, time-consuming, and ultimately useless work of dragging them uphill and meticulously assembling them into architectural formations?

"There are two theories bandied about," explained Dee Dee, "which sound rather dismissive when you hear them. They're called the village idiot and the senile old man."

In both cases, the theory goes that able-bodied but mentally challenged members of the village were given a task to keep them away from people who had real work to do. Nobody on our outing was buying that explanation. This site is one of several hundred found in the Northeast. The notion that primitive occupational therapy could result in literally thousands of artifacts like these seems too far-fetched.

As for when these rocks were placed there, that too is a mystery. No literary works, letters, or paintings from the colonial period mention odd rock piles in this part of the country. The oldest reference seems to date from an 1822 travelogue about a trip across New York State from New

1700s. A colleague of his excavated a similar site in northern Georgia and found pottery inside one cairn dating from around 500. But Muller urges caution before jumping to any conclusions. He'd recently made a long trip to see a pair of backyard cairns very much like the ones in Georgia, and they turned out to have been constructed in the 1960s by the homeowner's grandfather.

Nevertheless, Norman believes that the Pennsylvania site may have been a sacred place to the Susquehannock Indians once living in the area. The signs are there: Many ancient cultures treated sites with springs or large rocks as sacred. There is a

York City to Niagara Falls. It mentions "stones piled in a pyramidical fashion" in the Binghamton area. More recent accounts tell of poor Irish farmers building hilltop cairns in the early 1800s, though the sources for these accounts are unreliable. Most likely, these stories derive from the tale about Billy Welch, an old Irish eccentric in New Milford who had built such cairns on his Harmony Road farm in the late 1800s. But whether he and his countrymen started the custom or merely continued it is open to debate.

Norman Muller, our expedition's Princeton scholar, believes that the cairns were probably built long before the influx of Europeans into the colonies in the 1600s and

huge rock perched at the top of the hill, split and scored with horizontal lines. And partway down the hill is a natural spring that's delineated by rocks in a Stonehenge-like manner.

But nothing about the site is conclusive, and very little has been written about these particular cairns. All we could find were a couple of articles in Binghamton newspapers from the 1980s. The piles are not easy to find, and we're not going to give away their location. But if you know where they are, we suggest you take along only trusted friends to see them until they can be properly studied. Just one piece of advice, though: Don't do it in the summer. The flies are everywhere.

Indian Steps

In Center County, a steep ridge called Tussey Mountain cuts a swath through the Pine Grove Mills area near the town of State College. Centuries ago, long before the advent of cars, the native inhabitants would hike a trail called Standing Stone Path through a pass between two ridges. That path has since been paved and expanded into Route 26.

The Standing Stone Path is well documented and is a logical place for a trail. But there's another old trail, several miles to the west, where a series of stone steps was constructed through a much steeper and harder route over the mountain. Now called the Indian Steps, the stones form part of a hiking trail used by outdoorsy folks and day-tripping Penn State students.

But why bother to build steps there? The location makes little sense. The steps are too far from the Standing Stone Path to be part of a regular route. In fact, to get there from the path, you need to take a miles-long detour through the valley or hike up the highest part of Leading Ridge. And take it from one who has scrambled up the crumbled remnants of the steps—the trail is too steep for comfort. Why, then, would anyone build steep steps that go nowhere at a significant distance from a well-traveled trail?

Some believe that the Kishacoquilla tribe built them about three hundred years ago. Others point out that there is no record of the steps before 1911, though it's not unusual for an obscure artifact to slip under the radar. Probably the most realistic explanation stems from the fact that the steps stop at the boundary of the state forest line. It's possible that the stones were never intended to be steps at all, but rather a boundary marker. One theory is that they were laid out in the nineteenth century as a demarcation line separating the settlers' territory from that of the native people. But whatever their reason for

being there, they're still worth the strenuous uphill hike. The Leading Ridge side is in decent condition, but the downward slope, to Henry's Valley Road, is in poor shape. If you do go, take some sturdy hiking boots, a stick, and a companion to argue with about the origins of the steps.

Pillars of stone standing upright are an inspiring sight. Some of them are geological in origin, such as the standing stone in Wysox in the Endless Mountains. But there are other, more mysterious, ones that Europeans called dolmens, which were erected by humans and served some unknown religious purpose. Pennsylvania has its fair share of those.

Huntingdon's Missing Stone

Filed away in the Library of Congress is a 1756 map of the "Province of Pensilvania" [sic], showing the prerevolutionary state of our state—its rivers, borders, mountain ranges, and towns, plus a smattering of Indian settlements. Just a little to the left of center on this map, on the Juniata River, is a place called Standing Stone. Comparing this old map with AAA's finest, you realize that Standing Stone was on the site of the current town of Huntingdon. And sure enough, in downtown Huntingdon there is an old megalithic monument at the corner of Penn and William Smith streets. But that monument is only a replica of the one indicated on the 1756 map. The original stone disappeared twice, and after the second time nobody knows exactly where it went.

Before the first white settlers came to the area, that stretch of the Juniata River was occupied by Indians of the Oneida tribe. The Oneida, or Onyota, means the "people of the Standing Stone," and they moved their villages every decade or so, when hunting became scarce and the soil depleted. Their oral tradition tells of a stone mysteriously appearing outside each new settlement, a stone too large for even twenty men to move. The stone became a symbol of the tribe and was inscribed with representations of the nation's history.

When the earliest European settlers came to the area in 1754, they were impressed by the fourteen-foot-high granite column—and they were not the only ones. A neighboring tribe of Tuscarora stole the stone for a brief time, but the Oneida fought the thieves and regained their tribal treasure. But soon the Oneida realized there was a battle brewing that they would not win. Once a few English settlers appeared and charted the area, the Oneida knew it was only a matter of time before the intruders established a permanent settlement.

Like many tribes, the Oneida distrusted the English and allied themselves with the French. So when the provost of the University of Pennsylvania, William Smith, set his sights on developing the area, the Oneida moved on. By the time Smith established the town of Huntingdon in 1767, the Standing Stone and most of the tribe named after it had vanished. The Oneida pressed on westward, and their giant stone—too big to be carried by people on the move—disappeared without a trace. Did they hide it somewhere before they left? Or did it mysteriously rematerialize outside their new villages, as tradition holds.

Partly to commemorate the tribe, and partly to create a sense of cartographic continuity, the townspeople of Huntingdon created a replica of the original stone. It still stands today in the historic section of town. But the whereabouts of the original stone remain a mystery. The remnants of the tribe keep a large inscribed stone at the Oneida Reservation on Lake Oneida in New York State. Perhaps that is the old Juniata River stone, or perhaps that too is a replica of the original sacred stone. We modern descendants of the distrusted English will never know.

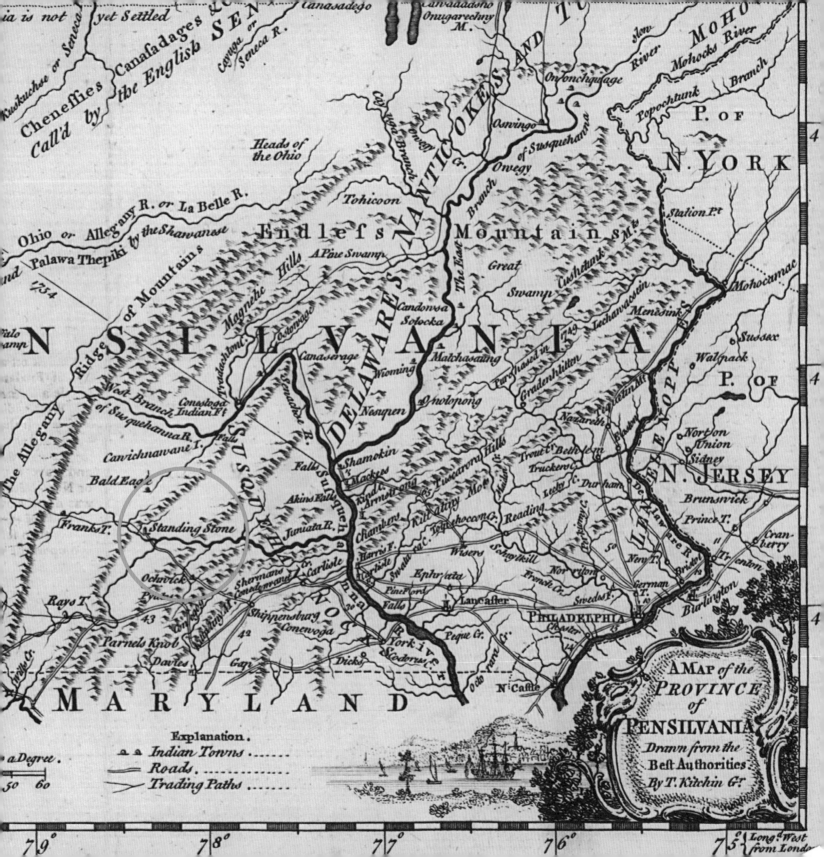

Radnor Henge

Driving west along Lancaster Road through the string of upmarket Philadelphia suburbs called the Main Line is slow-going, even though this stretch of Route 30 was once part of the original national road, the Lincoln Highway. But the pokey traffic and a long red light at Airdale Road give drivers a tantalizing glimpse of an imposing circle of stone monoliths by the roadside.

If you stop and walk around, you'll find that the rocks are built in a perfect circle on a well-tended lawn in Unkefer Park. But you'll get no clues as to what the stone circle is all about. Only two permanent markers stand at the site: two headstone-style carved stones that mark the border of Radnor Township and show the date 1682 beneath the spreading canopy of a tree.

The lack of information imparts a romantic aura to the circle of monoliths, as if it were an ancient relic thrust into the modern world. However, it is actually a relic of modern civilization. The stones were removed from the ground when Interstate 476 (the Blue Route) was built, and the township of Radnor decided to use them for beautification projects to mitigate the ugliness of a major highway on the outskirts of town. The stone circle is only one of several projects Radnor undertook with the leftover rubble, including a rock garden and a large griffin built into the grassy slope at the Blue Route's northbound exit. It's not exactly ancient, and it's not really mysterious, but it's one town's classy protest against suburban blight—and for that, we salute it.

Ringing Rocks of Bucks County

Today's lesson, class, is about the earth's crust. It's made up of a rock called diabase, which contains many hard minerals and a fair amount of iron. You can sometimes see the iron in the form of brown-red streaks in the gray rock. And you can see seven acres of the stuff in a boulder field in Bucks County that cuts through the middle of a forest. When you go, take along a hammer, because at the Ringing Rocks Park in Upper Black Eddy, you can whack the exhibits to your heart's content. About a third of them will resound with a clear tone, like that of a blacksmith's anvil.

The ringing-rock phenomenon isn't unique to this part of Pennsylvania, but the way the locals have reacted to it is. A nineteenth-century local character by the name of Dr. J. J. Ott sought out rocks with specific tonal qualities and played a concert on them, accompanied by a brass band. Local percussionists jam on the rocks even to this day, and since Bucks County made the place a park, it's become a very popular destination for families.

It's hard to say what's so strange about Ringing Rocks Park. It's both cool and puzzling to be able to knock bell-like tones out of rocks—cool because of the unexpected sound the rocks make and puzzling because, though all the rocks are chemically the same, only about a third of them ring out. Most just make the dull chain-gang thud you'd expect. Perhaps stranger than the phenomenon itself is the sight of nice suburban parents giving their kids a hammer and saying, "Go hit something with this."

But one thing trumps the ringing tone and hammering kids: It's the way the place looks. Both sides of the boulder field are heavily wooded, and the contrast between the greenery and the barren field is awe-inspiring. The abundant life of the forest seems to shy away from this place. The only other natural phenomenon that keeps trees this far apart is a river, so many people assume the area is a dried-out riverbed. But rivers don't pile up jagged rocks like these; they wear them down smooth. So as you look at this strange place, with its soundtrack of clangs from children with hammers, you begin to wonder, What put these rocks here?

Where there are no easy answers, fantasy floods in. Tales have circulated about a curse on the place that drives away all living things, including animals and insects. At face value, there seems to be something to that assertion: Several members of the *Weird Pennsylvania* team are bug magnets, but surprisingly few mosquitoes bit anyone during our trips to Ringing Rocks Park.

But science can explain that away easily enough. Rocks get much hotter in the summer sun than do trees in the forest, so anything that sticks around too long will get fried. The rocks go down about ten feet, providing nothing for plant life to take root in. So why would anything be attracted to a dry, hot place with no food and water, especially when there's a lovely forest all around?

Yet the science of Ringing Rocks Park doesn't spoil the weirdness. If you turn off your analytical mind long enough, you start to feel the fear of an ancient and mysterious place surrounding you. Then some kids will bang a tune out of stone, and you'll forget all about that fear.

To get to Ringing Rocks Park, take Route 611 to Route 32, drive a few miles, and then take a right onto Narrows Hill Road. Take a left onto Ringing Rocks Road. The park is a few miles along the road.

Fabled People and Places

The dark woodlands, steep mountains, and verdant fields of Pennsylvania are home to many groups of people, some living in the mainstream, others living on the fringes of society. Some are religious communities that keep outsiders at arm's length, while others probably don't exist at all except in the overactive imaginations of people who are hell-bent on a scary late-night ride to a local place of legend.

We celebrate all these fabled people and places, whether real or fictional. Like William Penn, we welcome them with open arms though some with a polite nod from the other side of the street. And others we welcome with a cloud of dust as we accelerate in the other direction. But that's only when they start throwing things at us.

The Quest for Midgetville

While doing field research for this book in the Greater Philadelphia area, *Weird Pennsylvania* found that one subject kept cropping up. Usually, people would preface their comments with "I know this sounds dumb, but I've heard of this place," and then they'd trail off, as if they were too embarrassed to say more. It got to the point that we'd finish the sentence for them. "Midgetville," we'd say.

Midgetville is a legend across the United States. Just outside a settlement of regular-sized people, it seems, there exists a community populated with undersized people, living in housing that's made to their scale. It's perfectly proportioned but built somewhere between half and three quarters the size of even the tiniest conventional housing. The only troubling thing about this story is its location: It's always in the home state of whoever is telling the tale, although exactly where is vague.

The eastern Pennsylvania Midgetville, they say, is about twenty minutes south of Philadelphia. You can drive to it on I-95, past the airport, getting off at the Ridley Park

Just outside a settlement of regular-sized people . . . there exists a community populated with undersized people, living in housing that's made to their scale.

exit. It's near a hospital on Chester Pike. That's about as clear as the directions get. In the interests of research, we drove around there for hours, and the closest we came to housing for little people was a collection of garden sheds near the car park of a municipal swim club.

So we dismissed Ridley's Midgetville as just another urban legend. But that skepticism ended when we met Karen at the Ridley Township library. She overheard the conversation we were having with a library assistant about the Land of the Little Folk and interrupted us. "I've been to Midgetville," she said. The room was stunned. Everyone within earshot stopped and listened. This wasn't a case of "a friend of my cousin's"; it was a firsthand account, the only one we'd ever come across. Then another woman said, "Did I hear you say Midgetville? My husband went there back when he was a kid. But he'd never take me there, because they threw rocks at him."

Karen is not a tall woman, but she reckoned that to get in through one of the doorways there, she'd need to duck her head. The road is so narrow and winding, you have to turn into a driveway to get out again, and that's when the residents start to get angry. When pressed for directions, Karen called her husband to get the story straight. He was the one who had taken her to that little cluster of houses years earlier.

We tried, but we never did find the place. Nevertheless, Karen's tale allayed our skepticism. It also reminded us of how annoying it is when people hang around outside your house after dark. So let's leave the little folks of Ridley to get on with their lives undisturbed. And as a side benefit, you'll avoid getting rocks thrown at your car.

Little Details Count

We have a Midgetville here in Ridley, across from Taylor Hospital. Trespassing is prohibited, but there are ways of getting inside. Once inside this small town, there are streets of tiny little houses; even the mailboxes are tiny. It's a must-see.—*Carol*

There's No Place Like Gnome

Midgetville isn't hard to find. It's off a narrow little driveway opposite Taylor Hospital on Chester Pike. The road's very narrow, and there's no outlet, so you have to turn around in a driveway at the end. But you can't miss it. If you go, just click your heels together three times! —*Pete S.*

I Knew a Resident

I've been to Midgetville, and I knew someone who used to live around there. She'd get really mad with us when we talked about the place. She kept telling us that it was just an optical illusion because the houses were set down at an angle. But I'm telling you, those doorways were definitely too small for a regular person.—*DCas*

Weird Ways of Worship

The United States is one of the few countries in the world that was founded on the principle that its citizens should be free to worship however they see fit. It's a mandate that owes a lot to the liberal ideas of Pennsylvania's Quaker settlers, who had suffered enough persecution by state religions to decide that when they were in charge, things would be different. The early Quaker-influenced government of the colony welcomed settlers from many countries to worship God in their own way without hindrance. As long as their spiritual rituals didn't involve human sacrifice, pretty much anything was okay.

Of course, not everybody is as accepting as the early Quakers were. Fear and ignorance have twisted other people's ways into some warped and exaggerated tales. Fueled by rural superstition and the magic effect of moonlight over the woods, people's imaginations have interpreted other people's practices in some interesting ways. Here, then, are tales of the commonwealth's fringe religions, all of them true.

Bucks County Pyramids

By the side of a small road between Quakertown and Dublin in Bucks County, near Nockamixon State Park, stands a memorial garden that's no longer open to the public. It used to be a place of quiet reflection and peaceful meditation, but the group that ran it closed it down and painted NO TRESPASSING signs all around it. Much of the garden is now hidden by overgrown shrubs, but poking through the undergrowth are two large pyramids—and a mystery that goes back hundreds of years.

The land is owned by a Christian mystical sect called the Fraternitas Rosae Crucis, literally translated as the "Brotherhood of the Rose Cross." Better known as Rosicrucians, they have been a secretive but major presence in Pennsylvania since before the Revolutionary War. The Bucks County property is a place of worship and a training facility, but nobody outside the order really knows what goes on there. From the roadside, you can sometimes hear chants and catch a tantalizing glimpse of people in robes, but apart from that, the place is veiled in mystery. Anyone wandering around the property without permission is reportedly chased away.

Like many secret organizations, the Rosicrucians deal in symbols. Pyramids loom large in their symbology, and even their name contains two powerful ciphers. The cross obviously reflects their Christian beliefs, but the rose has more ancient pagan origins. In Roman times, this flower was a symbol of secrecy. The legend goes that Cupid gave Harpocrates, the god of silence, a rose in exchange for keeping Venus's secrets. Roman banquet rooms were decorated with roses as a reminder to keep silent about any confidences revealed there under the influence of wine. And so we have the English word for something done secretly: sub rosa, "under the rose."

This veil of secrecy means that it's hard to get any solid details about the Rosicrucian order, but one or two things are known. The order arose in Germany with the 1614 publication of a book called *Fama Fraternitas,* describing the travels of a mythical figure, Christian Rosenkreuz, through Damascus, Egypt, and other biblical places. In the course of these travels, he gathers the secret wisdom of the order whose true origins and nature are now lost to outsiders. The book attracted many mystical Christian groups, such as the Gnostics, the Pythagoreans, the Magi, and the Freemasons, into an umbrella organization, sharing many secret symbols. The most obvious is the pyramid, which features prominently in Rosicrucian architecture.

By the roadside in front of the Bucks County Rosicrucian garden is a three-foot-high pedestal that looks quite normal at first but on closer investigation turns out to be a topless pyramid. It's lined up perfectly through the shrubs with a second pyramid, more than five feet tall. This pyramid, in turn, lines up with a large pyramid-shaped mausoleum with bronze plaques commemorating members of the order.

The mausoleum provides tantalizing hints as to the structure and nature of the order. Those commemorated include members of Supreme Councils of nine, seven, and three, with such titles as Supreme Grand Master, Member Sublime Third, and Hierophant. The organization seems more egalitarian than most, since many of those named are women. And there have been some very influential members, including Benjamin Franklin and Abraham Lincoln.

Looking inside the pyramid, you get a clearer idea of the symbols of the order. Over the gated doorway stands a circular plaque with a winged world crowned by a skull and crossbones, with the word TRY underneath it. The torch, anchor, and triangle in the design only confuse the uninitiated further. Peeking through the gate into the pyramid, however, one sees familiar designs that give one a jolt of recognition: On one wall is an unfinished pyramid topped with an eye and on another is an eagle holding an olive branch and thirteen arrows. These form the two sides of the Great Seal of the United States, as depicted on the dollar bill.

So why are these seals hidden inside a Rosicrucian monument? Is the order tipping its hat to the United States? Is it worshiping the mighty dollar? Or is this country actually branded with the seal of a secret society?

One piece of evidence at the Bucks County site leads to an inescapable conclusion. It is cast in bronze and screwed to the outside of the pyramid. It is the name of a prominent council of nine member—Benjamin Franklin. If one of the founding fathers of the country was a celebrated Rosicrucian, why wouldn't the symbol of the new nation and its currency reflect that affiliation?

So next time you look at the all-seeing eye in the sky on a dollar bill, remember that there's a similar eye inside a pyramid near Nockamixon State Park. And take the time to wonder what other secrets might be hidden there beneath the rose.

The Pyramids of the Rosy Cross

Pyramid Gardens is a mysterious templelike area in the middle of nowhere that, after years of investigation by frightened high schoolers, turns out to be a Rosicrucian temple. The truth was weirder than what we imagined. The place is actually documented in half a sentence in Time-Life Books' *Mysterious Places.* —*Marko*

I spent about a month researching our local cult, a band of people up in the woods who dress in medieval-looking robes and perform strange rituals at night. Turns out they're a church of Rosicrucians, a Christian mystical sect started in Europe with the Knights Templar and brought to the New World by German immigrants. A band of them have set up shop right in my backyard! Their church and grounds are hidden back in the woods and have a lot of beautiful, if bizarre, buildings on the grounds: a gray stone pagoda, a tiled pyramid that may be a tomb for a founding member, and a utility shed with a giant lightning rod. They have a huge white Greco-Roman temple way back in the woods. I and others have visited the temple a few times. At the summer solstice, they stand around the pyramids in ceremonial robes and chant loudly. I have seen this and was subsequently chased away by these people. They are strange and unfriendly, but not really dangerous. —*Amy McCormick*

I have seen three pyramids around my area, off a small road near Nockamixon State Park. The rumor is that they're for some cult or the KKK. —*Melissa*

The Littlest Church

The Quakers, the Amish, and the Mennonites all flocked to various parts of Pennsylvania to build large congregations of like-minded worshippers. Francisco Cannella had humbler aspirations. Nevertheless, this native of Palermo, Italy, did build his own church in the Keystone State. Since 1928, it has stood at the corner of Marshall and Creek roads on the outskirts of what is now Marsh Creek State Park in Chester County.

Most people drive past it without even knowing it's there. The building is so small that you can walk around the outside in twelve paces. Its thick stone walls mean that the inside is even tinier, probably no more than thirty-five square feet. Except for the blue glass cross on the white door and the tiny cast-iron bell mounted next to the door, it could be a toolshed. Even the church sign is unassuming. Its hand-painted lettering is brief and to the point: the little church.

The origin of this tiny house of worship is a heartwarming tale of the faith and hard work of a poor immigrant. Cannella emigrated alone, leaving his family back in his hometown until he could afford to bring them to America. He vowed that if God would provide him with enough to reunite him with his wife in a new home, he would attend church every day. He worked in a nearby quarry until he earned enough to bring his family across the ocean.

Cannella intended to be as good as his word, but his sincerity was sorely tried by the harsh winters in the area. Snowfall and ice made it hard to trek to the nearest Catholic church, which was in Downingtown, nine miles away. So he did the next best thing: In the corner of the large vineyard that used to skirt Creek Road, he built his own church. It was small and windowless, just large enough on the inside for an altar and a congregation of one or two people. For the next twenty-four years, until his death in 1952, he would go there on any day when he couldn't get to the church in Downingtown.

Cannella's family still owns the property on which the little church stands. It used to be open to the public, until thoughtless people began to trash the place, but sincere visitors are still welcome. The owner of the gas station across the road remembered a wedding there a few years ago. "The couple wanted to run away and get married," she said, "but the bride's mother persuaded her to have a real church wedding. The priest stood inside, and a little circle of family and friends gathered around the door. It was real pretty. Afterward, the mother turned around and said, 'Now you got a weddin' you'll remember.' "

So there you have it. A family reunited. A monument to faith and hope. All topped off with a small, intimate wedding. It's not often that the weird and the heartwarming go hand in hand in this state, so make the most of this story while it lasts. Things can only get weirder from here.

Celestia, God's Own Country

Many people who look at the woods and rolling mountains of this fair state take a deep breath and declare that this is God's own country. But as far as we can determine, the Divine Being only held the deed to six square miles of Pennsylvania, and even then, some of it was repossessed after years of failure to pay taxes. The land in question is located on top of a mountain in Sullivan County, near the county seat of Laporte. It's now mostly overgrown, but in the late 1800s it was known as Celestia, a religious community devoted to true believers of the Second Coming of Christ.

The city of Celestia—once called Celesta—was the vision of a fervently religious Philadelphia papermaker named Peter Armstrong. In the 1840s, he had fallen under the influence of the Millerites, a group of Adventists who believed that the Messiah would return on a particular date in the 1840s. When the Lord failed to make the deadline, many left the faith, but Armstrong was not one of the fainthearted. He held fast to the belief that when a series of prophecies came true, the End of Days would indeed take place.

One of Armstrong's favorite verses was Isaiah 2:2: "And it shall come to pass in the last days that the mountain of the Lord's house shall be established in the top of the mountains." So in 1850, he bought up some land in the Endless Mountains of Pennsylvania and set about assembling the people and materials necessary to create a new Zion.

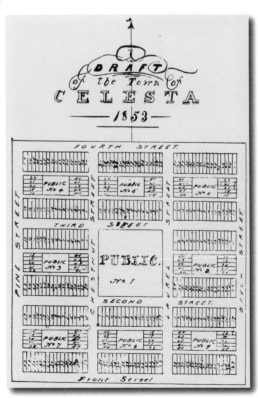

Armstrong filed draft layouts of the town at the county recorder's office in Laporte. The plan's nine-block grid was arranged around a ten-thousand-square-foot block reserved for the temple, where the town's most prominent resident, the Divinity Himself, was to reside. With such a neighbor, Armstrong and his wife, Hannah, insisted that anybody else who came to live there should be sincere in their faith.

Things progressed slowly at Celestia until the Civil War broke out, when something happened that changed the place forever. One member of the community, Brother Charles Russell, was drafted into the Union army. Armstrong saw this encroachment of the world as an

intrusion on the community's faith and promptly wrote a letter to President Lincoln asking that Brother Russell be excused on religious grounds. Lincoln granted the exemption. This gave Armstrong the inspiration to make a bolder request of the government—not only exemption from military duties but also exemption from taxes. He petitioned the House of Representatives to treat the worshippers at Celestia as "peaceable aliens and wilderness exiles from the rest of the Commonwealth of Pennsylvania."

However, it turned out that Armstrong and his wife held the deed to the land in their names, and this self-interest was a stumbling block to the tax exemption. So on June 14, 1864, Peter and Hannah Armstrong registered a deed of conveyance, transferring ownership of the land to the "Creator and God of heaven and earth, and to His heirs in Jesus Messiah, for their proper use and behoof forever."

Once the land was legally God's country, Celestia fell under a veil of silence, and little is known of what happened over the next few years. But the place became the equivalent of Canada during the 1960s—a place where people could avoid the draft and taxes, at least for a while. Unfortunately, the world encroached on Celestia again when Sullivan County tax collectors came knocking. God, they reasoned, may be the landowner, but that didn't grant Him tax exemption. The officials petitioned His representatives at Celestia for back taxes.

Peter Armstrong was struggling to make ends meet at the time and refused to pay. The county was left with one option: repossession. So in 1876, 350 acres of the property were placed on the auctioneer's block at a sheriff's land sale. The property went for $33.72, including $30.10 in back taxes. The buyer was Peter Armstrong's son.

Even with the land back under the control of the Armstrong family, Celestia failed to thrive. In the early 1880s, two other visionaries moved to the town, eroding the authority of the aging Armstrong, and with the twin incentives of tax-free living and freedom from military draft removed, Celestia's population dwindled. The dream vanished completely when, in 1887, Peter Armstrong died in the almost deserted community. In a few short years, the area became a wilderness again.

You can still visit Celestia by driving along Route 42 from Laporte toward Eagles Mere. The land that was once literally God's country is now woods, with a few stone foundations, owned by the Sullivan County Historical Society. Stop by the society's building on Route 42 before your visit—you'll need a map to interpret the remains.

The Lost Hills of Eternal Youth

Interested in holding on to that youthful glow forever? Then you may want to consider looking for a couple of hilltops in Oil Country. The Seneca tribe told of a place that guaranteed eternal youth to whoever saw it. The legend describes the appearance of the place: Through the woods, you can see two adjacent mountaintops. But only a handful of descendants of the Indians know its exact location, and they're not talking.

Naturally, there's a legend behind this mystery site. It concerns a brash Seneca brave, who often boasted about his running skills, and a bizarre Seneca deity called Flying Head. This odd god had a huge fanged head—with wings and a mane that trailed behind it like a kite tail, but no body. Flying Head ate constantly because of a gnawing hunger it could never satiate, since it had no stomach to fill. On hearing the Seneca brave's boasts, Flying Head challenged him to a high-stakes race: Whoever won would kill and eat the loser. Because the odds were in Flying Head's favor, he sweetened the deal by offering to show the brave the secret of eternal youth if the latter won.

The race began, and lasted for many days. By agreement, both rested and slept after the sun set, then began the next leg of the race at sunrise. Sometimes Flying Head was in the lead, sometimes the brave. But as the end of the world approached, it was clear that the brave would win. When he did, the tricky god was prepared to pay the price of failure—but only if the brave picked a weapon that could do the job on the first try. The choices were a dull, rusty blade and a bright, keen dagger. The brave picked the dull blade, which, legend tells us, was the right choice.

Before meeting his fate, Flying Head told the brave to look around. From the end of the world, the brave could see two adjacent mountaintops. Flying Head told his executioner, "As long as you look at this, you will never grow any older. This is the source of youth." Then he was slain. The brave stared for a long time at the mountains, then began his journey home. When he finally arrived at his village, nobody he knew was left there. He had stared at the mountains for generations, never aging.

If this sounds like a fate you'd like, start looking over your shoulder in Allegheny State Park. Some believe the site is in Mercer County near the historic Quaker Bridge. But like eternal youth itself, the precise location is elusive.

The Amish: Just Plain Folks

Why include the Amish in a book about weird things? The Amish are a perfectly normal group of plain-living Anabaptists, speaking a seventeenth-century rural German dialect and driving horse-drawn buggies within striking distance of Three Mile Island. What's so weird about that? They don't behave outrageously. They just peacefully farm their land and want to be left alone. So let's move along, right? There's no story here.

However, there is one weird thing about the Amish: For decades, tourists have driven to Lancaster County to gawk at the men, with their Honest Abe beards, straw hats, and high-water pants. They've stared at the women, with their long form-concealing dresses and old-time bonnets. And they may have watched the movie *Witness* to get some idea of what these people are all about. But despite this exposure, very few outsiders have any idea of what makes the Amish tick. So maybe a few words on the subject are in order.

First, let's dispel a few misapprehensions. The Amish do not all dress and act alike, they don't avoid all technology developed after the eighteenth century, and they never paint quaint circular designs on their barns. They don't even call themselves Amish. But their determination to stay separate from people who don't share their ways opens the door for all kinds of misinterpretations and makes it hard to correct wrongheaded ideas.

The fact is that, unlike many of the German and Swiss immigrants who settled in Pennsylvania (a group called the Pennsylvania Dutch or, more properly, Pennsylvania Deutsch), the Amish are determined to live plain lives. They grew out of a group of German Anabaptists called the Mennonites, who rejected the icons and rituals of the established churches, reasoning that it was the same as worshipping idols and graven images. The Mennonites had been around for about a century when, in the 1690s, a charismatic leader named Jacob Amman began to expand this suspicion of anything decorative from the church into the home and daily life.

Amman preached plain living, not just plain churches. Humility, modesty, and devotion to God were the watchwords of the group. They returned to the New Testament practice of washing one another's feet to

reinforce humility and were avowed pacifists. Being ostentatious was a sign of false pride, so they wore similar plain clothes. Because buttons were often used as decoration, especially on military uniforms, they began to use hook-and-eye fastenings on their coats.

Amman realized that strong beliefs and rigid customs seemed strange to outsiders and that mixing with nonbelievers could erode their way of life. So he imposed a strict set of rules, called the Ordnung, and encouraged his followers to keep to themselves. The idea of being separate led to many regulations. Amman's followers would look different, for one thing. Women's hair would be twisted at the temples and tied back in a bun. Every man's hair would be cut in a Moe Stooge style. Unmarried men would be shaved; married men would grow beards, but mustaches would be forbidden. (Moses had a beard, Jesus had a beard, but the Bible doesn't mention mustaches, so they're out.)

That said, the Amish "uniform" does have a lot of variations—brightly colored shirts and petticoats are not unusual. The size of men's hat brims varies a great deal, and the number and style of the straps in suspenders (Amish men never wear belts) also set them apart. Among young people, who are given some years of leeway in the outside world before settling down, lurid socks and sneakers are common. Many young women wear really outrageous footwear beneath their long skirts. As long as they don't show, flashy clothes are fine.

The focus on humility leads to some strange customs. The Amish finish school in the eighth grade, because too much study leads to swelled heads. Most orders won't hire lawyers for anything. They avoid portraits and photographs and anything self-consciously artistic. Mothers make dolls for their daughters, true, but they are made from scraps and have no faces because of the commandment about graven images and idolatry. Their sole concession to art seems to be the intricate quilts that the women make, and even these are abstract in design and created in groups so that no single person can feel too proud of the results. Quilts are also practical, and they are a good use of scraps of old clothing, which avoids wastefulness. The fact that tourists buy them for $800 apiece is immaterial. Like all farmers, the Amish get whatever they can for their products.

Like any group that's been around for three hundred years, the Amish have different communities with varying customs. Some orders are stricter than others, with different dress codes, behavior, and standards on how far they can push the technological envelope. Many orders of Amish use telephones, ride in cars, and have electricity in their homes. They won't buy cars or tractors, though. Frugal German farmer habits take over here. Horses work the farms, and they produce manure and other horses, both of which a farmer can use. By contrast, motor vehicles are wasteful and dirty. But if their Mennonite cousin or neighbor happens to be driving one into town, the Amish will pay for the gas in exchange for a ride.

The one thing the Amish won't do is hook up to a power grid. Electricity must come from generators, and phone lines are forbidden in homes. That's because of the Amish prime directive to keep separate from unbelievers.

And as with any group that has survived for centuries, the Amish have a way of enforcing their strict rules. It's called shunning, which is an extreme form of excommunication. When a church excommunicates its members, it forbids them from taking communion or attending church. Many Amish hold church ceremonies at home with their neighbors, so their excommunication is more extreme. A transgressor is banished from eating with anyone, talking with anyone, and living in the community. This is much more serious than merely getting the silent treatment from your neighbors.

The Amish don't have insurance policies or Social Security—the community takes care of itself by pitching in with money, time, and effort when the need arises. If you're shunned, you lose all of that. Small wonder, then, that people toe the line and repent quickly when the community feels they've broken the rules.

Amish on the Lam

Not all the Amish are community-building, God-fearing folks. Some of them hang out with motorcycle gangs and get into trouble. In 1998, two Amish men were arrested on drug charges. Abner Stoltzfus, twenty-four, and Abner King Stoltzfus, twenty-three years old and not related, were tried for conspiracy to distribute more than a million dollars' worth of cocaine and methamphetamines they had bought from the Pagan motorcycle gang. The two Stoltzfus boys had apparently been selling speed at Amish hoedowns for years before the bust and had got in over their heads. During their trial, which was covered in the *Washington Post, Time,* and other publications, the Pagan gang came off as the real heavies. One of the Pagans, from a chapter that operated out of nearby Chester County, broke one of the defendants' legs with an ax handle and knocked out the other one's teeth when they failed to toe the line. I don't know about you, but after a run-in like that, I'd certainly reconsider living in a community whose most dire punishment is shunning. Is it any wonder that the Amish reject the outside world?–*RubyWednesday*

Manners Maketh Amman

The Amish are plain folks, alright. Plain speaking, too. Old Order Amish, the really strict sub-sect of the group, seem pretty rude if you're not used to it. They almost never say please or thank you and will just walk off without saying good-bye. It took me a while to realize it was just their way. They consider well-groomed manners a fancy thing, not the plain and simple way they consider the way of righteousness. It can be fun to be really polite or complimentary to them at farmers' markets. They really don't know how to react to it.–*Yoda Leahey*

A Matter of Breeding

One thing that you can't ignore about the Amish and Mennonites is that they are a small population that marries within its community. Over hundreds of years, this inbreeding leads to all kinds of genetic ailments, some of which cripple or kill them in slow and painful ways. One tragic condition that occurs is commonly called maple syrup disease because of the sweet smell of the urine and earwax of its sufferers. A child with this condition reacts very powerfully to normal childhood illnesses, like colds and ear infections. Temperatures spike very high, which causes seizures and brain damage. Almost invariably, a series of minor childhood ailments will lead to severe brain damage, spasticity, and ultimately death.

Another ailment that's rife is a liver defect that causes a chronic jaundice that usually kills sufferers before they reach their mid-teens. It's called Crigler-Najar syndrome, and it can only be held at bay by ultraviolet light treatments for up to 14 hours per day. Many women suffer from a deformed chromosome that leads to a condition called chicken breast disease. The deformed gene hardens and expands the muscle fibers in the chest, making the sufferers barrel-chested.–*Galen8*

Where Do I Sign Up?

If the Amish are weird, I wish everyone in my town were as weird. When someone in the Amish community needs a barn, everyone gets together and builds it. The children really belong to the community and enjoy a great sense of responsibility from joining in with the chores. When an Amish buggy rider gets hit by a speeding car (and it happens all the time on Lancaster highways), their Ordnung takes care of any medical bills that they can't afford to pay for themselves, no questions asked. Everyone chips in something practical to help a sick person's family in time of need. They don't carry insurance, because they don't need it. They have each other as their insurance policy.–*ICL*

Beyond the Pale

Tales of strange people bonded together in self-policing communities are common throughout the States and, indeed, throughout the world. Pennsylvania is no exception. These communities can include anybody out of the ordinary, but a favorite candidate for such campfire scare stories is albinos. There's nothing like a lack of pigmentation to send the overactive imagination into a tailspin. Realistically, pale skin and pale blue or red eyes may be just an anomaly of genetics, but it has become the stuff of some very creepy stories.

If any communities of albinos do exist in the mountains of Pennsylvania, let's inject a sense of civility into the proceedings here. Driving around people's homes at night with the intention of disturbing them is a form of persecution. Let's treat these stories as what they are — good fun — and not a call to single out any group for unpleasant treatment.

Albino Cannibals of Ghost Mountain

Every rural area in the country seems to be inhabited by a reclusive band of albinos. We here in Sellersville, have our own. This particular cannibalistic, child-stealing, rock-salt-shooting, circus-escaping, inbreeding clan of albinos is said to live high up in the woods on Haycock Mountain. They're said to waylay unwary travelers and eat them. They supposedly sometimes raid local farms for livestock and leave gruesome evidence behind. Local police know of their existence and are scared to go up the mountain.

They live in a huge concrete house with no windows and throw firecrackers at passing cars in the middle of the night. They block back roads and perform unspeakable rites on moonlit nights. Sightings of them flitting from tree to tree and being mistaken for errant specters even supposedly gave one local road its name: Ghost Mountain Road.

My own investigations into this have turned up plenty of stories and supposed eyewitness accounts, with some proof in the form of rock-salt residue blasted into the cheap paint jobs of local high schoolers' Camaros. But of the albinos themselves, not a trace. A search of local newspaper archives has revealed a depressing lack of corroborating evidence here. But hey, not all the news gets reported, y'know?
—*Amy McCormick*

Albinos Under Glass

There's a place we call Ghost Mountain
[actually Haycock Mountain], near an old
covered bridge, where local legend has it that
someone had hanged himself. It's also said that if you
turn your car on and off three times, your car will cease to
start. You can really get a sense of bad vibes around that area.
There is a glass house near there where albinos live. The story with
them is that if you dare go on their property, they will chase you away
with a shotgun in hand. A couple of my friends found this out to be true.
—*Melissa*

And a Glass Deck Too

The Albino Glass House . . . is there anywhere you can't find a place dedicated to
caring for criminally insane albinos? I never saw the actual albinos myself, but did see the
house. It's pretty strange. You have to go down a dirt road, and just before you reach a cool
old-timey red-covered bridge, there is a huge gate, a la Beverly Hillbillies mansion, and off the dirt
road behind the gate is an asphalt road which goes up to a large house with an all-glass deck hanging
over the side of a hill. On the way to the place, down the bumpy dirt road, are little doors in the side of a
hill, strange tunnel complexes, hobbit holes, and other freaky stuff. It turns out they are really root cellars, but
who the hell knows what a root cellar is anymore.—*Marko*

Plague of Peculiar People

Who knows whether any of these creatures ever actually walked through the Keystone State? Whether they're based in reality or are just a projection of the collective subconscious, we'll probably never know. And frankly, we don't care that much. They're just terrific tales for a camping trip in the twilight zone.

First up is a tale of misdoings in freakish greasepaint. Let's face it—deep down inside, we all always suspected that clowns were up to no good. Whether it's the frightening wigs, the garish outfits, or the nightmarish face paint, a clown is enough to give the heebie-jeebies to children and adults alike. In 1981, that actually happened as a rash of evil clown sightings swept across the nation.

Round the Horn

If you want skeptics to believe that Pennsylvania was once home to a race of deformed giants (and who doesn't?), you'll need to provide evidence that respected antiquarians can believe in. As luck would have it, three academics back in the 1880s found just such evidence in Sayre, Bradford County. In an ancient burial mound just outside of town, the then state historian of Pennsylvania, Dr. G. P. Donehoo, and two professors—A. B. Skinner of the American Investigating Museum and W. K. Morehead of Phillips Academy in Andover, Massachusetts—uncovered human bones. At least, they looked almost human. But the men to whom these skeletons belonged were seven feet tall, and their skulls were oddly deformed. Above the eyebrows were strange hornlike protuberances sticking out about two inches.

Of course, the best way to prove the existence of prehistoric horned basketball players is to show off their remains in a museum. That's where Donehoo, Skinner, and Morehead failed in their duty as scientists. They lost their evidence after shipping it back to Philadelphia. The bones went missing, apparently stolen, and were never seen again. So for now, all we can do is imagine what creatures may have been practicing dunk shots at the dawn of time. They can't have been any weirder than Dennis Rodman, surely?

Ape Boy of the Chester Swamps

My grandparents were born in Chester in Delaware County more than a hundred years ago. It's one of the oldest towns in Pennsylvania, where William Penn first landed in the country. They were the ones who first told me the legend of the Ape Boy of the Swamps.

The tale went like this: There was an ugly boy who lived in Chester back in the early days. He was tall, thin, gangly, red-headed, and really unspeakably hideous. His peers taunted him so mercilessly that he ran away into the swamps around the Delaware River, not too far from where the Commodore Barrie Bridge now crosses over to Gloucester County, NJ.

The boy was never seen again—at least not as a boy. But he roamed through the swamplands and woods during the War of Independence and the subsequent skirmishes with the British. Gradually, he mutated into a half-ape, half-human creature with thick reddish fur and an appetite for any small mammals or fish or birds he could catch with his bare hands. Think of him as a cross between two movie characters—Gollum from the *Lord of the Rings* and Chewbacca from *Star Wars*—a gross, hairy basketball player that eats its food raw and wiggling. That's the Ape Boy. Oh, and he's also immortal, or at least, he's still being spotted today, some 250 years after he first moved into the swamp.

As towns sprang up, the swamps were drained and the woods cut down. Heavy industry moved in, and the Philadelphia International Airport was built. Each development ate away at Ape Boy's habitat. But there's still one area in the region where animals can run wild—the Tinicum watershed wildlife preserve. Many herons, egrets, and a zillion Canada geese roost there, and according to some, so does Ape Boy. Every so often, you'll hear tales of people boating on the Delaware or fishing at Tinicum, and seeing something covered in matted red-brown fur, scrabbling around in the undergrowth.—*R. Skillman*

Unexplained Phenomena

In a normal world, there are no mysterious lights darting around in the night sky. Fields of wheat and corn grow straight up, and never flatten spontaneously into strange patterns overnight. People do not suddenly explode into flames for no readily apparent reason. And brown mud and red lizards do not fall from the sky. That is how things are in a normal world. Aren't you glad that's not the world we live in?

Twinkle in his eye

If the world of the weird ever adopted a patron saint, the obvious candidate would be Charles Hoy Fort. In the early 1900s, Fort was a journalist, writer, and, some might say, satirist. His main interest was anomalous phenomena—things that were a matter of public record but that scientists of the time could not explain. With true journalistic zeal, he collected tens of thousands of reports from newspapers in the reading rooms of the New York Public Library and the British Museum.

But Fort's real genius was not in merely researching these matters; it was in the humor and wit with which he brought the information to public attention. He seemed to have had a twinkle in his eye when he introduced each nugget of the unexplained, as if challenging the rational world to come up with a good explanation. The humor of Fort's books *The Book of the Damned, Lo,* and *Wild Talents* is often missed, which makes the protestations of the serious skeptics rather amusing.

Here are just a few of Fort's findings for the Commonwealth of Pennsylvania.

On Creatures Falling from the Skies

In a 1924 letter to the *Philadelphia Public Ledger,* Fort appealed for evidence and eyewitness reports to back up a story he had read in the *Ledger*'s July 23, 1866, edition. After a severe storm at Hobdys Mills, Pennsylvania, the ground was scarlet with hundreds of inch-long red lizards that crawled out of sight within two hours, never to be seen again. Strange creatures appeared again in the commonwealth on March 2, 1892. On that wintry morning, residents of Lancaster awoke to find that the surface of the snow blanketing their town was itself blanketed with tiny worms or larvae.

On Mystery Lights in the Sky

In his book *New Lands,* Fort writes of an aurora glowing in the northern area of Pennsylvania that was not visible only a few miles farther north across the state line.

On Mud Falling from the Sky

On April 12, 1902, showers of mud fell from the sky in several locations in Pennsylvania, New York, New Jersey, and Connecticut. The only major geological or meteorological phenomenon reported that day that could have been related was an earthquake in Siberia.

On Spontaneous Human Combustion

In *Wild Talents,* Fort included a *Toronto Globe* report dated January 28, 1907, in which the Pittsburgh home of one Albert Houk was stricken with a mysterious case of human combustion. The body of Houk's wife was discovered on a table "burned to a crisp," with no signs of fire on the table or anywhere else in the house.

Not all of Fort's reports were written up during his lifetime, but fortunately, a band of like-minded colleagues calling themselves the Fortean Society carried on his work. The group was founded while Fort was alive and to this day continues to publish tales of the weird and wonderful—sometimes from Fort's research, sometimes from their own. The *Fortean Times* is the foremost publication of the unusual, but with the advent of the Internet, many more sources are cropping up. And to keep the Fortean camp honest, a contrarian publication called the *Skeptical Inquirer* has arisen. Anytime the Forteans get too gullible, the skeptics step in and poke holes in their arguments.

Here at *Weird Pennsylvania,* we don't take sides. Whether the incidents we report about are real or bogus, we can't say. Somewhere between the credulity of true believers and dismissive responses of the critics lies the truth, and the truth can sometimes be pretty weird.

A Hunka Hunka Burnin'

Imagine walking into a room and being assaulted by the acrid smell of smoke. You look around expecting to see charred ruins on all sides, but the room seems to be mostly intact. But wait! There, in the corner, is a square yard of scorch marks. The floorboards have been burned away, revealing the basement below. As you move closer to the gaping hole, another smell reaches your nose, something foul. You recoil from the smell but move closer, and as you do, you see something else, something horrific. At the end of a charred stump is what's left of a human foot. You have just walked into the site of one of the most dramatic cases of unexplained phenomena: spontaneous human combustion, or SHC.

SHC is a favorite subject of both the fans and the debunkers of unexplained phenomena. It taps into one of the most dreaded human fears: a deadly fire that you can do nothing to prevent. Often SHC victims are almost completely reduced to ashes. The site of the fire is usually very contained. In most cases, the flames spread no more than a few feet from the body, leaving furnishings, paper, and other obviously combustible materials unscathed. It looks as if the victims had suddenly grown unbelievably hot and burned, then, as their bodies vaporized, cooled down before a real fire could take hold.

What would cause a sudden intense fire to consume just the person in a room and leave the rest of the place intact? Fortean analysts have come up with some pretty far-out explanations for these peculiar pyrotechnics. Some of them postulate the existence of a new subatomic particle called a pyrotron, which releases sudden bursts of energy within the human body. It's a nice enough hypothesis, but it falls outside traditional scientific thought.

Skeptics point out that many of the victims are either infirm or alcoholic and smoke, a combination of factors

that can lead to fire accidents. And the classic "stop, drop, and roll" response to burning clothes could contain a fire in a small space, preventing its spread through a room and making its victims burn all the more fiercely. It's possible, the naysayers claim, for falling hot ashes to ignite synthetic-fiber clothes or matchbooks in pockets and cause a more extensive fire. But experienced firefighters sometimes find the so-called rational explanation inadequate. Some pyro-professionals are willing to call such incidents the result of SHC. So why shouldn't the rest of us?

One of the foremost writers on the SHC phenomenon is a native Pennsylvanian: Larry E. Arnold, author of *Ablaze!: The Mysterious Fires of Spontaneous Human Combustion.* He has explored two of the most significant SHC stories, both of which took place in the Keystone State.

The Burning of Dr. John

On December 5, 1966, in Coudersport, Don Gosnell let himself into the house of retired Dr. John Irving Bentley to read his meter. Because the ninety-two-year-old physician had limited mobility, Gosnell, a part-time firefighter, had permission to enter the home to take the readings. He made his way down to the basement, and there he noticed a strange sweet smell. He thought nothing of it until he found a cloud of light blue smoke and a pile of ashes on the dirt floor. Looking up, he saw a hole in the ceiling, revealing the ground-floor bathroom.

Gosnell ran upstairs to investigate and found Dr. Bentley's bedroom filled with smoke. In the bathroom, beside a hole measuring two and a half by four feet burned into the floor, lay the walker that the good doctor needed in order to move about. Beside it lay all that remained of Dr. Bentley—the lower half of his right leg, with the foot intact, still wearing an undamaged slipper.

What could have caused this gruesome scene? Gosnell thought at first that the frail old man might have had a pipe-smoking accident, since his robe was dotted with tiny burn marks from hot tobacco ash. But the doctor's pipe was still on its stand in the bedroom.

Perhaps there was another explanation. There were remnants of a broken water pitcher lying at the scene of the conflagration. Perhaps a small clothing fire had started in the doctor's room and he had gone to the bathroom to douse it but had not made it in time. His pockets were often filled with wooden matches that could have sparked the fatal blaze. As the fire took hold, he might have resorted to a "stop, drop, and roll" in a last-ditch attempt to quell the flames. At that point, his burning clothing could have ignited the linoleum on the bathroom floor, spreading to the hardwood flooring and wooden beams of the basement ceiling. Such a fire

would draw fresh air from the basement to feed the flames, which would keep the fire burning.

Such arguments don't win over the true believers. If the linoleum and floorboards were as combustible as this explanation argues, why did the fire not consume it all? The hole in the floor was not large, and there was plenty of combustible material elsewhere in the small bathroom. Why did that remain unscathed by the fire?

Whatever the actual cause of Dr. Bentley's fatal fire, it remains one of the most celebrated cases in the annals of SHC. And so does the earlier tale of Delaware County resident Helen Conway.

The Flames of Helen

The case of Helen Conway's death by fire in November 1964 is so intriguing that it became the focus of a television documentary filmed by the British Broadcasting Corporation (BBC). But at first glance, the demise of this resident of Upper Darby Township looks more like a case of death by misadventure than of spontaneous combustion.

Mrs. Conway was a firefighter's worst enemy. She was a heavy smoker whose room was dotted with evidence of small cigarette burns. She was known to be somewhat careless. And shortly before her death, her granddaughter had brought her a new book of matches. So . . . case closed, right?

Not necessarily. When the firefighters made their way through the thick smoke on that November morning, they found very little of Mrs. Conway. All that remained was a greasy pile of melted flesh and her two legs intact below the knee, as if she had been sitting down when consumed by the flames. But Fire Chief Paul Haggarty, who was present at the scene, has gone on record saying he believed that this was a case of spontaneous combustion. And his opinion is shared by one of the first volunteer firemen on the scene, Robert Meslin, who later became fire marshal. The key factor in their conclusion is the speed at which the fire took hold.

Larry Arnold's book *Ablaze!* describes Meslin's line of reasoning. Meslin estimated that Mrs. Conway's granddaughter had made the emergency call to the fire department within a few minutes of talking to her grandmother. The call came in around eight-forty a.m., and firemen were on the scene within ten minutes. Conservatively, this would mean that the fire lasted no more than twenty minutes, and some estimates go as low as six minutes. The idea that a fire started by a match could consume a body so completely and so quickly does not sit well with firefighting professionals. The most likely type of fire that a seated woman like Mrs.

The Evening Bulletin
Monday, November 9, 1964

Widow Burns To Death in Drexel Hill

A Drexel Hill widow w
burned to death shortly afte
A.M. yesterday as she sat
chair in her home at 527 A
road.

The victim, Mrs. H
Conway, 51, was pro
dead at the scene by
Shore, Upper Darby. The
police surgeon. The
confined to the s
room in which her
found.

Two of Mrs. Co
children, Stephan
eight, and her b
six, of 2641 A
Havertown, we
weekend with
the house at t

The little
elevision o

Conway would experience from natural causes would be a "wick effect" fire, in which flames melt the body fat, which fuels the fire. According to experiments made by the makers of the BBC television documentary, such a fire would take at least seven hours to consume a human body.

The so-called reasoned analysis by the *Skeptical Inquirer,* the anti-Fortean magazine that appeals to science and reason, pooh-poohs the results of the BBC's approach. If the fire had started at the base of Mrs. Conway's seated body, they say, it would have been more intense and would have consumed the body faster. Perhaps so, but are they seriously suggesting that Mrs. Conway accidentally sat on a lighted match to precipitate that fatal fire? That seems less likely than the existence of a subatomic particle that spontaneously bursts into flames.

Whose side does *Weird Pennsylvania* take in these mysterious cases? We're inclined to sit on the fence and nowhere near any lighted matches.

Pennsylvania Fires Spread to Florida

The most famous case of spontaneous human combustion in the world happened in St. Petersburg, Florida, but it does have a Pennsylvania connection. A 67-year-old widow, Mary Hardy Reeser, turned into ten pounds of ash overnight between July 1 and 2, 1951, leaving her apartment undamaged except for the chair she was sitting on. Her remains, which consisted of one foot, bits of vertebrae, some organ tissue, and a mysteriously shrunken skull, were buried in the Chestnut Hill Cemetery outside Mechanicsburg, Pennsylvania.–*Mal Dooley*

The Bloodstains of Grumblethorpe

Sometimes, trying to quell a revolution puts you in the history books. Sometimes it creates a permanent record of your death on the floor of a house in Germantown. General James Agnew falls into both camps.

In the fall of 1777, this British general, by all reports a dignified and kindly man, was leading his troops up Germantown Avenue when he was shot by a sniper. Mortally wounded, he was carried to the summer home of John Wistar, a place that would later be called Grumblethorpe. Agnew died shortly afterward, but not before his blood became permanently embedded in the parlor floor.

Even now, more than 225 years later, the faded stains of the general's lifeblood are clearly visible. Centuries of scrubbing cannot remove the stains, which became a point of pride with the family. In 1826, when William Wister—the name somehow evolved into this spelling—wanted to marry a Quaker girl named Sarah Logan Fisher, both sets of parents refused to bless the union. William's uncle, Charles, took pity on the couple and offered Grumblethorpe as the venue for a civil wedding. The happy couple exchanged vows in front of a justice of the peace in the bloodstained parlor. Now that's one weird kind of wedding!

Grumblethorpe, however, is not only known for its gruesome memento mori. This historic house has exhibits ranging from a colonial kitchen to a ledger marking the rent paid by a newly arrived Bostonian lad called Ben Franklin. It also has the writing desk where Wistar's descendant Owen Wister wrote *The Virginian.* But let's not deny it—the real draw is the grisly Rorschach blot on the parlor floor.

The Ghostly Handprint at the Carbon County Jail

Every day in the town of Jim Thorpe in Carbon County, a hanged man proclaims his innocence in the only way a dead man can. Since 1877, his hand has been raised in protest in the last home he ever had—Carbon County Jail cell number 17. This permanent marker on the cell wall has resisted cleaning, repainting, and even replastering. A couple of days after every attempt to cover it up, the handprint comes back, and a story of persecution by evil mine owners comes back with it.

The coal barons of the late 1800s were an unscrupulous band who kept the mostly Irish and Welsh workforce squashed firmly under their thumbs. As the miners chipped away at the anthracite deposits in the Pennsylvania mountainsides, they earned only pennies, and the coal barons took the cost of their supplies out of that meager pittance. It was a social situation that often leads to revolution, and the revolutionaries here were the Molly Maguires. This secret society of coal miners committed acts of sabotage and, according to the coal barons, murder (something the management knew plenty about, since they themselves stooped to murder if their profits were threatened). Of course, the plutocrats had money, power, and therefore the law on their side, which made it easier to dispose of troublemakers. In a series of trumped-up trials, the death penalty was routinely handed down, gradually eroding support for the troublesome proto-union.

During one of the Molly Maguire trials, the inhabitant of cell 17 vehemently proclaimed his innocence, but he was sentenced to death anyway. On hanging day, before he was taken from his cell, he slapped his hand, dirty from the cell floor, on the wall and exclaimed, "This is the hand of an innocent man!"

In those days, innocence was no defense, so the prisoner died that day. But his handprint remained and came back even after it was scrubbed off. Over the next century, the cell was cleaned, repainted, and replastered, and always the hand reappeared in a day or so. It's still there to this day and can be seen at the Old Jail Museum, housed in the old Carbon County Jail.

The Ghostly Hand Foils a Camera

The most significant happenings at the Carbon County Prison were the Molly Maguire executions that began in 1877. Seven members of the Molly Maguires, a secret union of coal miners, were convicted of murder and hanged. Most of the men protested their innocence but apparently none more vigorously than the prisoner in cell 17, who placed his hand upon his cell wall and declared that this impression would forever remain there as an enduring sign of his innocence. Sure enough, his handprint can still be seen there to this very day! On the day of my tour, a film crew was trying to do a story on cell #17, but the high-tech camera equipment inexplicably stopped functioning. Try as they might, the camera just would not work. The crew left the jail and decided to try again, with some exterior shots of the building. Voila! As suddenly as the problem had appeared, it was gone. Everything once again functioned perfectly. Were mechanical gremlins at work here, or was something deeper, more ominous, interfering with the equipment? I'll leave that for you to ponder.—*Jeff Bahr*

Crop Carvings
Grain of Truth or Circles of Confusion?

In M. Night Shyamalan's film Signs, strange crop circles begin to appear mysteriously in the fields of a Pennsylvania farm, owned by Mel Gibson in the unlikely role of the farmer. Like most of Shyamalan's films, *Signs* is set within striking distance of suburban Philadelphia, where the director grew up. But the commonwealth has a much longer history of what crop-circle fans like to call UGMs, short for unusual ground markings.

Though many crop circles are pranks, hoaxes, or concept art pieces, not all of them are so easy to explain away. Some of these nocturnal formations register extreme levels of magnetic or nuclear energy that cause headaches, dizziness, or nausea — or, in some cases, bring temporary relief to sufferers of chronic health problems.

So what causes the phenomenon? The Pennsylvania Dutch, who observed crop circles early on, have long attributed them to witches dancing on Walpurgis Night (May 1). In their distinctive German dialect, they call the ceremony Hexen Danz ("witches' dance") and use the term to refer to crop circles as well. Such stories hearken back to the old European concept of fairy rings — dead or discolored circles in grass, or round clusters of mushrooms, all supposedly caused by the fancy footwork of supernatural creatures.

But fairy rings have a clear scientific cause — underground fungal growth. That's not the case with crop circles, which are geometric patterns of bent wheat stalks with "knuckles" at the bend that cannot be attributed to microorganisms.

Naturally, the commonwealth's many UFO enthusiasts show a great interest in UGMs, and their investigations have corroborated (and dismissed) a number of incidents over the past few decades. On May 25, 1992, in a wheat field in Limerick, north of Philly, at least a dozen matted-down areas appeared overnight. One of the areas was T-shaped, and three of them were circles about five feet across, arranged in a triangular configuration. The owner of the land explained that this kind of

Some of these nocturnal formations register extreme levels of magnetic or nuclear energy that cause headaches, dizziness, or nausea . . .

thing happened every year, but UFO investigators suspected a hoax. Soil samples and Geiger counter readings at the site showed no irregularities. However, an investigator from Ursinus College in Collegeville found some interesting facets in the samples from the circles. Wheat and oats from the Limerick site and nearby Linfield showed some irregularities at the growth nodes—the place where leaves and stems branch out. There was some odd cracking and redirection at the nodes that do not occur normally.

But perhaps the most interesting case of crop circles in recent history happened in Linesville, Crawford County. It was there that several sources reported a strange series of events on a forty-acre farm. Early on the morning of July 31, 2000, the Beitz family heard a humming noise, like snoring but without any pauses. They discovered that a formation had appeared in their field, but their video camera suffered ill effects when they tried to capture evidence of it—a fresh battery pack reportedly drained completely when it was taken into the field. Moreover, their compasses would not work there either.

According to a report on the Web site of Lucy Pringle, a British crop-circle expert, Kevin and Trina Beitz were inside the crop formation at their farm for about two hours, and after this, Trina noticed a temporary remission from a debilitating condition she suffers from called fibromyalgia. For several days, the fatigue and the twelve-hour sleep sessions that she normally needed were replaced by increased energy, good spirits, and lessening of her usual chronic pain. Kevin experienced relief of symptoms from a long-standing neck injury, and visiting relatives suffering from migraines and asthma attacks also experienced relief from their conditions.

Whatever caused the Beitz crop configurations, it was clearly not a couple of pranksters. We'll probably never know the cause, but if the results are anything to go by, it was not a malicious entity—which is odd, really, considering that this takes place in *Signs* country. Just goes to show you that you can't believe everything you see in movies.

Unidentified Flying Objects

If movies reflect the attitudes and hopes and dreams we have in real life, then many people are willing to entertain the possibility of extraterrestrial aircraft floating through the earth's atmosphere. Some of the most popular films of our time include UFOs. Just think of *E.T., Close Encounters of the Third Kind,* and *Independence Day.*

But UFOs are more than mere grist for popular fiction. They have also been the subject of a prolonged study by the U.S. Air Force during the cold war. Between 1947 and 1969, Wright-Patterson Air Force Base in Ohio tracked a total of 12,618 reports of strange objects in the sky. Over its twenty-two-year history, Project Blue Book, as the mission was called, explained away most of the objects . . . most, that is, except for 701 cases that remain mysteries to this day. Sixteen of those unsolved cases were from Pennsylvania, spread out over fourteen years in towns across the state:

Case number 1273: June 13, 1952 Middletown

Case number 1351: June 26, 1952 Pottstown

Case number 1409: July 9, 1952 Kutztown

Case number 1494: July 19, 1952 Elkins Park

Case number 1554: July 23, 1952 Pottstown

Case number 1567: July 23, 1952 Altoona

Case number 1938: August 20, 1952 Neffsville

Case number 2085: September 13, 1952 Allentown

Case number 2093: September 14, 1952 Olmsted AFB

Case number 2923: March 2, 1954 [town unnamed]

Case number 4348: August 27, 1956 Juniata

Case number 6089: October 2, 1958 Stroudsburg

Case number 6317: March 26 or 27, 1959 Corsica

Case number 8839: May 26, 1964 Pleasant View

Case number 10739: July 11, 1966 Union

Case number 10798: July 31, 1966 Presque Isle State Park

When the air force dismantled Project Blue Book, it stated that none of the flying objects it had tracked posed any threat to national security and that there was no evidence that any were of extraterrestrial origin. Well, they would say that, wouldn't they?

None of the UFOs that Project Blue Book tracked ever landed in Kecksburg, the epicenter of one of the biggest UFO stories in recent history. What was the mysterious acorn-shaped object that fell from the sky that night in 1965? Read on, and decide for yourself.

The Night the Sky Fell in Kecksburg

Roswell, New Mexico, may have staked its claim as America's mecca for UFO buffs, but the small town of Kecksburg in rural western Pennsylvania has its own claim to the title. Kecksburg may have experienced the crash of an extraterrestrial craft forty years ago and subsequently been part of a long-term government cover-up.

On the night of December 9, 1965, residents of Canada, Michigan, Ohio, and Pennsylvania witnessed what they described as a "fireball" that seemed to be under "intelligent control," streaking through the dark sky. This fiery object, about the size of a Volkswagen Beetle, crashed into a wooded area outside Kecksburg, in Westmoreland County, forty miles from Pittsburgh. Some eyewitness accounts described this object—whatever it was—changing course to avoid mountain ridges and slowing down as if it were gliding. But its impact was still powerful enough to register on a seismograph 320 miles away in Detroit, Michigan.

Nearby residents contacted the state police, who arrived and searched the woods for the crashed object, but not before some locals decided to have a look for themselves. Accounts of the size vary, but these intrepid witnesses agree that they had seen a bronze or gold–colored object that looked like a large metallic acorn. Some said it appeared seamless, as if it were cast as one solid piece of metal, without rivets or welds. The object had a slightly raised lip on its blunt end, encircled by a band that contained writing that looked like ancient Egyptian hieroglyphics. After the state police searched the woods, the U.S. military was contacted. Members of the U.S. Army and Air Force descended upon the scene a few hours later. Some residents said that NASA personnel were also present, but this could not be confirmed.

Crowds of curiosity seekers came to the crash site, determined to have a look at the fallen object after hearing reports on local radio and television stations. Witnesses said they saw a state police fire marshal and a man toting a Geiger counter heading into the woods toward the crash site. Military personnel also arrived at the scene. Armed with heavy equipment, including a flatbed tractor-trailer and a crane, they declared the woods "off limits" and "under quarantine." The site was sealed, and citizens were banned from the area.

Once the military was in place and the crash site secured, they apparently went to work recovering the object. Later that night, some locals saw a military flatbed truck, carrying a large object covered with a tarpaulin, leaving the scene at a high rate of speed.

What was concealed under that tarp? Why did it require a military escort? The air force's official statement concluded that the fireball that had crashed in the woods was a meteorite, but some witnesses reported that other theories seemed a better fit for the metallic

object. Many were convinced it was really a man-made space probe with stable reentry capabilities, or a misfired Nike missile, or perhaps an extraterrestrial craft. Serious consideration was given to the theory that it was a Soviet-made Venus space probe. The Kosmos-96 had failed and reentered the earth's atmosphere that same day, though the Russians stated that their probe had crashed down in northern Canada.

Later on, more outlandish stories came out. One claimed that the object had been transported to the Wright-Patterson Air Force Base, where bizarre bodies were seen soon after. But just because a few unsubstantiated rumors surround this event, let's not discount it altogether. If this truly was a meteor, why hasn't the public seen any photographic evidence or any published studies of such a find? There's nothing to gain from secrecy over a fallen chunk of space rock, and scientific study of such a find could add to our knowledge of the universe. And if it was a man-made object, surely its classified status would have lapsed by now. So the question remains to this day: What kind of object could have crashed into a wooded area in rural Pennsylvania and force those who investigated it into four decades of silence?

Today, almost forty years later, a monument to the acorn-shaped object sits upon a lighted display platform behind the Kecksburg Fire Station. It was made as a prop for an episode of *Unsolved Mysteries* in 1990, and years of exposure to the elements have taken their toll on it. But it can still turn heads and raise questions as people drive by on Route 982 through the small town of Kecksburg.

—*Patrick Wetherby*

Mystery Lights of Hansell Road

Between two cornfields near Buckingham, Bucks County, a gravel track called Hansell Road once led into the woods. For years, drivers would park there at night and switch off their headlights to see a strange set of lights in the distance. One or two sets of lights, sometimes red but more often green, would move around in the woods and occasionally onto the road.

Lights in the woods are nothing extraordinary. It's easy enough to explain them away as flashlights, lightning bugs, or even marsh gas. But the ones near Hansell Road didn't act like lanterns or flashlights. Several witnesses on different occasions saw them move through the woods, sometimes swinging or dipping as if they were being carried, sometimes slithering more smoothly. When they reached the road, most accounts have them either suddenly drop to the ground and form a ball, or rear up into a shape that then made its way swiftly toward the car.

Such behavior is hard to explain away, especially because so few people hang around long enough to see what would happen next.

Sadly, the march of progress seems to be closing the book on the Hansell Road lights. In the late 1990s, Buckingham Township widened and paved the road to accommodate new housing developments. The woods have been thinned out, and in 2000, the township opened a park at the edge of the woods. If, as the stories go, the mystery lights appear only when everything is still and all the lights are out, they won't appear often anymore. Although the park closes at dusk, there's plenty of suburban traffic along the roadside on dark summer nights, and the houses nearby cast a glow over the road until the wee hours of the morning. We can only hope that the Hansell Road lights won't fall victim to suburban sprawl.

The Red Eyes of Hansell Road

I am well able to take care of myself and am not generally afraid of anything or anyone! Maybe sharks and God, but that's it! That all changed one dark September night.

I was working in Newtown, Bucks County, and had made friendships with some co-workers. We heard some of the younger employees talking about a road in nearby Buckingham called Hansell Road. You were supposed to go there and park along the road, which was long and dark and only had a few houses that sat far off the road. After you parked and waited for a while, you would see green mists appear and cross the road, followed by a "darker" or "black shadowy" entity. These are said to be the spirits of some youths who were murdered by an evil landowner for trespassing on his property.

So one night in early September, four friends and I took a ride to Hansell Road. It was very dark and cloudy, with no moon to be seen. The road ascended on a slight incline and had large cornfields on either side for about a quarter mile. Dark woods loomed ahead and grew along the whole rest of the road on either side. The trees were old and grew over the gravel road like a dark canopy. We parked the car on the grass shoulder on the right, about fifty feet from the tree line. We sat there on the car hood and waited for about twenty minutes before I got antsy and strolled up the road. What happened next I will never forget for as long as I live.

The rest of the gang (one guy and three ladies) were sitting or leaning on the front of the car. I was walking up the road slowly and was about fifty feet from them in the wooded section of the road, when a red glowing orb began coming out of the woods from the left side of the road. It was small and bobbing slightly up and down and was about fifty feet ahead of me, so about a hundred feet more or less from them. It was bright enough that they could see it from the car. The girls started yelling, "What the hell is that?" I shushed them and watched as it neared the road, as if it were going to cross the road from left to right.

Then when it exited the woods onto the road, it became two red glowing orbs that floated about six feet from the ground. They bobbed until they stopped directly in front of me, then just stayed there stationary. The hairs on the back of my neck stood up.

The girls were yelling for me to come back, and my buddy was asking what the hell it was. Now, bear this in mind: We were not drinking, smoking, or doing any kind of drugs or taking medication. The sky was overcast, and it was extremely dark under the tree-lined road. There were no lights at all, anywhere. So the deer-eye-reflection theory doesn't hold up, and besides, I never saw an animal with bright red eyes.

I took two steps forward, and the "eyes" started to move off the road into the woods, then disappeared. I heard no foot or hoof on the gravel road or in the woods.

I swear this account is true and that it happened exactly as described.—*Jim Bechtel*

Getting a Green Light on Hansell Road

I've never seen the Hansell Road lights myself, but a trusted friend of mine has. They parked next to a field facing the woods, turned off the lights, and waited, telling each other scary stories. Then a green light made its way through the woods smoothly, like a flashlight across the surface of water. It's hard to imagine what could cause that slithering motion in a wood, but not as hard as figuring out what happened next. At the edge of the road, the light kind of stood up in the shape of a large cylinder about the size of a man and began to make its way up the road. What happened next nobody knows because the driver slammed the car into reverse and got out of there. I don't think anybody in the car had any problem with his decision!—*OctoberTree*

Scared Witless on Hansell Road

I moved from Connecticut to Bucks County, when I was a sophomore in high school. Initially, I found this place to be a bit on the boring side, but I soon came to be fascinated by the stories many of my classmates would tell me about an extremely haunted place known as Hansell Road.

There are a few different tales that explain why the road is haunted. Most people say that the road was the site of at least one gruesome murder. There was a patch of woods along the road; you were supposed to park your car at the edge of it and turn off your engine and lights. From there, a strange light would emerge from the woods and approach you. This was the ghost of Hansell Road. Many believe that the ghost on Hansell Road is that of a slave. I've heard that he was captured and killed on the road after trying to escape from his master.

For a long time, I brushed off the stories as mere folklore. I didn't believe in ghosts at all, let alone one right in my own backyard. Then one cold fall night about eight years ago, I was proven very, very wrong.

My friend Derek was a couple years older than me, which meant he got his license and would drive me around pretty much every weekend night. This increased mobility also allowed us to pick up girls and ride around with them. But when you're living in Bucks County, you run out of places to take said girls pretty quickly. So even though we thought the stories of Hansell Road were a bunch of bull, we often found ourselves out there. Because it was someplace to go, not to mention we quickly realized that scaring the girls meant they would cling to us and all that good stuff.

The first few times we were out there, we didn't see anything unusual. We got to scare the girls with some hokey stories, we'd act like brave little big shots, they'd cuddle up to us, and we'd be on our way—mission accomplished. The fifth time we pulled this stunt, though, we didn't look like big shots at all. Instead we looked like a couple of scared little kids, which is exactly what we were.

Well, on this particular night, we had our car parked by the border of the woods. Derek was in the front seat scaring his girl, and I was in the backseat scaring mine. After a few minutes of telling stories about runaway slaves and whatnot, I noticed that

she was really scared—I mean, totally spooked. At first, I thought my stories were doing the trick once again; then I turned my head and realized that I was in a bit too deep for my own good.

Hovering in the trees was a green glowing light. I shouted just about at the same moment everyone else in the car started to freak out as well. The light reached the edge of the road when it did something totally unbelievable: It dropped out of the treetops and landed in the road, as if someone had dumped a bucket of the stuff. It was rolling around on the road haphazardly for a moment. Then, much to our terror, it seemed to stand up—it wasn't in the shape of a man, but it was about the height of one—and began heading in the direction of the car. It was a pale green light but definitely had a form and was moving.

Derek had already started the engine and was in the beginning stages of a K-turn. The light was still coming at us, slowly but very clearly intentionally. Derek gunned the engine, and we left the thing in the dust.

Derek and I were screaming worse than the girls, and needless to say, we didn't look brave or heroic that night. For a long time, I avoided Hansell Road. Other friends of mine would head there looking for adventure, and I became known as a bit of a square for warning them that they were tampering with forces beyond their control.

These days, Hansell Road is a lot different. Developers have moved in on the area, and there are now houses along the road, especially at the entrance. It has been paved over, so it's no longer a cracked, pothole-ridden dirt road. But still, when I go down that road, I can feel the presence of that glowing green whatever-it-was we encountered there many years ago.
—*Jeff Salerno*

Mud from Above in Paradise

Back in 1998, Paradise Township in York County fell victim to a mysterious deposit that fell from the skies, and to this day, nobody knows what it's all about. It happened only once, and it happened only at Rose Snell's house.

Mrs. Snell was returning home one dark Sunday evening in January. Walking up to her house in the dim light, she found something the color of mud splashed on her side door. She dismissed the deposit as the remnant of a mud fight between her teenage son, Marc, and his friends and called him to task.

Marc protested his innocence, saying he'd come back an hour earlier and found similar stains on his car. He tried to clean them up with cleaning fluid, but the waxy brown splashes proved very difficult to remove. Mrs. Snell called the police to investigate what she now took to be an act of vandalism. When an officer of the Northern York County Regional Police illuminated the scene with his industrial-strength flashlight, everybody was shocked at the sight.

The brown splashes covered everything on Mrs. Snell's property—all the walls of the house, the roof, and the driveway and everything on it. The pattern of the splashes hinted that the substance had fallen from the sky, and the Snells feared that it was the obvious type of brown substance that falls from the sky out of an airplane restroom. But it wasn't. Leaking pipes in an airplane would spread any substance wider, and it would be frozen in blocks of blue-colored water. This substance, however, was uniformly brown, odorless, waxy or pasty, and not gritty or offensive in any way except for the fact that it covered the Snells' property.

Also, the deposit was spattered over a very small area. When the investigating officer checked the neighbors' homes, nothing out of the ordinary was found. So the matter was turned over to insurance adjusters. They found that pigment from the material had stained the house in places, but could not identify the goop itself or come up with a good hypothesis about its origin. According to a report in the following week's *York Daily Record*, Rose Snell had only one solution for finding the answer: "I think we should call Scully and Mulder," she said. Seems that the daring duo of *The X-Files* are the only ones who can solve this mystery.

This lady must know exactly how Mrs. Snell felt.

Bizarre Beasts

What makes a creature weird? Is it that it's so rare that only a few people have ever seen it? Or that it doesn't look or act like anything we're familiar with? If so, the world is filled with weird creatures. Once upon a time, the kangaroo, crocodile, gorilla, platypus, and rhinoceros were such unbelievably exotic creatures that the folks in Europe were reluctant to believe they existed at all.

Even now, when time and science have broadened our horizons, many people can't believe that unknown species could forage through our state. They dismiss the reports of hairy bipeds in the woods, enormous birds overhead, and underwater monsters in Pennsylvania's deep lakes as nothing more than tall tales.

But there's another possibility. These strange sightings could be the first evidence of animals that may one day become commonplace in zoos and in *Animal Planet* documentaries. But until hard evidence of bizarre beasts comes our way—something that scientists at UPenn or Carnegie Mellon can label with a genus—these tales will remain a guilty pleasure. Guilty because part of us wants to believe but part of us can't quite buy into it. And a pleasure because nothing's better than hiking through the woods in one of Pennsy's vast national parks and imagining that each rustle in the undergrowth is from Bigfoot and every breeze overhead is the flapping of a giant thunderbird's wings.

Bigfoot Stalks the Keystone State

Since the mid-1800s, Pennsylvania has been awash with sightings of hairy apelike creatures lumbering around leaving huge footprints. Although the beast almost always gives off a nauseating smell that, one would think, would put off most observers, the fascination with this deodorant-challenged creature remains, and new reports keep surfacing.

The longest series of encounters with a Bigfoot in Pennsylvania is described by author Jan Klement in his short 1976 book *The Creature: Personal Experiences with Bigfoot.* Starting in the summer of 1972, Klement's cabin in the southwestern part of the state was visited many times by a seven-foot-tall creature that was neither ape nor man. Klement affectionately called him Kong and befriended him by giving him apples. The creature's short brown hair covered his whole body, including most of his expressive face. His arms were long, but did not reach below the knees, and his feet were slightly larger than a man's—about thirteen inches long. Klement met the creature frequently over the space of four months, until he found him dead in January 1973 and buried him in the woods near his property. However, he was never able to find the burial place again.

The case for the existence of a big biped in the woods wasn't helped by one piece of news in 2002. It was then that Ray L. Wallace died. Wallace's employees had been the first to uncover physical evidence of a Bigfoot—some tracks at a building site near Eureka, California, back in 1958. After his death, Wallace's family revealed that he had rigged all the "evidence" as a prank. It would seem that this news item would put a lid on the whole Bigfoot phenomenon. And yet the reports keep coming in, albeit the creature itself remains elusive.

You would think a biped more than seven feet tall would leave some evidence behind, including its skeletal remains. But nothing like this has ever come to light. *Weird Pennsylvania* spoke with a hunter who claims to have seen Bigfoot. (This man declined to give his name, as Bigfoot spotters often do. They are worried that their reputations will suffer if they're known to have seen strange hairy creatures lurking in the dark.) We asked our informant how he thought such a creature could evade detection.

"It's obvious, really," he said. "These are really smart creatures. They keep out of the way because they don't trust humans, and I don't blame them for that. I know enough guys who'd put a hole in one just for fame and money."

That sounds reasonable enough, but why have no Bigfoot remains come to light?

"They must be socially organized enough to bury their dead," he said. "Or maybe they live underground and know enough to crawl back there to die."

But even if an individual Bigfoot goes underground to die, the tales of the creature live on.

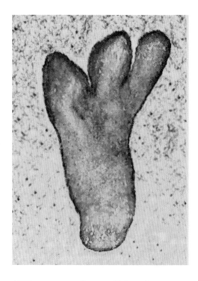

Klement's cabin in the southwestern part of the state was visited many times by a seven-foot-tall creature that was neither ape nor man.

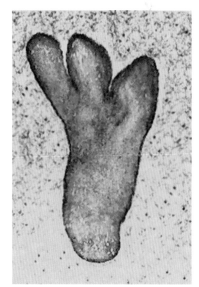

Appalachian Bigfoot Lacks Underarm Charm

Draw 30-mile lines from Harrisburg, Sunbury, and Pottsville, and the lines will intersect at the Appalachian Trail. It's around there that I saw—and smelled—a tall hairy creature in the woods. We were hiking, and at the end of the day, we'd pitch pup tents, eat dry food, and go to sleep. Well, like all hikers, we needed to go out into the woods alone sometimes to answer nature's call. One time, as I was standing there behind a tree, I heard a loud rustling in the trees around me. A really sickening smell wafted my way; it smelled like latrines and stale sweat and something left dead for a week in the summer sun. I could barely control my gag reflex. The rustling came closer, and I hurried to finish up so I could hightail it out of there. I never got a clear view of whatever it was, but through the branches, I saw the outline of something very tall. Its head was covered with black hair, and it either wore dark clothes or had dark fur. I can't swear it was fur, though I'd like to, because I didn't get a good look. How tall was it? I'm a bad judge of that, but it seemed taller than most people I know. My friends thought I had just spotted a big bearded hiker who'd been at it for a while; after all, we were all pretty ripe-smelling after a week's hiking. But this was different. I know it was.—*Fred Nicholas*

Kong Counterpoint

Jan Klement's book *The Creature* is tough to believe. It's a great story, full of interesting detail, and that's part of the problem. It's a little too good to be true. The obvious objections are dealt with quickly. Kong shied away from metal objects, cameras, and anybody except Klement, so there's no pictorial evidence or other witnesses. The story ended neatly, with Kong dying and being buried, but a little too conveniently: Klement couldn't find the burial spot when he returned there later. The book leaves us thinking that Kong had been dug up—a nice little cliff-hanger. Then there's the author himself: Klement describes himself as an earth sciences professor, but like Watergate's Deep Throat, nobody knows who he is. Nobody by that name taught anywhere in that part of the state. Maybe he used a pseudonym to protect his reputation, but thirty years later, the silence goes on. According to the most recent biographies, he too has died. So why is he still anonymous?—*Also anonymous*

I Used to Tell Werewolf Stories . . .

Back in the early 1970s, there were rumors of werewolves in the mountains of Adams County. Every so often when we went up Mount Holly we'd run into somebody retelling the tales, sometimes saying that they'd just met someone who had seen one, sometimes saying that they'd seen one themselves. Naturally, we thought they were just telling the adult version of campfire ghost stories to scare the townies who were up for a week's trout fishing. The place was always packed with teens, especially up at Hammonds Rock, where they held parties nearly every weekend. One year, we were going up to one of the parties (going to it, so we were stone-cold sober) when a huge hairy creature leaped out in front of our car. I want to call it "he," though who knows what species it was, let alone what gender. Anyway, he was bigger than a man and more upright than an ape, and jumped across the road in a couple of leaps. That night, we were the ones telling the werewolf stories, and I bet nobody believed us. —*SkyWalker*

But I'm All Right No-ooooooooow

I've hunted deer throughout Indiana County, and I've never seen any Bigfeet or wild apes or anything. But I have heard something pretty strange. I was deer hunting when I heard a big rustling in the brush. The noise stopped awhile, and I started to line up my sights in case it was something that was in season. I waited quietly for something to happen; then I heard something else way off to my left—a quick glance told me it was a good-sized buck coming out onto the trail. I swung around too fast and made a noise that spooked the buck. It took off, and that must have spooked whatever it was I'd heard before, because there was an almighty ruckus in those bushes and the most terrifying scream I'd ever heard. I never saw what it was, but I've never heard any animal in the woods scream like that before or since.—*Mick L.*

An Interview with a Bigfoot Hunter

Several members of the *Weird Pennsylvania* research team have seen large hairy creatures wandering the hiking trails and byways of our great state, and some of these creatures grunted and smelled pretty bad. Unfortunately, all of them were definitely human.

So where could we turn for the definitive word on Bigfoot's comings and goings? Where else but the Pennsylvania Bigfoot Society, which has been collecting evidence of sightings since 1999. The society's director, Eric Altman, was kind enough to answer our questions.

People use the terms Bigfoot, Sasquatch, and Yeti interchangeably. Are they the same thing?
Eric Altman: They may be the same species, but the terms have just been lumped together. Yeti is the name the Sherpa gave to a creature in the high mountainous terrain of the Himalayas, as well as in the dense jungle forests in the valleys. It seems to be a more violent type of animal. Sasquatch is one of many different names that Indian tribes call the animal. The term Bigfoot was first introduced to modern pop culture in the late 1950s by the *Humboldt Times* newspaper, after road construction workers in the High Sierras of California discovered large humanlike footprints around the heavy machinery. Jerry Crew and the other construction workers who found the footprints made plaster casts and presented them to the media. The *Humboldt Times* called the animal responsible for the footprints Bigfoot, and it stuck.

Isn't Pennsylvania way up there in the number of Bigfoot sightings?
Eric: Pennsylvania has the greatest number of collected reported sightings. That could be due to several factors. During the early 1970s, particularly 1973 and 1974, a slew of sightings occurred across Pennsylvania. Bigfoot/UFO researcher Stan Gordon and his organization investigated over three hundred cases. Stan and an independent Bigfoot researcher, Paul Johnson, have collected hundreds of reports. The Pennsylvania Bigfoot Society has collected over a hundred reports.

The most interesting one I investigated occurred from June to August 2003 in central Pennsylvania. A farmhouse near Dubois was visited almost nightly for two months. An unknown animal would scream and crash through the woods and leave foul odors in the air. Farm animals disappeared, a burn barrel was destroyed, and several fish vanished from the pond. When we showed up to investigate and hang game cameras—motion-detector cameras with an infrared beam that takes pictures whenever anything trips the beam—the activity quit. However, I witnessed the odd behavior of the family dogs as nighttime approached. They would whine, cry, and act very scared as the woods got dark.

What kind of equipment do you use for your investigations?
Eric: All kinds. We have audio equipment with parabolic microphones, shotgun microphones, digital recorders, twelve-hour recorders. We broadcast predator calls, supposed Bigfoot calls, primate calls from apes to see if they attract anything. We have 35-mm cameras, digital cameras, infrared cameras, Night Owl Optics equipment, and game cameras.

Have you ever seen Bigfoot yourself?
Eric: No, I have not. I hope I will someday, but I have better odds of winning the lottery. Some longtime researchers have not. But several members of our organization joined because of having a sighting and want to learn more about what they saw.

What common themes emerge in the reports you get of Bigfoot sightings?

Eric: Not every report is the same. Some include odors, while others don't. Some include animal vocalizations, others don't. The most typical information shared by most reports is the description of the animal: usually standing between four and twelve feet tall, weight usually estimated between three hundred and eight hundred pounds. The animal is almost always described as walking on two legs, with hair covering most of its body, about three to four inches in length. The hair color is most typically described as brown, dark brown, reddish brown. Some of the reports indicate facial features closely resembling those of humans.

We don't have live animals or fossil records or bone remains of a dead Bigfoot to categorize a species or even more than one species of Bigfoot. Except for eyewitness accounts, what evidence do we have?

Eric: The only thing I can point you toward are the casts taken of footprints. There have been three-, four-, and five-toed footprints collected. Forensics specialist Jimmy Chilcutt from Texas has studied footprint casts that show dermal ridges. Humans have dermal ridges. They are found on your hands, fingers, feet, and toes. The dermal ridges Jimmy has studied have convinced him that these animals do indeed exist. If someone were to have faked them, they would have to have extensive knowledge of human anatomy. Also Dr. Jeff Meldrum, associate professor at Idaho State University, has several of these casts in his possession.

Some people say that Bigfoot isn't a matter of belief—if you look at the evidence, the conclusion is obvious.

Eric: I agree with that.

So what Bigfoot evidence convinces you?

Eric: There are several things that convince me—hair samples that come back with DNA matching no known animal, footprints with dermal ridges found all across the country. But to me the most compelling evidence is the thousands of sightings reported by people from all walks of life—from doctors, lawyers, police officers . . . from blue-collar workers to white-collar workers. People from all backgrounds have reported seeing these animals. I do not believe that all these people are lying or making it up. If just one report is true, then these animals do indeed exist.

I'm going to play devil's advocate here. We're talking about a creature seven or eight feet tall. How come it's been so successful at evading detection and capture?

Eric: Well, people say they have a more acute sense of smell and eyesight than we do. They see us coming, and they get out of there. Also, they're generally brown in color, which is a natural camouflage. You could probably step past one and never know it was there.

What advice do you have for people who are interested in investigating Bigfoot for themselves?

Eric (laughing): I warn everybody who's interested and writes in. I tell them, "Run away now! Run away, and don't look back," because once you get hooked on it, you have to get the answer. No matter how long it takes, you've got to know.

So that's the expert's opinion. Alternatively, you could visit www.pabigfootsociety.com and run the risk of getting hooked. But don't say you weren't given fair warning.

Monsters of the Deep

Probably the most famous legendary animals live in the water. Tales of the kraken, the Loch Ness monster, mermaids, and other creatures of the deep fire the imagination, and overzealous fishermen stoke that fire with their tales of the ones that got away.

Pennsylvania has its share of watery weirdness, from the deep lakes and rivers of the eastern mountainous region to the shores of Lake Erie. Here are a few stories that have risen to the surface.

It Came from Lake Erie

Only a small portion of Lake Erie borders Pennsylvania, but it's a mighty big lake with some mighty big tales attached to it. Without a doubt, the most famous concern South Bay Bessie, a serpentlike fish that's seen most often from the Ohio shores. Most people who live or spend a lot of time at the lake have seen something that they can't quite identify, and the details of the sightings seem to be fairly consistent.

South Bay Bessie is cigar-shaped, measuring about twenty to thirty feet in length and two feet in diameter. The creature is dark in color—maybe black, blue, brown, or green—and it's seen in calm waters, sometimes showing humps above the water. It has been reported dozens of times since the first recorded encounter in 1960.

That said, most sightings of this sea serpent can easily be explained away by a quick study of the lake sturgeon, a fish that was very common in the region until dam-building projects in the 1850s interfered with its spawning grounds and supposedly destroyed the population (or maybe just dramatically reduced it). The lake sturgeon has bony plates on its back and belly and four barbels dangling from its lower jaw, and it grows up to four feet in length and reaches a weight of up to two hundred pounds. It's a much larger fish than most people are used to seeing, and it has a bizarre prehistoric look to it.

Whether Bessie is a strange lake monster or something already known, it's Lake Erie's most famous bizarre beast. But it's not the only freak show in those chilly waters.

Face to Face with the Monster of Lake Erie

I have a boat on Lake Erie, and I can tell you that there is a monster in that lake called Bessie. Many people have seen it over the years, and I am one of those people.

I am a fishing fanatic. I've got an 18-foot Boston Whaler that some friends and I use constantly in the summers. Two summers ago I was out on the lake more than usual.

In early July, I was having one of those nights where I was just cruising the lake. I anchored the boat a few hundred yards offshore and was just lying on my back.

This particular night, I was awakened from my slumber by something rubbing against the bottom of the boat. I immediately heard a noise that I find hard to describe. It was the rushing of water followed by the slap of something against the surface of the lake. I sprang up and grabbed the lantern, which I always left burning in the bow of the boat so that no other vessels would plow into me at night. Then I lunged to the gunwale and held the light over the water to have a look. What I saw I will never forget.

Before I go any further, let me say that I was not drunk when I saw what I saw.

I am sure what I am about to describe is in no way the product of any alcohol-induced hallucination.

There was a long, thick creature a few feet beneath the hull of my boat. All exaggeration aside, this thing was at LEAST twenty feet long. It darted with incredible speed away from my skiff as I struggled to make out its form beneath the inky black surface of the water. When it was about 30 feet away from my vessel, the beast reared its body up out of the lake. Although it was still dark out, it was a clear night with a full moon shining down on the still surface of the lake. Because of this fact, I was able to clearly make out the long serpentine body of the animal and its large, round head. That was all I saw before it submerged again and disappeared forever.

There is no doubt in my mind that that thing intentionally slammed into my boat. The first instinct I had when I saw it was that I had invaded its territory and it was letting me know. Perhaps like a common eel, it had been attracted to the glow of my lantern. I cannot say for sure, but that was the last night I ever spent alone on Lake Erie. I've only gone fishing at night a few times in the past two years and never by myself.

Thankfully, since then my life has returned, more or less, to normal. I've remarried, see my kid often, and have a new job, much better than the one I was so worried about back then. When I think back to that summer, the only really terrifying aspect of it I haven't managed to reckon with is the mystery of what I saw that night.—*Franklin P. Wainwright*

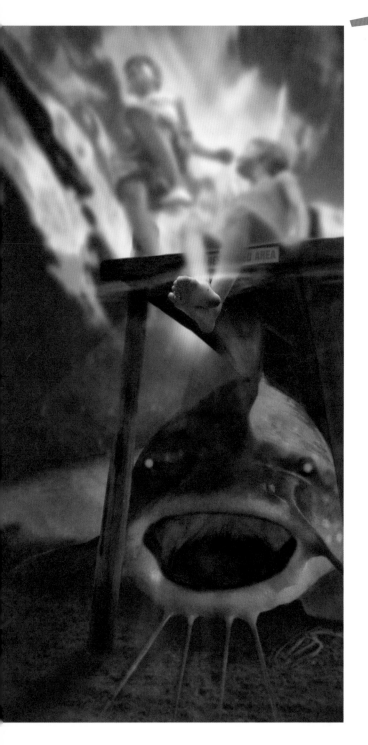

The Giant Ogua of the Monongahela

Since the earliest settlement along the Monongahela River, legends of the mighty Ogua have been whispered from generation to generation. Native Americans told one another of the beast, and early European settlers sent letters back to the old country describing some monstrous amphibians they had killed. No evidence of their kills remains, perhaps because the creature apparently grows to twenty feet in length and weighs five hundred pounds dripping wet. Those early settlers would be hard-pressed to build a fireplace mantel large enough to hang a creature that size above it.

At any rate, they said that the Ogua lurks in the waters until some unwary deer comes by for refreshment, whereupon it lashes the deer with its tail and drags it underwater. Once the prey is drowned, the Ogua swiftly consumes it.

Some people believe that Ogua stories are a primitive public-safety announcement dreamed up to scare children away from the more dangerous parts of the river, where they were more likely to fall in and drown. The tales could pertain to another river monster that supposedly swims in the waters of western Pennsylvania—namely the giant catfish. Stories of huge ugly fish ten to twenty-five feet long in the Monongahela, Allegheny, and Ohio rivers are quite common. These beasts are much larger than the largest catfish measured so far, which top out at around five and a half feet and a hundred pounds. The tales go on to say that a creature as big as the giant catfish could easily swallow a diver—and therefore, of course, that's exactly what these monsters do.

There are some elements of familiar urban legends in these catfish stories, not least of which is that they've never been caught or photographed. However, there are enough firsthand accounts of giant river leviathans to keep the stories fresh. And if you had ever seen the Monongahela in the 1970s, you could just about believe there was something mixed into the water that could mutate your average catfish into a triple-sized diver-swallowing cryptid (that's the scientific term for a bizarre beast)—if you'd read enough of the right kinds of comic books, that is.

Pittsburgh's Alligator Population

Stories of giant sewer alligators abound in many cities, especially New York, and they're universally dismissed as urban legends. However, there are a few verified reports of what the U.S. Geological Survey calls nonindigenous aquatic species, including a 1935 sighting of an alligator escaping a New York sewer. The USGS lists no Pennsylvania sightings in its database.

Nevertheless, reports have been flying about since 1927 of *Alligator mississippiensis* in the western part of the state. Cryptozoologist Loren Coleman obtained an old newspaper report from September 28, 1927, in which a highway worker wrastled a yard-long alligator below Royal Street on the north side of town. Nobody could account for its being there, but the worker in question displayed the three-foot reptile in his home. Yikes!

In 2002, two reports of alligators appeared within a couple of days in the *Beaver County Times.* On August 2, *Times* staffer Bob Janis wrote about three fishermen who had spotted a prehistoric-looking reptile swimming around in the Beaver River. It ate their bait and bit through their lines four times before they finally landed him in a net. Like Steve Irwin, the Crocodile Hunter, they bound its mouth for their own protection and then took it to their favorite bait shop. It turned out to be a rather skinny alligator just short of three feet long that an expert at the Pittsburgh Zoo estimated was two years old. Two days later, Janis reported a second gator sighting by several reliable witnesses in Beaver River, just below the Townsend Dam at Big Rock Park in New Brighton. This one, however, got away.

Gators aren't indigenous to the northern states. Unlike some of Pennsylvania's big cats, they never roamed in the state before they were brought here by humans. And right there is a big clue as to where these specimens came from. Pennsylvania has not forbidden the public from keeping gators, so they're traded at pet shops and swap meets. But only people who don't know anything about these critters buy them. At first, they seem like cute little lizards, though maybe a bit nippy. But after five or six years, they can be more than ten feet long and eat a hundred pounds of meat at a sitting, so it's not surprising that they turn up periodically in the wild after they get to be too big to live in a suburban bathtub.

Too bad Pennsylvanians haven't mastered the New Orleans art of turning the big monsters into a Cajun sausage. Gator sausage is a little fishy-tasting for some gourmets, but experts agree that it's better to bite into one of them than have it be the other way around.

Fish Stories from "Down There"

When I was a kid, I heard some stories about Harveys Lake north of Wilkes Barre. Some scuba divers went down and said they would never do it again. There were supposed to be fish with razor-sharp teeth down there and some kind of huge monster at the bottom. The man who owned the diving school there, Tommy O'Brien, used to mock the idea. He'd say things like "Whenever I see a big cloud of mud down there, I know it's a lake trout, and the biggest I ever saw was a four-footer." Tommy taught scuba around there for more than thirty years—if he didn't see anything, there was nothing to see.—*CousteauX*

The Ones That Got Away

I remember some Susquehanna River fish stories from Exeter Township in Luzerne County. Some old fellow in town said he caught something that was half lizard, half fish. It had razor teeth that bit clean through the line, so it kept getting away. I don't know whether to believe him or not.

But one guy I did believe was a diver I saw but didn't actually know. I was hiking around Blue Heron Lake (Pike County) when he came out of the water faster than butter off a hot knife. His eyes were wide open, and he looked terrified. He said to his buddies, "Let me outta here—that was the biggest catfish I've ever seen."

This was a few years back, but I remember it clearly because the man was terrified and I thought it was weird to be that scared of a fish.—*Legsmith*

Bizarre Beast of Helltown

About 12 years ago, three friends and I were driving around about 12:30 at night in an area I know as Helltown, in a farm area in Westmoreland County, near Irwin. We were driving down a bumpy and rutted road with woods on the left and a fenced-in pasture on the right. A few hundred feet ahead of the car, we caught a glimpse of something in the headlights as it crossed the road. My friend put the car in reverse to see what it was. The headlights hit it just as it was approaching the woods. It was walking on four legs and was about the size of a cow, but much thinner. It was entirely black, with white near its feet. As it neared the tree line, it stood on two feet and proceeded to walk into the woods, just as a person would. On two legs, I would estimate it to be seven feet tall.

The next afternoon, some of us returned to the same spot. All of the trees were shredded from about six feet down to the ground, and there were heavy footprints embedded in the damp ground.—*Susan Wallace*

Alien Big Cats

We all know that cougars and other feral cats are indigenous to the Americas, but scientists tell us that the last of the wildcats in Pennsylvania died out in the mid-1800s. The Pennsylvania Game Commission maintains that there are no wild cougars or other big cats in the state. That's what makes the people who research weird animals call these felines ABCs—alien big cats.

They're not going X-Files about the matter; they don't mean that the cats are extraterrestrial. But if the cougars or leopards weren't born here, they're clearly the animal kingdom's equivalent of resident aliens. And they've been seen across the state off and on since the 1940s.

In his 1996 book, *Strange Encounters,* Curt Sutherly describes two feline encounters from the 1980s. In 1983, a Dauphin County woman who lived at the base of the Blue Mountains was searching her eighty-three-acre property for hemlock seedlings when a large dark cat crossed her path. It looked like a jaguar, with almond-shaped eyes, a black pelt, and a long, thick tail. But a Lebanon County big-cat breeder, Danita Wampler, was present at an interview with the woman, and one part of the cat's description led her to conclude it was a puma. The cat's coat was pure black, with none of the faint spotting you see in black jaguars. Other evidence of cougar came to light in 1984, when an Armstrong County farmer discovered tracks in the mud on the family farm. The paw prints, which were more than three inches wide, were asymmetrical and featured a squared heel pad—characteristics that match cougar prints.

More recently, cougars have been spotted in the east and west of the state. In September and October 2003, a large cat was seen in the vicinity of Bensalem and ten miles north, around Tyler State Park. The beast was tan-colored and about four feet long. By November, it was apparently comfortable enough to lie around in plain sight. On November 7, at least three reports came in of a large cat sunning itself on one of the Holland Elementary School's fields in Northampton Township. Numerous sightings also occurred in Lancaster County in 2003 and 2004, and some townships held well-attended meetings to develop cougar safety plans. In February 2004, more sightings occurred in Beaver County, near Pittsburgh.

Are all these sightings legitimate? If so, there's precious little hard evidence. More than a hundred Pennsylvania bobcats are killed by cars every year, but not a single cougar or leopard. Assuming that their rarity makes them harder to find, where have these alien big cats come from? It's illegal to own an exotic animal in the state without a permit, so it should be easy to track escaped animals through pet records. Of course, animals could be brought into the state illegally.

Perhaps the creature's huge stomping ground plays a part in tracing its origins. A cougar can travel up to a hundred miles from its birthplace to establish its own territory, which could point to places in Delaware, Maryland, West Virginia, and Ohio as the origin of these wild animals. Delaware does have some documented cougars living in the wild; perhaps they roam north. Wherever they hail from, one thing is important to know: Cougars and leopards are best left to their own devices. If you spot one, don't approach it; just write to *Weird Pennsylvania* and let us know.

Beasts on the Wing: Death from Above
Pennsylvania's Fabulous Thunderbirds

Forget the car. Forget the 1960s TV show and 2004 movie. And if you can, forget the hard-rocking Austin band featuring Jimmie Vaughan on guitar. To anyone with an interest in the unusual, thunderbirds are something completely different. They are enormous predatory raptors that have been reported throughout the world since the early 1800s and play a particular part in Native American legends. And if recent eyewitness reports are anything to go by, they are alive and well in at least one eastern state.

The original thunderbird was a Native American mythical creature so large that its wings, when flapped, caused the boom that we know as thunder. Its eyes shot bolts of lightning. It created fear everywhere it went, and during the past forty years, one of those places has been Pennsylvania.

In June 2001, two Mercer County neighbors spotted a flying object that at first glance looked like a twin-prop or microlight aircraft. After twenty minutes of observation, however, it was clear from the wing movement and feathered body that this was a living creature about five feet long, with a fifteen-foot wingspan. It perched in a tree, which bent severely under the great mass of its body. After a quarter of an hour, it took off toward the south. Witnesses agreed it was the largest bird they had ever seen.

The bird reappeared that July in Erie County, according to a report in the *Fortean Times* magazine. It was described as being dark gray, with little or no neck and a circle of black on its throat. "Its beak was very thin and long—about a foot in length," the report went on, and it had a wingspan between fifteen and seventeen feet.

Two months later, in September 2001, the beast reappeared over Route 119 near South Greensburg in Westmoreland County. A young man in his late teens heard a sound resembling the flapping of a flag in a windstorm.

He looked up to see the creature beating its enormous wings in a slow and menacing way as it glided past the big rigs on the road. It had a wingspan of somewhere between ten and fifteen feet, a head about a yard long, and such vast bulk that when it landed on a nearby tree, the tree nearly broke.

Stan Gordon, Pennsylvania's czar of the weird, has been collecting reports of all kinds of cryptids for decades. Sure enough, less than a year after these sightings, he received reports of more huge flying creatures over northeastern Pennsylvania. According to a report that has since appeared on many Web sites devoted to crypto-zoology (the study of unexplained animals), a pair of these birds appeared in late June 2002 between Tunkhannock and Nicholson in Wyoming County. Too big to be herons and with legs too short to be those of a crane, these birds perched awhile on the top of a tall evergreen tree. Their wings were wider than the span of the branches and had a batlike appearance. The two family members who saw these birds thought they resembled a black cormorant but scaled up to enormous size.

No reliable photographs or videos exist of these sightings, so scientists and birders have little to go on beyond eyewitness descriptions. But if these birds are from a recognized species, it's not easy to figure out which one. The largest known bird is the wandering albatross, a creature with a twelve-foot wingspan, but the descriptions of the thunderbird don't mesh with that of the albatross.

Jerome Clark's book *Unexplained!* lists many more sightings of a mysterious bird across the country. In the early 1940s, a writer named Robert R. Lyman spotted a massive bird sitting on the road near Coudersport, Potter County. When disturbed, it took to flight, with each wing measuring about ten feet. And the following year, in

Lycoming County, several people saw a gigantic bird "soaring toward the Jersey Shore. It was dark colored, and its wingspread was almost like an airplane."

All these bird sightings tap into long-told fearful tales of monstrous birds. Big-bird hysteria probably began in the mid-1800s on the slopes of the Swiss Alps, when a five-year-old girl was carried off by an eagle. Her remains were found two months later in the bird's aerie, alongside goat and sheep bones. Some fifty years later, the big birds were encountered closer to home—in the desert of the Arizona Territory. Two cowboys shot a gargantuan featherless creature from the sky and used their horses to drag it into Tombstone. According to the April 26, 1890, edition of the *Tombstone Epigraph*, the wingspan measured a mind-boggling 190 feet, and its body was 92 feet long. Its skin was smooth and its wings "composed of a thick and nearly transparent membrane."

In short, it was more like a pteranodon than a bird, and the newspaper report reeks more of the tall tales of the Old West than of an accurate account. Still, the story breathed new life into the legend of the thunderbird in America. Long may this creature hover over the roads and rivers of Pennsylvania—just as long as it doesn't swoop down and grab anybody else.

Local Heroes and Villains

The Doors had the right idea when they recorded a song called "People Are Strange." People are strange, and they've been that way for a long time—long before The Doors came on the scene. Pennsylvania has seen a succession of oddballs since it was first settled by persecuted religious extremists back in the 1600s. Some of the Quaker State's local characters have been harmless, and some have been extremely dangerous. And some have actually made their corner of the world a better place to live in.

Whichever camp these local heroes and villains fall into, their contributions have helped make Pennsylvania the place it is today. Here's hoping that we always get our share of the heroes who inspire us and the pranksters who bring smiles to the faces of passersby. As for the others—well, their evil deeds will catch up with them in the end. So here are a few choice specimens from both sides of the fence.

Death on the High C's

Most of us celebrate our love of music by singing in the shower or belting out duets in accompaniment to our car radios. But real singers spend years in the single-minded goal of building an audience. It takes commitment, persistence, and enthusiasm. And it is these qualities that brought Wilkes-Barre socialite Florence Foster Jenkins fame and still keep her memory alive today, sixty years after her death.

Florence Foster Jenkins was convinced she had a gifted operatic talent, and she wanted to share it with the world. In the early twentieth century, she hired ballrooms at the Ritz Carlton in New York City to stage annual recitals; she played numerous smaller gigs as well. She commissioned original songs to show off her range and even wrote her own lyrics—a rarity for any operatic singer in the 1930s. She tackled demanding operatic arias, like Mozart's "Queen of the Night" aria from *The Magic Flute*—a piece that taxes the vocal cords of the most dedicated divas. And she designed her own costumes, at least three for each performance. Yes, Florence had persistence and enthusiasm in spades. And that's just as well, because she had no musical ability whatsoever.

Florence Foster Jenkins's voice was appalling. Thanks to nine of her recordings that survive, modern audiences can hear her tortured attempts to find the beat and the key. It's not a pleasant experience. By comparison, a bunch of crows sounds like a barbershop quartet. Playing a rendition of Flo's "Like a Bird" falls into the category of cruel and unusual punishment, and that track is only one minute and twenty seconds long.

Yet oddly enough, the audiences of the time seemed to love her. The fact that she was a well-connected socialite and a music patron probably didn't hurt but it does not account for the genuine affection she seemed to engender. Although reports of her concerts and recordings were very carefully phrased, the audiences clearly relished her singing with good-natured indulgence. *Time* magazine described her performance of the "Queen of the Night" aria in its June 16, 1941, issue with great deftness, capturing the spirit of her fans.

Mrs. Jenkins' nightqueenly swoops and hoots, her wild wallowings in descending trill, her repeated staccato notes like a cuckoo in her cups, are innocently uproarious to hear. . . .

With a characteristic lack of self-criticism, Mrs. Jenkins judged her first test recording of the aria as excellent and beyond any improvement. When she listened to playbacks later, however, a tiny doubt seems to have entered her mind about "a note" at the end of the piece. The director of the recording studio assured her, in a masterly example of doublespeak that "you need feel no anxiety concerning any single note."

On October 25, 1944, Florence took the bold step of appearing in Carnegie Hall. The event was a runaway success. Not only was the auditorium sold out, but more than two thousand people were turned away. A local columnist suggested that her next concert should be at Madison Square Garden or the Polo Grounds. Sadly, this was not to be. A month after her greatest triumph, Florence Foster Jenkins died at the age of 76.

Death, however, could not silence her. When her recordings were re-released in the 1950s, they sold for years and were subsequently uploaded on sites all over the Internet. At the 2001 Edinburgh Fringe Festival, playwright Chris Balance celebrated her in a play entitled *Viva La Diva*. And in 2003, the Naxos record label released her entire recorded output on CD. This is a fitting tribute to the personality and drive of a woman who did it her way. She even wrote her own epitaph, which sums up her life perfectly: "Some people say I cannot sing, but nobody says I didn't sing."

Lawrence Schoen: Klingon Guy

Alumni of Chestnut Hill College, West Chester University, and Widener University may remember Dr. Lawrence Schoen as a psychology professor, specializing in cognitive psychology and psycholinguistics. Others may know him from his consultancy work with Philadelphia's Wedge Medical Center, which treats patients suffering from mental illness and substance-abuse problems. But to anyone who's seen the 2004 documentary movie *Earthlings: Ugly Bags of Mostly Water,* Dr. Schoen has another identity—that of the Klingon Guy.

Schoen, an outwardly normal-looking science-fiction writer and academic, started the nonprofit Klingon Language Institute in 1991 between academic assignments. He isn't one of those obsessed *Star Trek* fans, though many of the people he deals with are. He's a real enthusiast for language in general and finds Klingon fascinating. "It's an agglutinative language, so people who know German assume it's based on German," he explains. "But it also has a topic marker, so people who know Japanese assume it's based on Japanese." It also involves a lot of throat clearing, but it's not based on dogs eating peanut butter either.

In fact, Klingon was created by a Berkeley linguist, Dr. Marc Okrand, so that the scriptwriters for the 1984 movie *Star Trek III: The Search for Spock* would have realistic dialogue for the movie's many Klingon scenes. And according to Schoen, Okrand used many different sources for the alien warrior language. "Whenever he found he was taking too much from a language, he'd switch." But Okrand only invented the language, published a dictionary, and moved on.

Like other constructed languages, such as Tolkien's

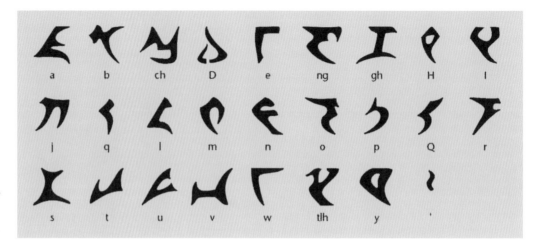

Elvish and the nineteenth-century global language Esperanto, Klingon needed people to study it and use it to help it grow. That's where Schoen's work fit in. His language institute actually teaches and expands the language. He provided a forum at www.kli.org for like-minded people to explore the language together, and they came. "We have superior court justices, trash collectors, and everything in between," he told *Weird Pennsylvania.* He has also published more than fifty issues of a journal called *HolQeD* to consolidate their studies. Schoen's institute sponsors a language course and an annual convention, which is what director Alexandre Philippe filmed for the documentary mentioned above. In the movie, thirty-three people get together in a Philadelphia hotel to explore the language together. One of them (not Schoen) wears a prosthetic head and hams up the Klingon experience. Schoen clearly enjoys the hammy playacting element, but that's not what he's all about: "We have no

illusion that there are really Klingons who are coming to earth to take over. That's the fluff. The language is very exciting. We've never had a constructed language grow out of popular culture, or a worldwide culture that makes it instantaneous and readily available. Plus it's just cool."

Though Schoen's interstellar linguistic work continues, he balances it with research and his own science-fiction writing, most of which is in English. So if you happen to come upon an erudite-looking bearded gentleman in the Greater Philadelphia area who sounds as though he's coughing up a fur ball, give him the benefit of the doubt: He could be Schoen on his cell phone conjugating Klingon verbs.

Del or Donna?

Back in the 1950s, eastern Pennsylvania and western New Jersey were invaded by a series of explosive and incendiary illusionist acts. Three stage magicians cornered the local market for stage conjuring and fire breathing. There was local Philly boy Delbert Hill, the Buffalo Bill–style Colonel Don Q, and Donna Delbert— "the celebrated English fire-eater and magician." The three stars were very different: Hill tended to be a bit raunchy, the colonel was a down-home bearded gentleman, and Donna Delbert was a plump and impeccably dressed middle-aged woman.

Not surprisingly, these three were never on the same bill, but that's not because their acts were similar. It's because all three of them were the same person. Larger-than-life Philly showman Delbert Hill adopted many personas both for his stage act and his real life, and whatever persona he adopted, he played to the hilt. Whoever hired him—the Elks, the Lions, the American Legion, the Boy Scouts—would witness a breathtaking act of incendiary tricks and stage conjuring and be completely taken in by the performance. If he was in his Donna persona, they might not even have known he was a man in drag.

Socially, things could get a little dicey with Del. Invite him to dinner, and you'd never know if Del or Donna would show up. More than one Philadelphia hostess had to hastily redo her seating plan to accommodate a guest of an unexpected gender.

Donna Delbert was "born" in London in the spring of 1945 at the age of around thirty (a lady never tells), shortly after Delbert Hill had deserted from the U.S. armed forces. Hill had been sent to Great Britain in 1942 with the Air Force Special Services with a mandate to entertain the troops. And that he did enthusiastically. Not even Hitler dropping bombs around the London theater

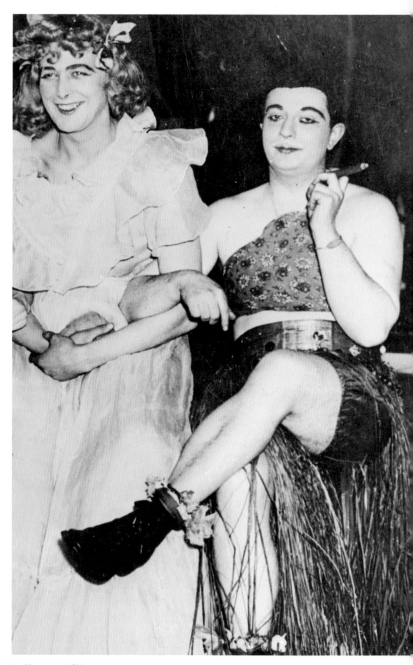

Delbert E. Hill, *right, then a Private First Class in the U.S. Air Force, is shown in one of his female impersonations, as he appeared in the 8th Air Force show "Skirts."*

district could keep Delbert Hill off the stage. But then the armed forces had yanked him from his favorite venue and redeployed him to normal military duty. Ill suited to drilling and swabbing out latrines, Hill went AWOL and stayed underground for four years, during which time Donna emerged.

Billed as "America's Outstanding Lady Magician and the Only Lady Fire-Eater in the World," Donna used a whip to snap out candles, then filled the stage with flames blown from her coyly smirking lips. Music-hall audiences throughout England were enthralled by the fire-breathing lady magician. She also had a couple of girlfriends, and that proved to be her—er, his—undoing. One friend, Betty, discovered Del's real identity, and the two began a clandestine affair. But when Betty found Del cheating on her, she ratted him out to the police, and Delbert served two years' hard labor in the United States for desertion. After his release, he resumed his stage career.

For a while, all went well. Del/Donna continued to work his/her magic, with the homey Colonel Don Q thrown in for variety. But as the years wore on, the acts grew less lucrative, and Del and Donna were forced to turn to new lines of work. He sold ice cream, worked at the Magic Fun Shop, and briefly ran Del's Diner on Philly's South Street. Presumably, Donna filled in on days when Del was busy at his other jobs.

Unfortunately, Del went out without a bang. When he contracted cancer in his mid-seventies, his only contacts with the outside world were social workers from Graduate Hospital on South Street. He died in his home in 1991 and is buried in an unmarked grave in Merion Cemetery. Sometime later, a crate of memorabilia from this remarkable man's career appeared in Marshall, Michigan, in the American Museum of Magic.

Monks of Wissahickon

Around the large green belt of Philadelphia's Fairmount Park, not far from Wissahickon Creek, are a cluster of streets named after solitary folks. There's Hermit Street, Hermit Terrace, and Hermit Lane. The story behind the street names dates back to June 1694, when a brotherhood of German mystics set up shop on the banks of the Wissahickon. Under the leadership of a twenty-one-year-old pietist named Johannes Kelpius, they practiced medicine, music, and good old-fashioned magic. Deep in the Wissahickon woods, even to this day, stands the only remnant of the order: the stone-gabled cave where the master of the order is said to have practiced his solitary ways.

This brotherhood of university-educated men studied, tended the sick, prayed, and used their musical skills to help the Anabaptists and Lutherans in Germantown and Philadelphia to assemble a liturgy for their services. The brotherhood was an extreme and solitary religious sect, absolutely convinced of the imminent return of Christ.

The group called itself by many names, one of which was Woman of the Wilderness, after a character in the Bible's book of Revelation. No doubt the name of the neighboring city of Philadelphia appealed to the members of the brotherhood. Most people know that Philadelphia means the City of Brotherly Love, but they may not know that the city got its name from William Penn's reading of the book of Revelation, which speaks of a faithful church in the ancient Middle Eastern city of Philadelphia.

But these mystics avoided cities. They stayed in their small community near Wissahickon Creek, awaiting the end of the world. There, they used astrolabes and telescopes to watch for signs of the impending Rapture. They also practiced numerology, astrology, and alchemy. Near the monastery was a tabernacle with a cross within a heart, which many took to be a Rosicrucian symbol. On the eve of St. John the Baptist's Day, around the time of the summer solstice, they celebrated a festival, during which, some sources believe, they witnessed visions of angels.

But the hermit Kelpius should have paid more attention to worldly concerns. The freezing-cold winters and his cave-dwelling ways eventually gave him pneumonia. In 1708, he became terminally ill. As he lay on his deathbed, the legend goes that he handed his assistant Daniel Giessler a locked box full of magical artifacts, with strict instructions to throw the box immediately into the Schuylkill River. In a tale reminiscent of Arthurian legend, Giessler thought that the artifacts would be valuable for future generations and, without any thought of personal gain, chose to keep them for posterity. He hid the box on the bank of the river and returned to his dying master.

Today, little remains to remind people of the hermits except for street names. There's a Pennsylvania historical marker commemorating the brotherhood. And if you walk through the woods near Hermit Lane, you may stumble upon the stone hut that legend calls the Cave of Kelpius. They say that he had lived and meditated here, apart from the other monks. Or it may mark his burial place. Either way, the Rosicrucian Society erected a monument beside this stone hut back in 1961.

A side note: Some people claim that on night walks on the trail next to Wissahickon Creek, you can sometimes see six men in brown hooded robes walking through the woods. Are these six figures the ghostly reminders of those who had stayed faithful after Kelpius's death? Or are they just perfectly normal Rosicrucians paying homage to Kelpius's memory? Who knows? But it's no coincidence that the pedestrian walk beside the Wissahickon Creek is unofficially but universally known as Forbidden Drive.

But Kelpius knew Giessler had not done as he was told, and Kelpius again commanded him to go and do it. On his second trip, Giessler threw the box into the river. A mighty explosion issued out of the water, with flashes of lightning and a crash resembling thunder. Naturally, because of the group's reputation, some believe that the box contained the philosopher's stone—the holy grail of alchemy that existed, if only in legend, before Harry Potter. If so, it still rests at the bottom of the Schuylkill.

After Kelpius's death, the brotherhood dwindled dramatically, and worldly concerns almost destroyed it. But the monks still provided services, some of which seem out of place for religious men. One monk, Conrad Matthai, cast horoscopes, exorcised demons, and could travel outside his body. According to Julius Sachse's book *The Pietists of Provincial Pennsylvania,* a captain's wife in 1740 asked Matthai when she could expect her husband's ship to return. Matthai lay down in his chamber for an hour in a trance. Then he awoke and returned with the news that her husband was at a London coffeehouse, getting ready to set sail for Philadelphia. When the captain returned and met Matthai, he claimed to have seen the hermit in the London coffeehouse. He remembered the encounter because the old man had come up and berated him for not writing to his wife.

Hallowed Be Thy . . . What's Your Name

When Connie Muir was driving home from work in Hazleton a few days before Halloween in 1999, she spotted a long-haired bearded man dressed in a robe. Naturally, she assumed it was a costume, but then she saw his bare feet. People don't take their Halloween costumes that seriously in Luzerne County. She realized that there was something more to this man than met the eye, although what met the eye was quite enough in itself.

Connie told her son-in-law about the odd-looking man and he drove back to offer him a ride. The strange fellow returned to the Muir duplex, said "Peace be with this house," and ended up staying there for months.

The Muirs learned that their guest had initially dressed like Jesus just to attract attention, but then switched the focus to a message of harmony and faith. He was so intent on keeping the focus firmly on God that he wouldn't even give his real name, so he became universally known as What's Your Name. The local pastor, Gerard Angelo of the Shrine of the Sacred Heart of Jesus, came calling and discovered that the man, who was about forty at the time, had taken a vow of poverty and had been on a missionary tour since the early 1990s. He carried only his few possessions—the clothes on his back, his sandals (when he had any), and his Bible. His strong religious faith resonated with the pastor, and that was all the locals needed to take What's Your Name to their hearts.

If you're looking for miracles, that's one right there. Hazleton is blue-collar country, not generally warm and accepting to weird-looking people. And folks there have little truck with fringe religions either. Yet What's Your Name quickly became a local celebrity. After attending Mass at St. Joseph's Church, he would be surrounded by members of the congregation, seeking solace and advice. He received invitations to speak at local churches, hospitals, schools, and nursing homes, where he would attract audiences in the hundreds, including those who hadn't set foot in a church for decades. When local talk-show host Sam Lesante invited him onto his show, What's Your Name got such a positive call-in response that Lesante invited him back three times in the next two months and eventually secured him his own broadcast show. This television slot spread the word further, attracting attention from such diverse groups as Polish priests, journalists from Great Britain, and representatives of the mainstream U.S. media, such as *20/20* and *Time* magazine. The strange preacher was always tight-lipped about himself but spoke freely about God.

Naturally, when the news media became involved, some facts emerged. It turns out that What's Your Name's real name is Carl Joseph. Originally from Ohio, he's been traveling around since 1990 with only what he could carry and without money. Any money he has come by, he has given to local churches. The single blot in his past is an arrest in Ohio for assembling and failing to disband a disorderly crowd—apparently, a group had gathered to hear him speak (not unusual) and got a little rowdy when police came to break the group up. Before arriving in Hazleton, he had been in forty-seven states and thirteen countries, though nobody's entirely sure which ones.

When asked about his odd way of dressing, What's Your Name would usually say something about simple and practical clothing (although a robe and bare legs are hardly practical in mountainous country in winter) and not supporting exploitative clothing manufacturers. But some of the wilier people who have interviewed him have gotten him to admit that the clothes drew crowds, which meant more people would hear what he had to say. He'd say this with a smile, as though he didn't mind using a gimmick if it were for a good cause. And few people disputed that the cause was good. To Hazleton, a town in recession like many of Pennsylvania's coal, lumber, and oil towns, any message of hope and consolation was welcome. Certainly, people did warm to What's Your Name's religion in the cold winter of 2000. People would congregate in the open air, even in the dead of night, to hear him talk of a personal relationship with God and of the mystery of Christ.

Most people were anticipating that after wintering in Hazleton, What's Your Name would use his television forum and local following as a base for a larger-scale mission. But he surprised everyone: He left town. One day, he was just . . . gone. He's resurfaced in various other places since then: New Jersey, Virginia, Michigan, and then New Jersey again. Reports come filtering back through various Web sites set up in his honor. Because the most recent sightings show that he appears to be circling back toward the Keystone State, many of his fans are hoping for a second coming. We'll not be waiting in the wilderness looking for signs, but if he shows up again, we'll mosey on over and hear what he has to say. We may even take a spare pair of sandals in case he's worn out his current pair.

He Is What He Is

In May 2000, some of my religious aunts told me that a man who dressed like Jesus spoke at the Presentation BVM Church in Montgomery County. Apparently he was very charismatic and spoke to people during and after the meeting about the spiritual life, the mystery of Christ, and other spiritual hot buttons. They were suspicious about how evasive he was about his real name, thinking that What's Your Name sounded a bit too close to "I am that I am," one of the holiest names for God. But they think that you know people's intentions by the fruits their works bear and that even if he's not doing great works, he doesn't seem to be doing any harm.—*Titus*

What's Your Name Gets His Kicks En Route 1

I've seen a man who dresses like Jesus wandering down Route 1 near Granite Run Mall in Delaware County. I saw him several times just strolling down the middle of the road, talking to people in cars stopped at the red light there. People told me he's a preacher who had been living up in the mountains, and now he's on a walking mission. What kind of person would stand there barefoot in the rain talking to people for 20 seconds until the light changed? How much could you hope to communicate in that time?
—*Sparky*

Pennsylvania Turnpike Killer

In the years following the Second World War, there was something romantic about trucking. The Kerouac mythos of the open road made life behind the wheel amid an ever changing landscape seem like another version of the American dream—the one about freedom and adventure. But on July 25, 1953, the death of a thirty-year-old trucker named Lester Woodward changed all that. As Woodward slept in his cab near the Irwin interchange on the Pennsylvania Turnpike, he was shot to death and robbed.

Three days later, thirty miles farther east along the turnpike, near Donegal, Harry Pitts suffered the same fate. Three days after that, on Route 30 eighteen miles west of the turnpike, the same weapon wounded, but did not kill, trucker John Shepherd in his cab. At least one of these shootings was believed to have been a sniper killing from an overpass or other distant vantage point. The brief reign of terror of the Turnpike Killer had begun.

The FBI and police began an investigation, but frightened truckers took matters into their own hands. These determinedly independent characters began toting their own weapons, including guns, baseball bats, and crank handles. They began to travel in convoys, park together at a Howard Johnson's or other well-lighted parking lots, and take turns standing guard as their buddies slept. Both the Teamsters union and the Pennsylvania Motor Truck Association offered a $5,000 reward for the capture of the killer.

The police investigation was progressing, albeit slowly. Investigations ranging as far afield as St. Louis turned up dead ends. A thirty-four-year-old ex-con confessed to a Philadelphia priest after the second killing, but the police determined that although he was a "dangerous mental case," he had no connection with the murders. A young Ohio farmhand arrested for assault three weeks after the third killing also confessed, but police dismissed him as a screwball and released him. They were right about this second confession: He was a screwball. But he was also the Turnpike Killer. John Wesley Wable, a Fayette County resident, had turned twenty-five just a few days after the third shooting and appeared on the police scope again a week after his release.

A watch stolen from the third shooting victim, the one who survived, appeared in a Cleveland pawnshop. The pawnbroker's records led police to a rented room containing a .32-caliber pistol and to Wable's girlfriend. A nationwide search for Wable himself ended two months later with his arrest near Albuquerque, New Mexico.

During questioning, Wable admitted to owning the gun used in the murders, but claimed he had given it to a man in Pittsburgh. The man could not be found, but Wable stuck to this story through his trial and conviction and the years-long appeals process. Despite that, late in the evening on September 6, 1955, he was taken from his cell at Rockview State Penitentiary near Bellefonte and executed in the electric chair.

Even though Wable's purported crime spree occurred half a century ago, the fear of a highway sniper attack still persists. Police discourage anyone from sleeping at the side of roads, and few professional drivers even consider it. That's a lot of kickback from a one-week shooting spree.

The Shadow of Death

A Pennsylvania historical marker near Shade Gap in Huntingdon County has a chilling title, Shadow of Death, but gives almost no other information. It tosses out the name of one of the early surveyors of the area, but doesn't describe why the place once went by that ominous name. The plaque ends with the written equivalent of a shrug of the shoulders: ITS LOCAL SIGNIFICANCE IS NOW UNKNOWN.

Weird Pennsylvania drove through the valley of the Shadow of Death to get the scoop from a chatty clerk named Deborah at the local filling station. She soon filled us in on the details.

In the days when Europeans first passed through the area, she explained, it was a prime location for ambushes by local Indians and bandits, given the fact that the heavily wooded mountains are peppered with caves, making it next to impossible to track down attackers. In May 1966, this fact was brought home forcibly to the townsfolk. The events of that May brought the FBI and state police together to mount what was, at the time, the largest manhunt in history. For a week, some two thousand people from the FBI, the state police, and the National Guard, along with fish and game wardens and volunteers, hunted through the Tuscarora Mountains for William Hollenbaugh, who had abducted a seventeen-year-old girl named Peggy Ann Bradnick.

Hollenbaugh, who was euphemistically described in the area as "special," went by the nicknames Bicycle Bill and Mountain Man. The reclusive fellow had developed an obsession with Peggy Ann and had snatched her one spring afternoon as she made her way home from school. When the two of them were discovered missing, local law enforcement jumped to the obvious conclusion, and the feds came in.

Hollenbaugh hid Peggy Ann in one of the local caves and took potshots at anyone who appeared to be hunting for them. . . . One of the people he shot at was FBI Special Agent Terry R. Anderson, who died from his wounds.

Hollenbaugh hid Peggy Ann in one of the local caves and took potshots at anyone who appeared to be hunting for them. On May 17, 1966, one of the people he shot at was FBI Special Agent Terry R. Anderson, who died from his wounds. From that point on, Hollenbaugh was a doomed man. Deadly accurate marksmen had him in their crosshairs, literally as well as metaphorically. After an eight-day hunt, Bicycle Bill was shot to death, and Peggy Ann was found alive and rescued.

After hearing the story, told very effectively by Deborah, we returned to take a picture of the historical marker. As the camera snapped away, a creeping sensation of evil seemed to hang in the surrounding scrubby woods. Perhaps it was just the name of the place. But most likely it was the knowledge that somewhere out there, a deranged kidnapper had shot at anyone who came near the object of his obsession. Whatever the reason, *Weird Pennsylvania* was happy to get back on the road.

FBI Special Agent
Terry R. Anderson

Taking Potshots with Bicycle Bill

I know an actual moving-car-killer site. Shade Gap was the home of Bicycle Bill. He used to sit on the hillside and shoot at cars going by on the highway. He was apparently a very good sniper, and he positioned himself so that the cars he hit lost control and went over the side of the ridge. No one found the bullet holes, because the cars and bodies were so banged up that nobody looked for them. People didn't figure out what was up until he kidnapped a woman and she escaped and told the police. This is not a legend. My mother routinely drove that route during her pregnancy with me while Bicycle Bill was still active.—*Ali Davis*

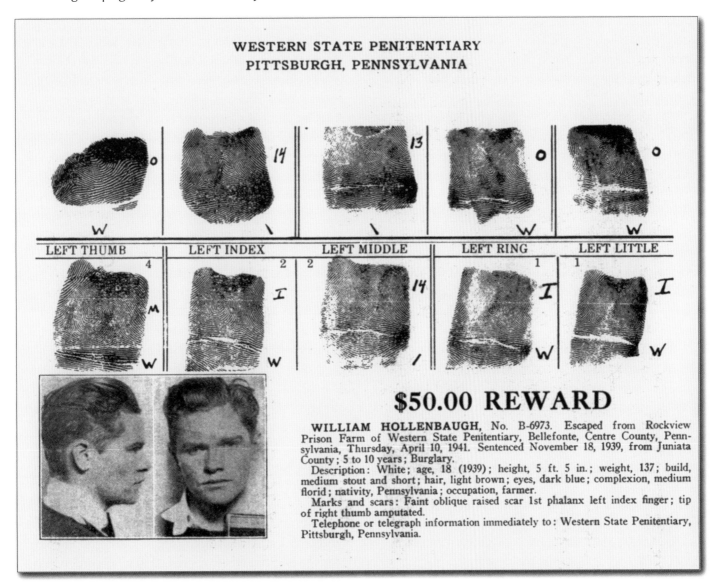

WESTERN STATE PENITENTIARY
PITTSBURGH, PENNSYLVANIA

LEFT THUMB | LEFT INDEX | LEFT MIDDLE | LEFT RING | LEFT LITTLE

$50.00 REWARD

WILLIAM HOLLENBAUGH, No. B-6973. Escaped from Rockview Prison Farm of Western State Penitentiary, Bellefonte, Centre County, Pennsylvania, Thursday, April 10, 1941. Sentenced November 18, 1939, from Juniata County; 5 to 10 years; Burglary.

Description: White; age, 18 (1939); height, 5 ft. 5 in.; weight, 137; build, medium stout and short; hair, light brown; eyes, dark blue; complexion, medium florid; nativity, Pennsylvania; occupation, farmer.

Marks and scars: Faint oblique raised scar 1st phalanx left index finger; tip of right thumb amputated.

Telephone or telegraph information immediately to: Western State Penitentiary, Pittsburgh, Pennsylvania.

Ridley Creek's Witch

These days, the town of Eddystone in Delaware County is a fairly typical blue-collar neighborhood. It has a power-generating plant, a concrete works, some greasy spoons, and a Wal-Mart. But back in the late 1600s, the area was all farms and plantations, mostly owned by Swedish immigrants. For centuries, one of them, Margaret Mattson, was the subject of many fireside tales. Few people know of her now, but she was once infamous as the Witch of Ridley Creek, the defendant in the only witch trial ever to be held in Pennsylvania.

Margaret Mattson and her husband, Nils, were already established Pennsylvania landowners when in 1670 they were granted one of two large land grants in what is now Eddystone. For the next eleven years, they lived there in relative peace, but in the early 1680s, a new wave of English landowners swept into the area, no doubt eyeing the Mattson property with some jealousy. Nils Mattson owned several hundred acres elsewhere in Pennsylvania, and this fanned the flames of jealousy even more. The fact that the Mattsons barely spoke English did little to endear them to their neighbors.

Before long, dark mutterings began circulating about the now elderly woman. Whenever a cow went dry, they said the old Swedish witch on the Mattson plantation was responsible. Given the witchcraft hysteria that was then sweeping England and spreading to the New England colonies, it was only a matter of time before someone accused Margaret Mattson outright in a court of law. And in 1684, that's exactly what happened. She appeared before the council in Philadelphia that January before Judge William Penn and two separate juries. Amelia Mott Gummere's 1908 book, *Witchcraft and Quakerism,* detailed the trial.

She appeared before William Penn, his Attorney General, a Grand Jury of twenty-one persons, all apparently English, and a Petit Jury of twelve persons, one of whom was a Swede. . . . There were various accusations of a vague sort against the poor woman, as that she had bewitched calves, geese, cattle and a few persons.

The trial's minutes go into greater detail. One witness, Henry Drystreet, attested that he had been told twenty years before that Mattson was a witch who had bewitched several cows. This was, rightly, dismissed as hearsay. Another witness, Charles Ashcom, had more sinister testimony. He claimed that he had heard from Mattson's own daughter-in-law (her son Anthony's wife) that Mattson had conjured "a great light" and a threatening apparition, frightening the poor daughter-in-law (whose previous feelings for her mother-in-law are not recorded). Margaret Mattson denied everything as hearsay and said that her daughter-in-law should come herself and tell the apparition story if it were indeed true.

This is all the evidence that appears in the public record, but according to the legend recounted in Gummere's book, Margaret herself gave some damning testimony. The trial was held in English, a language she needed an interpreter to understand fully. As Gummere tells the tale, William Penn asked her the crucial questions outright: "Art thou a witch?" "Hast thou ridden through the air on a broomstick?" Possibly because of language difficulties, the old Swede answered, "Yes."

This boxed Penn into a corner. The Witch of Ridley Creek trial had all the hallmarks of a nuisance lawsuit borne of malice or ignorance, and besides, as a liberal and well-educated Quaker, Penn had serious doubts about the witchcraft hysteria spreading across Christendom. But Mattson had essentially confessed to witchcraft, which was against the law of the land, so Penn had to think quickly to salvage the situation. And that he did. His exact response does not appear in court documents, so there's probably some embellishment going on, but this is how Gummere described it: "He said that she had a perfect right to ride upon a broomstick, that he knew no law whatever against it, and promptly ordered her discharge."

Because she had actually admitted to being a witch in court, she could not be let off entirely, so the verdict was that Margaret Mattson was "Guilty of having the Comon Fame of a Witch, but not Guilty in manner and Forme as Shee stands Endicted." This bizarre guilty/not guilty verdict meant that Margaret's family had to post a substantial bond of 100 pounds to guarantee her good behavior for six months—which they promptly did.

The old woman lived the rest of her life without incident, though her husband continued to be the target of multiple nuisance lawsuits. But over the next two centuries, whenever people told scary stories to each other on long winter nights, there was always a tale or two about Margaret Mattson, the Witch of Ridley Creek.

Benjamin Franklin's Electrifying Moment

Few Pennsylvania scientists have achieved the heights of fame that Benjamin Franklin has. It must be said, however, that the man who charted the Gulf Stream and came up with daylight saving time sometimes went off the deep end.

It's well known that Franklin's experiments with thunderstorm kite flying advanced mankind's knowledge of the nature of electricity. But old Ben did more than just theorize about electrical flow. He hosted bizarre parties in which he would rig Leyden jars (an early type of battery, also called an electrical bottle) to drinking glasses to make a device he called an "electrified bumper." He would fill these with wine and hand them out to give drinkers a tingle as they drank. According to Franklin's notes, electrified bumpers worked best "when the party is close-shaved and does not breathe on the liquor."

Toward the end of the spring of 1749, after a season of unsuccessful electrical experiments, Franklin decided to kick off the summer with a huge electrical show on the banks of the Schuylkill River. In a letter to a fellow researcher at the Royal Society in London, he described his plan to electrify the whole river, electrocute a turkey and roast it with electricity, and set off cannons using electric charges.

History does not record whether he actually hosted such an event that summer, but it does note that he electrocuted poultry to entertain his friends. At least he did until the following Christmas, when he nearly killed himself in the process. The day before Christmas Eve 1750, he rigged up the equivalent of two car batteries' worth of electric charge in two Leyden jars to zap the bird for a social gathering. Because he was

deep in party-time conversation as he made the preparations, he distractedly grabbed the metal chain that formed one of the jar's terminals, and completed the circuit. He took the jolt that was intended to kill the turkey.

Now that the Leyden jars had lost their charge, that particular turkey strutted free that day. The memory of this event must have flashed back to Franklin years later after the Revolutionary War. The other founding fathers suggested that the bald eagle would be a fitting symbol for the new country. Franklin proposed a less predatory native bird as more suitable. Though the turkey was voted down as the national bird, Franklin had shown his kinship with this breed of Thanksgiving poultry, which he had forged some sixteen years earlier over a jolt of electricity.

Charles Redheffer's Fifteen Minutes of Perpetual Motion

Pennsylvania has had its share of hucksters and shysters, none more brazen than Charles Redheffer. In late 1812, he set up a machine on the banks of the Schuylkill River in Philadelphia for public display. He claimed that this machine could run forever without any external source of energy, and he displayed it without charge because he had a larger source of funding in his sights: the state government. Not one to think small, he applied to the

Pennsylvania legislature for funding to build a larger version of the machine for the benefit of mankind and the greater glory of Pennsylvania.

On January 21, 1813, a group of eight state-appointed scientists inspected his machine. One of them, Nathan Sellers, took his son Coleman along with him. When they got there, they found that the door that housed the marvel was locked and that they could examine it only through a barred window. But young Coleman Sellers spotted something suspicious even from this distance. The machine had a rotating table at its center, which supposedly provided the energy for the whole thing, with teeth that transmitted power to an axle. Coleman noticed that the teeth were worn smooth on the wrong side, indicating that the energy must have come from a mechanism hidden in the axle.

Instead of merely rejecting Redheffer, Nathan Sellers decided to beat him at his own game. He created his own model of a perpetual-motion machine—a carousel with a central pivot and two wooden cars on inclined planes around it. The cars had heavy stone weights on them, which supposedly moved the whole assembly around. It was actually a clockwork device with a hidden mainspring, but Sellers wasn't saying so when he demonstrated the device to several people, including Redheffer. The huckster was impressed and offered Sellers a share in his venture if Sellers would explain how it was done.

Sellers declined Redheffer's offer, and when the Pennsylvania commission refused to fund Redheffer's project, the con man moved on to New York City, where he met with a less playful crowd. In the Big Apple, the audience included an engineer named Robert Fulton, who noticed a wobble to the machine's motion and concluded that there was an irregular source of energy involved. He denounced Redheffer as an impostor and said that he could prove it. Redheffer had no choice but to rise to the very public challenge. Fulton removed a piece of lath from the machine's frame, revealing a moving string. The witnesses followed the string to its source, an adjacent room where an old bearded man sitting on a stool was turning a crank with one hand and eating a crust of bread from the other. Fearing a mob scene, Redheffer backed off quickly and disappeared.

After that, Redheffer vanished from the public eye. But well into the twentieth century, the prank perpetual-motion machine designed by Nathan Sellers was on display in the Franklin Institute. It's still owned by the institute, although it's now mothballed in favor of real science exhibits.

How Much Weather Would a Woodchuck Predict?

On the face of it, it's highly unlikely that a small Indian camp town between the Allegheny and Susquehanna rivers should become a national center for meteorological predictions. And when the forecaster making these predictions is a fat rodent from the squirrel family, the odds against it happening dwindle to almost nothing. But that's exactly what happened to the improbably spelled town of Punxsutawney.

Every February 2, calendars across America celebrate a creature the locals here call Phil, a *Marmota monax*, or woodchuck. Because the woodchuck lives underground and chomps down so much vegetation that it grows to an impressive size and girth, it's also called a groundhog. And when Punxsutawney Phil crawls out of his burrow at seven twenty-five on the morning of Groundhog Day, the presence of his shadow—or maybe all those TV cameras and reporters—is enough to make him crawl back again to hibernate for another six weeks.

How a group of Pennsylvanians dreamed up this bizarre ritual is a tale in itself. Naturally, the European immigrants in the Keystone State, being farmers, were obsessed with weather. Rhymes like "Red sky at night, shepherd's delight" came across with the English and Scottish immigrants. But in the harsh winters in northwestern Pennsylvania, the real interest is in how long the cold weather will last. Another European tradition foretells this, based on the ancient pagan festival of Candlemas, which occurs on February 2.

As the winter reached its bleakest, the Scots and the English would say the rhymes "If Candlemas is bright and clear, there'll be two winters in the year" and "If Candlemas brings clouds and rain, winter will not come again." It was the Pennsylvania Germans who came up with the idea of the groundhog predicting weather on that February day.

Back in the fatherland, German peasants would check out badger shadows during Candlemas. When they moved to Pennsylvania, they were as obsessed as ever with the weather, but the closest equivalent to the badger in their new home was the toothy burrowing creature that the Native Americans called Wojak. The European settlers misheard this as "woodchuck," by which name it's still known in many places today.

The earliest known reference to Groundhog Day in America dates from 1841,

in a diary entry by a storekeeper from Morgantown in Berks County. James Morris's entry for February 4, 1841, which appears at the Pennsylvania Dutch Folklore Center at Franklin and Marshall College, reads thus:

> Last Tuesday, the 2nd, was Candlemas day, the day on which, according to the Germans, the Groundhog peeps out of his winter quarters and if he sees his shadow he pops back for another six weeks' nap, but if the day be cloudy he remains out, as the weather is to be moderate.

In 1887, the editor of the *Punxsutawney Spirit* newspaper, Clymer Freas, whimsically referred to a group of groundhog hunters who had a beer-soaked party as the Punxsutawney Groundhog Club. Soon after, a few select townspeople in the Groundhog Club made the trek up to Gobbler's Knob, to check out the rodent's shadow and a tradition was born. History does not tell us why they chose this particular spot and this particular groundhog, but their descendants have faithfully trooped there ever since. Even in the insanely cold winter of 1961, the club braved a recorded temperature of twenty-five below zero to watch the creature in action. Of course, they had to down quite a lot of booze to keep warm.

Eventually the event was thrown open to the public, and the group cranked up the show a little. In time, Phil acquired a handler, Sam Light, a coalman and athlete. In the 1950s, he introduced the handler's costume of a top hat and dark morning suit—"the traditional dress for dignitaries greeting Very Important Persons," as he explained. In the run-up to the great prediction, the handlers call this titanic squirrel Punxsutawney Phil, Seer of Seers, Sage of Sages, Prognosticator of Prognosticators, and Weather Prophet Extraordinary. They make a show of talking with the creature in his native "groundhog-ese"

before delivering the weather verdict—usually to a chorus of good-natured (sometimes drunken) boos.

After the 1993 release of the Bill Murray movie *Groundhog Day,* the celebrations became more populous. The town of 6,700 hosted 35,000 visitors in 1995 and a staggering 38,000 in 2002. Nowadays, people are shuttled by bus from town to Gobbler's Knob to ease traffic. And of course, the whole event is an excuse for a big winter party.

Since 1974, Phil has lived in a climate-controlled zoo in the children's department of the Punxsutawney Public Library. His heated burrow staves off his natural inclination to hibernate, and his mate, Phyllis, apparently keeps him young. According to the local story, Phil is more than a century old, an unlikely age for any rodent, but it's not a statement we'll question.

He also has friends in high places. Phil visited President Ronald Reagan at the White House in 1986, after delivering a forecast of an early spring. And after a similar forecast in 1995, he appeared on Oprah Winfrey's show. And of course, his stunt double plunged to his death next to Bill Murray in 1993, only to be resurrected the following day.

One thing's for sure, however: No matter how revered Phil may be, he's a lousy weather forecaster. According to the records, between Groundhog Day 1887 and 2004, he has seen his shadow a total of ninety-four times. But less than half of these shadow winters have continued for six more weeks. In fact, Phil's been correct only 39 percent of the time. For a creature this well treated, most people would expect a little more in return. But to the people of northwestern Pennsylvania, he's a great excuse for a celebration at the dreariest time of the year. Who needs accuracy when you can dress up and hang out with thirty-eight thousand other partygoers on a freezing mountain?

Personalized Properties

Some people put in shrubs and lawn jockeys to set their homes apart from the ones next door. Others build extensions or install fancy fences. Then there are our kind of people, the ones who tear down their houses and build another in the shape of a shoe or a ship. Where others might fancy up their gardens with corkscrew topiaries, the weird folk take a chain saw to their trees to carve out a leering spider monkey. And while some people may beautify their neighborhoods by occasionally picking up the odd piece of litter, we applaud those who cover entire houses with mosaics made from broken mirrors and tile.

If, as they say, a man's home is his castle, we say bring on the castles made from railway cars, bring on the turrets adorned by bizarre handcrafted animal statues, and bring on the moats filled with cars from the 1950s. And after that, bring on the really weird stuff.

Along the Lincoln Highway

Any story of Pennsylvania's weird roadside architecture must start with the Lincoln Highway. This was the first paved transcontinental road in the United States, running from New York to San Francisco. It linked existing roads into a single system and became a heavily traveled motor route in the 1920s and 1930s. It's a rule of business that where there is traffic, commerce springs up, and a corollary to that rule is that where there is commerce, outrageous marketing will soon follow. In the days before neon lighting, strange buildings were a great way to catch the eye of the passing motorist. Some of the most bizarre buildings became the stuff of legend, sought out by tourists even after the Pennsylvania Turnpike took most of the through traffic away. Here are a few examples of Lincoln Highway personalized properties, past and present.

Coffee, Anyone?

Those Model T Ford motorists took their cups of joe seriously, and so did the folks who sold it to them. The two-story coffeepot west of Bedford is a testament to that. Built as an annex to a gas station in 1925, the eighteen-foot-high structure served lunch and stimulating hot beverages. Even after traffic on the Lincoln Highway declined, the coffeepot's location opposite the county fairground ensured some local traffic. Unfortunately, that traffic declined in quality as well as quantity. The place degenerated into a seedy bar, and seventy years after it had opened, it was a shabby abandoned mess next to a drive-through beer mart.

However, this tale of the coffeepot has a happier ending than some of its contemporaries. The state of Pennsylvania offered a grant for renovating the structure, and the Bedford County Fair Association bought the property for a token dollar in 2003. A nonprofit preservation group called the Lincoln Highway Heritage Corridor (www.lhhc.org) spent tens of thousands of dollars to move the building across the street to the fairground. Some serious reconstruction took place, and in the summer of 2004, the coffeepot reopened as a visitors center.

SAILING ACROSS ALLEGHENY MTS. ON THE S. S. GRAND VIEW POINT, 17 MILES WEST OF BEDFORD, PA.

SEE 3 STATES and 7 COUNTIES

ELEVATION 2,464 FEET

Ship Hotel

For close to seventy years, motorists cruising along Route 30 west of Bedford would catch sight of a ship halfway up the Allegheny mountain. A couple of double takes and a bit of swerving later, they would realize that they weren't crazy. There was indeed a two-funnel white steamship perched on a crag by the roadside. It was the S.S. Grand View Point Hotel, later known as Noah's Ark, a shipshape hotel and restaurant with a scenic view of three states and seven counties. And it was a classic of Lincoln Highway architectural carnival barking from the early 1930s.

The lookout point at Grand View was recognized as a tourist attraction long before the ship was built. From its elevation of 2,464 feet, you could see Maryland and West Virginia, as well as Pennsylvania, and postcards show that some entrepreneurs were cashing in on the view as early as the 1920s. The wiliest of them all, a Dutch immigrant named Herbert

Paulson, built a gas station and a small hotel there in the mid-1920s, then added the attention-grabbing Ship of the Alleghenies in 1932. This masterly work of promotion featured flags and pennants, a lookout point in the prow with a ship's wheel, and one of the few tourist telescopes that did not require a regular infusion of coins to keep working. The hotel fast became a necessary stop for tourists, a hot spot for

S. S. GRAND VIEW POINT HOTEL ELEVATION 2464 FEET
A Steamer in the Allegheny Mountain. 17 Miles West of Bedford, Pa. U. S. 30

dances, and an overnight stay for up to forty-nine guests at a time. And those guests included many luminaries. Thomas Edison, Greta Garbo, and Joan Crawford slept there (but not together, as far as the records go). The hotel flourished until 1940, when the newly opened Pennsylvania Turnpike stole much of the hotel's traffic.

The place changed hands in 1978, when the Paulson family sold it to Jack and Mary Loya, who gave it the biblical name of Noah's Ark. But even invoking the Old Testament didn't save the hotel from falling into disrepair and abandonment. It eventually closed, but it remained a must-see curiosity for anyone within striking distance, although littering and general decay put a bit of a downer on the whole experience. The Lincoln Highway Heritage Corridor tried to buy the place and turn it into an official landmark. However, the organization was unable to agree on a price with Jack Loya. So it remained abandoned, though Loya left lights burning and kept a television on at all times to discourage intruders. This practice is widely presumed to be the cause of the fire that destroyed the hotel in the early hours of October 26, 2001.

The fire removed every vestige of the mountain-faring vessel from the rock. Even when the ever-persistent Lincoln Highway Heritage Corridor offered to erect a twelve-foot mural of the hotel in its heyday by the road where it had once stood, the owner demanded rent for the space, something the nonprofit organization could ill afford. However, you can still pull over to the side of the road at Grand View Point and see the famous three-state and seven-county view, but to see anything of the flagship of the Alleghenies, you need to drive west to Route 30 Antiques and scope out an exhibit on permanent display there.

The Other Ship Hotel

The Ship of the Alleghenies may have sailed into the sunset, but if you still fancy a nautical night along the Lincoln Highway, there's another boat hotel in Amish country. The Fulton Steamboat Inn in Strasburg would look more in place sailing down the Mississippi, but it's named for the Pennsylvania farm boy who developed the steamboat, Robert Fulton, who was born in Lancaster County in 1765.–*Donna C.*

Haines Shoe House

As you head west down Route 30 through York County, near the small town of Hallam you'll catch sight of a building that's enough to make you swerve out of your lane and wonder what on earth was going through the mind of the person who built it. It's a giant shoe standing next to a tiny doghouse, also shaped like a shoe. This is the Haines Shoe House, the brainchild of Mahlon Haines, the most single-minded shoe salesman in Pennsylvania.

Haines arrived in York County in 1905, getting as far away from his native Ohio as he could on his bicycle. Though he was nursing a broken heart from a broken engagement, he was not the kind of man to mope about it. Instead, he hocked the engagement ring and used the proceeds to buy ten pairs of shoes. He sold these at a modest profit and bought twelve more pairs. Over the next forty years, he parlayed that rejected ring into an empire of forty shoe stores throughout Pennsylvania and Maryland. Haines gloried in self-promotion—he called himself Colonel, before the fried chicken guy, and kept a herd of bison near one of his stores to attract the attention of passersby. With his keen eye for a good marketing campaign, Haines hit upon a new gimmick in 1947, when he handed an old boot to an architect and said, "Build me a house like this."

The result was a three-bedroom house with a kitchen, a dining room, and two bathrooms. The forty-eight-foot-long, twenty-five-foot-tall house stands five levels high, with stained-glass windows on three levels, most of them depicting shoes. Ever the self-promoter, one window features Haines himself, holding up two shoes, with the legend SHOE WIZARD.

But Haines didn't stop at building a roadside attraction. He wanted to give back to the community, so he offered a week's free accommodations at the shoe house to newlyweds and the elderly. Each morning, a maid would bring breakfast to the visitors, and each evening, a chauffeur would drive them to a restaurant. Haines covered all expenses and it's not surprising that he got fantastic publicity in the bargain.

Since Mahlon Haines's death in 1962, the house has been several things—an ice-cream parlor, a museum, and a bed-and-breakfast. But it has always been an attraction. The current owner has kept its doors open to the public since she bought it in 2004, so the next time you're down Hallam way, you can see the Shoe Wizard window for yourself. Don't forget to wipe your feet before you go in.

Elephant Man

Maybe the twelve-mile drive west from Gettysburg softens you up a little as you whiz past monument after monument commemorating those who had died in battle against their countrymen. Or maybe the Lincoln Highway puts you in the mood for something odd and amusing. Whatever the reason, by the time you hit Mr. Ed's trading post in Orrtanna, you're ready for something lighthearted, and that's certainly what you get.

If Ed Gotwalt were any other trader, his trading post on Route 30 would be just another general store. He would sell peanuts roasted on the premises, hard candy, and knickknacks—the kinds of things you can get at a lot of places along the way. But Ed is no ordinary shopkeeper. He's a man with a sense of humor, a flair for the dramatic, and a vast collection of elephants.

Mr. Ed's Elephant Museum occupies a covered area between two roadside buildings. It is free to all comers, and it's crammed with more than six thousand elephants. Elephant pins, elephant statues, elephant toys, elephant bottles—you name it. If it's in the shape of a pachyderm, it has found its way to Mr. Ed's. There's even a small collection of Republican memorabilia, including a 1968 amber-colored liquor bottle touting Nixon for President. But the real appeal of this place isn't party politics; it's a love of jumbos and Dumbos, and it cuts across party lines, ages, genders, and social backgrounds. During our hour-long visit, everyone entering Mr. Ed's had the beginnings of a goofy grin on their faces. By the time they left, the grin had spread from ear to ear.

Mr. Ed began collecting elephants around thirty years

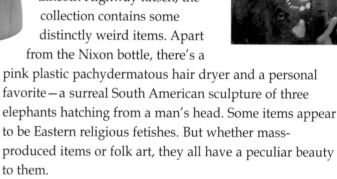

ago. In the early 1980s, about seven years after he had opened his store, he dragged the boxes of elephant memorabilia from his cellar and put them on public display. It's been a steady draw to roadside fans ever since. But even though the museum is mostly Lincoln Highway kitsch, the collection contains some distinctly weird items. Apart from the Nixon bottle, there's a pink plastic pachydermatous hair dryer and a personal favorite—a surreal South American sculpture of three elephants hatching from a man's head. Some items appear to be Eastern religious fetishes. But whether mass-produced items or folk art, they all have a peculiar beauty to them.

To demonstrate that he's a real lover of elephants, Ed doesn't trade in ivory items. In a small cabinet, he displays two tusks from a beast that had died of natural causes, and some donated ivory sculptures, most more than a century old. The cabinet contains the maxim "Only Elephants Should Wear All Ivory." This may be another example of Mr. Ed's self-promotion, but he seems too sincere and cheerful a man to condone cruelty to the animals he celebrates. As a result, his collection is something you can stare at for a happy hour in admiration and amusement, then grab a bag of his roasted peanuts. They are delicious, though the shells will make a mess in your car.

Staying at the Siding

The road to Paradise is lined with many distractions, but none are quite as strange as a serpentine railway siding filled with dozens of antique railcars, rejoicing in the name of the Red Caboose Motel and Restaurant. To find this bizarre stopover, turn off Route 30 at Paradise, about halfway between Gap and Lancaster, and follow Paradise Lane to its logical conclusion.

That conclusion is a rail yard with dozens of twenty-five-ton cabooses, plumbed and wired and furnished for overnight stays. For the past thirty-five years, this motel has been a haven for rail enthusiasts, families, and people wanting a sharp contrast from the Amishness of most of Lancaster County's attractions. And it all began on a lark in the summer of 1969.

Donald M. Denlinger, a museum president and a writer from Soudersburg, met an old friend at a sale at Mill Bridge. Carried away in a moment of camaraderie, he put in a lowball bid on some old railroad rolling stock. Six months later, during a January blizzard, he received a call to pick up his fleet of nineteen N-5 cabooses, or grimeys, as railway buffs call them. Grimy they were and weighed in at 475 tons, but Denlinger contrived to have them delivered to a place where they wouldn't block normal traffic. Then he began pondering what to do with them.

It takes a peculiar mind to look at rusty railcars

reeking of kerosene and think, "These would make a great hotel," but that was the kind of mind Denlinger had. So he secured funding from a bank and furnished the grimeys into family-style housing for up to six people per caboose, complete with bunk beds, potbellied stoves, and dinky little desks. Since it opened in 1970, the original nineteen cars have been joined by many others, not all of them red, and by a Victorian dining car serving three meals a day of decent farm fare. Visitors can read up on the history of the car they have stayed in. There's even a Thomas the Tank Engine running past the motel in season, shuttling folks between the towns of Strasburg and Paradise.

Many people who have visited over the years remember Denlinger, who was usually dressed up in a conductor's uniform. Nowadays he no longer runs the motel in his Mr. Conductor outfit. In fact, the place changed hands a couple of times and got some pretty poor reviews from guests along the way. It then spent a brief spell in receivership but has since been taken over by a Philadelphia hospitality management company. It may not be run by the same wide-eyed rail buff, but by all accounts, it has turned around and remains an eye-catching place to visit. If you're not sure about staying in a railcar, you can put a dime in a turnstile outside the restaurant and check out the furnishings in a walk-through guest room.

Another Dining Car

In the golden age of roadside diners, many were built to look like train cars. One example is the Sterling Streamliner model called the Penn State Flyer, which fed Allentown natives throughout the 1940s and afterward. It was moved to Scranton in 1956 and renamed Yank's Diner.

But a functioning diner in a real train car is a lot harder to find, unless you travel on the Lincoln Highway through New Oxford, between York and Gettysburg. There you'll find the Civil Bean Express, housed in one of two train cars in a V-shaped configuration, with a little garden between the two. It's not the first business ever to be housed in these trains, but we hope it'll stick around for a while. Its specialties—coffee and smoothies—are a welcome treat on the way to the battlefields at Gettysburg.

Stag Hog

This photo was taken outside a bar in Harrisburg. Incidentally, the name of the bar is the Stagg Inn. It is a real working motorcycle. I saw it on the road about 10 minutes before this photo was taken.—*Scott Wilson*

Home, Home on the Strange

Customized hotels and diners are all well and good, but it's fun too when people customize their own private homes. It's here that they feel free to express their inner selves, and boy, do they have some inner selves to express!

A Moister Kind of Water Park

Motorists traveling in Bucks County along Route 232 and passing through Wrightstown may wonder what they have just driven past. The town itself is a fairly typical Bucks County kind of place, but one property is a bit out of the ordinary. On a large multiacre lot, there is a gazebo, a concrete sliding board leading down to a grass-filled pond, and a bridge to nowhere. The lawn is enormous and open to the road. Tucked in back is a large Spanish-tiled building and a small gatehouse built in a similar style. All of this is visible from the roadside, but there are no signs indicating what it is.

Many people assume it was once a water park or a resort, but nobody seems to know when it was open, and since it's now a private home, it's not easy to find out. The *Weird Pennsylvania* research team dug up the story, and it's much more interesting than any tale of a closed-down commercial enterprise.

The lot was purchased in 1919 by Martin Moister, a thirty-three-year-old businessman, and his wife, Anna Francis Schoettle. Moister was born in Hazleton, in coal-cracking country, and moved as a young man to Philadelphia, where he built up his own steel company. The company thrived enough for him to buy six acres in Bucks County, where the couple set about making a home they could enjoy.

Within a decade, the Moisters had a family, so they added a playground

and a pool in the front garden for their children to play in. The other touches, including the gazebo and extensive decorative tiling from the nearby Mercer tile factory, were presumably for the grown-ups to enjoy. The family thrived, and by the time the matriarch and the patriarch had passed away, there were eleven grandchildren and twelve great-grandchildren in the clan. Anna died the week before Christmas 1969, and her husband, only a few weeks after.

The Moister estate was subdivided and sold. The gatehouse belongs to one owner, the gazebo to another, and the main house and playground to still another. Although they appear to be a little worse for wear, the seventy-five-year-old architectural follies on the divided estate stand as an unmarked monument to Martin Moister and his family. Next time you drive past, we suggest you respectfully stand by the roadside and salute the Moisters while keeping off the grass out of respect for the current owners.

Richboro Mystery Park

At the SW corner of 2nd Street Pike and Swamp Road in Richboro is the historic Eight Square School, which is neat in and of itself. However, across the street to the west, almost invisible to the eye, is what I call Richboro Mystery Park. It appears to be an abandoned water park, with slides and pools of concrete from the 1930s or 1940s. It's built in front of a home whose lawn appears to be cut but is rather ramshackle.

I saw a man who seemed to be living in this apparently private residence exit the rear dwelling as I took pictures. I tried to zoom in on the tower and waterslides. They're up in the trees! The size of the facility (and the waterslide) is clear: This was a big attraction at one time! The most prominent feature is a castle-themed pool with several slides in the center amidst crossover bridges akin to a moat. This is a large property, suggesting an old tourist attraction complete with motel. So what was Richboro Mystery Park in its heyday?–*Dr. David Feeney*

Cyril Griglak's Backyard Zoo

Perryopolis in Fayette County is a two-hundred-year-old town built on land owned by George Washington before the Revolutionary War. It boasts a gristmill that was once used in conjunction with a distillery and a barrel-building facility for the production of hooch. But the town's best attraction is a backyard sculpture garden built by a charming local character named Cyril Griglak.

In the spacious corner lot behind his home stand dozens of plaster animal sculptures with a rough folk-art look to them. On the lawn are a tiger, a lion, a cheetah, a bear, and a zebra. A little joey pokes his head out of his mother kangaroo's pouch. Suspended on a large spring tucked away at the back of the lot is a fabric-coated gorilla that bounces maniacally at the slightest provocation. And on a pulley system spanning the width of the garden is a smiling spider, chasing a delicately wrought dragonfly.

Here and there, you'll see a store-bought deer or alligator, but most of the animals are Cyril's own work, a hobby he began a decade ago. He was in his eighties at the time, and by the time *Weird Pennsylvania* came knocking on his door, he was ninety-five. He looked fifteen years younger, with eyes that twinkled like those of a man half his age. He was in his garage, surrounded by friends and tinkering with the carnival float that he enters into the Pioneer's Day parade every October.

Cyril is a man who likes to keep active. He began building the animal sculptures when he was forced to give up flying his Cessna light aircraft. "Before that, it was motorcycles," he reminisced. "I used to be able to stand up on the seat, with my arms out, like at a rodeo." We must have looked skeptical, because he launched into an explanation of the feat that was clear, detailed, and checked out as being accurate. "Well, you can set the throttle," he explained. "It has to be a good bike to stay straight. Then you just have to keep your balance. I wish I had a photograph, 'cause when I tell young fellows about it, they don't believe it."

So what makes an octogenarian take up animal sculpture? In Cyril's case, it was something to keep him occupied (the animatronic wirework that's built into some of the sculptures is quite challenging), but the real payoff is the entertainment his backyard zoo provides. Unlike many old-timers, he doesn't seem to mind neighborhood kids tearing around his lawn. In fact, he gets a kick out of it, as long as they steer clear of the pond, which is surrounded by model alligators to reinforce the point. He'll pull wires to make the animals' heads move, set the gorilla bouncing, and watch the glee unfold as he chats with any adult who'll stand still long enough. Most can't resist playing in the yard with the kids.

Where Edsels Rule

It's not unusual to hear of a collector with more than a hundred large items in his trophy case. When that collection is of vintage cars, eyebrows may go up. But the one thing that makes Hugh Lesley's passion really unusual is the make of car he favors: Lesley collects Edsels. He keeps more than 150 of Ford's least popular car, along with a sprinkling of Mercurys and Lincolns, on his wooded hilltop property near the border of Chester and Lancaster counties. He doesn't show his collection to the public. In fact, his property is widely posted as being private, but he graciously invited *Weird Pennsylvania* to see the cars one warm Saturday in June. And that's one invitation we didn't want to miss.

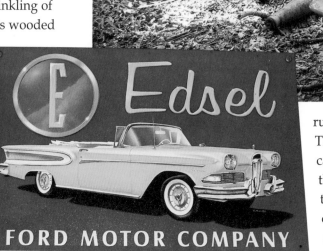

At the bottom of a dirt track, the Pennsylvania Game Commission had posted a sign banning motorized vehicles, so we parked the *Weird Pennsylvania* mobile— a nonvintage, non-Edsel—on a gravel shoulder near the local reservoir and hiked uphill. The steep climb up a narrow gravel driveway didn't seem right somehow. Would the leviathans that Ford made between 1957 and 1960 fit along this winding path? Even if they could, surely nobody would tow a couple of hundred of them there?

But then sure enough, large forms began to emerge through the trees—dozens of them—some wrapped in tarps, some exposed to the elements, some hopelessly rusted, doorless, and falling apart. The farther we walked, the more cars appeared, and before long, the house came into view. Next to it stood a long, barnlike garage containing what looked like several dozen of the better-preserved vehicles, with hundreds of hub-caps hanging on the walls. Nearby was a working garage with a peach of a vehicle sporting an aqua paint job. A man was leaning over the opened hood, tinkering with the engine.

Hugh Lesley fell in love with the Edsel in a Ford showroom in 1957, but he didn't fall in love with the price tag. "They were asking $3,500 for it," he told us. "So I decided to wait a couple of years until people started trading them in." Several years later, he picked up his first Edsel, a convertible. Soon after, he got a wagon and a sedan. Before long, Ford dealers knew whom to call when they had an Edsel to unload. "Dealers started to call me to come and pick them up from their back lot," he said. "They were charging $25, $50 for a three- or four-year-old car."

Although he hasn't lost his affection for the Edsel over the decades, Lesley has no illusions about the car. He pointed to a headlight dangling from its socket. "See that? They used to rust right through, and the headlights would fall out. They were real rust buckets."

Indeed, many of the cars were pretty heavily rusted, and a number were missing doors, engines, and other parts. Lesley uses some of the cars for parts to keep his few pristine models in good shape, and Edsel buffs from across the country contact him for help with their vehicles.

The Edsel was a big, ugly car and far too expensive. It featured huge imposing headlights and a central vertical chrome horse-collar–shaped grille measuring almost a foot high that split the front bumper in two.

"They used to call it a Lincoln sucking on a lemon," said Lesley. "See how they softened the horse-collar effect on this '59 model?" On this model, the horse collar was filled with a horizontal grille and a small insignia, with headlights that no longer bulged up the hood. "Now look over here at this '60." He pointed to a tiny insignia, only two inches high, on a car that could have passed for a Lincoln from the front.

The 1960 version was manufactured for only three months before Ford pulled the plug on the model. The three-year project had lost the company millions of dollars and so the 2,300 units of the 1960 Edsel were the very last to come off the assembly line. Hugh Lesley has about a dozen of them.

Lesley's Edsel collection hasn't always been tucked away in the woods. Up until a few years ago, it was scattered in barns on the family farm, but when that was sold, he had to haul them three miles to his current property. It took three solid months to relocate them. But in their new site in the woods, they certainly look at home. And it was when people saw all these Edsels among the trees that they gave the place its nickname: Lemon Grove.

Well, it's clearly not a cherry orchard, but it's a bit harsh to call it a grove of lemons. Even if most of the cars in it are only good for parts—or scrap—this secluded little wood stands as a testament to one man's passion for collecting. And for that, Hugh, we salute you.

Magic Garden of South Street

Philadelphia is home to hundreds of house-size urban murals, thanks to a long-standing civic movement called the Mural Arts Project. Originally praised because it stemmed the creeping blight of graffiti in the 1980s, the Mural Arts Project has turned many once bleak brick walls into colorful representations of hope and nature.

But even amidst this profusion of colorful walls, one property stands out. On South Street, a few blocks from Broad Street, you can find walls covered with tons of mirrors, ceramics, statues, bottles, bicycle wheels, and colored grout. The mosaics cover entire three-story houses between South and Kater streets and surround a property lot that's filled with odd statuary, a tiled floor, and all kinds of junk held together with cement. It's called the Magic Garden, and it's the vision of one tireless artist named Isaiah Zagar, who has lived and worked in the neighborhood since the 1960s.

It doesn't take much effort to appreciate the Magic Garden. It's huge and impressive in its scope, but if you turn your attention to any given square yard, you're rewarded with an absorbing level of detail. You could be staring at a statue of a man with three right arms (and wondering what on earth it means), looking at a cartoon painted on a tile, or pondering the origin of a broken piece of Mexican ceramic art. You might be reading a piece of poetry or taking in Zagar's slogan, repeated often enough in his work to qualify as a mantra: "Art is the center of the real world." Some of the elements in the garden look like slapped-together outsider art, but the scope and scale look like the work of a professional. And people who file past daily in a steady stream, snapping pictures through the locked gates, often have no idea of what's behind this spectacle.

But if you happen to come by at just the right time, you may catch sight of a gray-bearded man with a puckish smile and messy clothes who can explain what it's all about. If he's not in the middle of a project (which is rare) or if he feels like taking a break, Isaiah Zagar will step out of his

studio and welcome strangers into his house. He draws people into his cellar, which is covered from floor to ceiling in the same mosaic style, and describes his art. He'll show his paintings and those of his friends. He'll describe the ceramic pieces created by other people that were broken in transit on the way to his wife's gallery and wound up in his work. He may describe how he had moved to South Street on his return from the Peace Corps, when the neighborhood was a run-down slum about to be cut off from Philadelphia's civic center by a bypass. He may describe how the community had banded together to stop the plan, but he will usually stop short of saying what most people say, namely that he's largely responsible for reviving what was once a run-down rathole of a street and making it the cool place it is today.

Not everyone is a fan of Zagar's work. In early 2004, the owner of the Magic Garden lot, an absentee landlord in Boston who had ignored it when it was a rat-infested dump, gave Zagar notice to clear the lot for sale. The holding company that held title to the lot, GS Realty Trust, intended to sell the gap between two buildings for $300,000, a price the newly gentrified South Street market could probably support. Zagar, his lawyer, and his assistant— Allison Weiss—mounted a fund-raising campaign to save the garden. Using a collection bucket at the site, they raised several thousand dollars. Fund-raising events and "Save the Garden" specials on Zagar's Web site (www.isaiahzagar .com) raised more. But it wasn't until Zagar formed a nonprofit organization called Philadelphia's Magic Garden and secured a promise of $100,000 from an anonymous donor that the Magic Garden was saved from a bulldozer.

But the reprieve is only temporary. Zagar needs to raise another $200,000 before the end of 2006 to get the anonymous donor's money. So we suggest you get over to the Magic Garden and drop a few bucks in the collection bucket, because this is one of the few times when fans of the weird in Pennsylvania can make a concrete contribution to keep the weird alive. Go ahead. Be a part of the magic.

Stones of Columcille

Cruising around northeastern Pennsylvania on my motorcycle, I came across quite the oddity. Sticking up out of the ground like the proverbial sore thumb, the mysterious oblong stones of Columcille lured me in. In an instant, my life had changed. Columcille had found me!

So just what in the heck is Columcille anyway? Mostly, it's a bunch of rocks—BIG rocks. A profusion of them actually, and they're planted into the ground. If you get off on Stonehenge or the statues of Easter Island, or delight in nature's offerings and aspire to a higher level of being, then this crazy place may well interest you. I must warn you, it has a dark side as well, so be careful out there, solace seekers.

To begin your journey to enlightenment, just set your gaze toward the Blue Mountain ridge and the little town of Bangor. Columcille represents the offbeat dream of two highly spiritual fellows: Bill Cohen Jr. and Frederick Lindkvist. Their official line on the place reads something like this: Columcille was built to resemble an ancient spiritual retreat called the Isle of Iona, located off the west coast of Scotland, where 350 stones were set

into the ground to mark it as a place where "the veil is thin between worlds." While Columcille comes up woefully short in its number of stones, it nonetheless faithfully approximates the ancient design. In addition to the stones, there are chapels, altars, gates, and cairns, all made from stone and all open to everyone.

The site occupies seventeen acres of forestland and open meadow. More than eighty oblong stones are set in the ground, loosely interpreting the ancient design. Interconnecting trails run throughout and lead to a number of places set aside for meditation and reflection. Most notable among these is St. Columba Chapel. This wonderful building oozes feelings of the medieval. The structure is hexagonal in shape and constructed mostly of rocks. A heavy wooden door opens to reveal a large central stone holding candles, with benches encircling it.

No matter what your religious or spiritual convictions are, it's difficult not to feel the pull of this place. Perhaps it's important to note here that Columcille is nondenominational. In fact, its founders invite all to

On another visit, I was told by some locals that strange things occur here, particularly at night, and that Columcille attracts its share of kooks and lunatics. In fact, one woman seemed so nervous about pursuing our discussion any further, she curtly cut me off at midsentence, proclaiming, "Nobody has any need to go there at night—nobody!"

That ominous statement weighed heavily on my cowardly constitution as I extricated myself from the chapel. Carl Lewis himself couldn't have caught me as I bolted out of there. I've returned to Columcille since, but now limit my visits to daytime ones exclusively.

What is the meaning behind the stones? Why do the locals speak in such hushed tones about the happenings here? What scared me so at the chapel? I still can't answer these questions with certainty, but this I can tell you: By night, there is a very strange dynamic at work amongst the stones. It's a palpable feeling that something sinister is lying in wait, just off in the shadows. That feeling so unnerved me, I'm sorry I ever chose to tour it by twilight. From what I've learned, it has traumatized its share of local folks as well.

On the other hand, by day, Columcille is a land of enchantment, a remarkable place to behold. Filled with mystery and enticing in its beauty, it is easy to see how it can move people toward the spiritual and allow them to leave feeling cleansed and restored. You can meditate on it yourself by visiting Columcille at 2155 Fox Gap Road, Bangor.—*Jeff Bahr*

experience this peaceful place, whether to meditate, to reflect, or merely to form a firmer bond with nature. Other features include a bell tower, a stone gate, cairns alongside the paths, and many outlying sites intended to provide a quiet retreat—the better for each of us to pay heed to our "inner voices."

Columcille operates on a nonprofit basis. All funding for construction was provided by the founders and through contributions of friends and visitors. Many events are scheduled during the year, and a bulletin board with up-to-date listings greets visitors upon arrival.

But is there more than meets the eye here? Is there something else in this place besides its stone planters and chapels? Or am I perhaps a little on the neurotic side, with one-too-many conspiracy theories clouding my judgment?

As night descends upon the monoliths, eeriness hangs over the place like a pall. On my third visit there, at dusk, I stepped into St. Columba Chapel to satisfy my curiosity and immediately felt as if I'd made a huge mistake. I simply couldn't shake the notion that I was being watched.

Remembering the Railroad House

When we were in grade school, we paid for a trip to a house near the Haverford School. It was on the Main Line, just off Lancaster Pike. This place was a temple to the railroads. The driveway was lined with signals and lights and railway signs. The man who lived there had so many of them, they were lying in piles near his garage. He gave our class a tour of his basement, which had the most amazing train set I ever saw in someone's house. There seemed to be dozens of tracks and trains that kept disappearing into different rooms. There were galleries of train paintings, Amtrak uniforms on Amtrak hangers, British Rail uniforms, several ticket machines, and huge crossing signs. I remember wondering how he got all these things down the stairs. He was very hospitable to us little kids and kept doing funny stuff, like ringing bells and dropping money into the ticket machines. The funniest thing of all: His doorbell made a sound like a train whistle. –*ColleenBC*

Flight Delayed

This light aircraft appears to have landed in residential Derby, Delaware County, and remains there until cleared for takeoff. It still awaits clearance. You'd be better off taking the 113 bus along Main Street to get to your destination. When you do, look out the window to see whether the plane is still on its rooftop runway, eternally ready to taxi.

Shelter in a Tank

A couple of my friends and I traveled over to Shawville, in Clearfield County (Exit 123), where my friend has a 100-acre farm. We heard some stories from some of the locals there about a fallout shelter built by a crazy hillbilly near the bank of the Susquehanna River. We decided to go on a canoe trip to investigate a little further. We entered right next to the Shawville Power Plant.

While traveling down the river, on the right-hand side we noticed what looked to be huge tubes of sheet metal. After docking, we realized that they were actually 40-foot tanks from oil tankers. Through some bushes we saw the fallout shelter burrowed into the side of a mountain. Jackpot!

We slowly crept up to the entrance and tried to enter through the door. The door seemed to be locked from the inside. On the door, there was a peephole with a metal bar slid over it. While we were trying to pry the door open, I could remember thinking, "If that peephole slides open and I see a crazy hillbilly, I'm not going to need the canoe, because I'm going to run over the top of the river to get back home."

We searched all around and found out that there were actually several tankers welded together. We climbed to the top of the shelter and discovered manhole covers that were also welded in, but could not be popped open.

There were several smokestacks located on the top too—I guess to have the place heated. I got to talk to a local person in Shawville, and he said the guy who built the shelter is known as Crazy Maynard. The entire area seemed to be really weird.–*Mike S.*

Penn's Trees

What is it about Pennsylvanians and their trees? We all know that the state's name means "Penn's Woods," but that doesn't account for the bizarre things that the folks in this neck of the woods do to their spare tree trunks. It seems that when you put Pennsylvanians in front of a tree, their imaginations run wild. Where anybody else would see a birch or a maple or a hemlock, a Pennsylvanian sees a blank slate on which to create a bear, a totem pole, or perhaps a leering winged demon.

Given the hardy nature and logging background of many of Pennsylvania's mountain folks, it's hardly any surprise that every year the little town of Ridgway in the Elk Mountain region hosts an annual chain-saw carving convention. It's attended by power tool–wielding folk artists from across the world and celebrates the manly art of turning tree trunks into totems and bears.

We're not knocking totem poles and bears, but there are plenty of more unusual ways to carve your forestry by-products. Take, for instance, these prime examples of the tree-trunk chain-saw massacre.

Villanova's Chocolate Tree

Every spring, this tree stump, which lies between Villanova University and Villanova Law School off Route 320 in Chester County, receives gifts of chocolates and flowers. A throwback to druidical tree worship? A fertility rite? Just a bit of student fun? Who can say?

Bang! Zoom!

As you drive along Middletown Road in Chester County, you hardly notice that this odd rocket is mounted on a tree stump, but it is. Is it a tribute to cold-war brinksmanship? After all, Nike missiles were stacked around Pittsburgh and Philly. Seems the countryside had only folk art like this to save the day.

Memorial Tree

What kind of memorial is this? These parts from a Dodge Dynasty are nailed to a tree off Railroad Street in Windber, Somerset County. Right behind it lies a steep drop, which is perhaps where the poor unfortunate met her end? The gravel road on which the tree stands is past the residential areas in Windber and labeled with a snowmobile trail marker. It's easy to miss, unlike the drop behind it.

Big Smile for the Camera

How would you like to see this on your way back from Home Depot or Red Lobster? It's just what shoppers in Delaware County's town of Springfield encounter as they head out from the mall. This spider-monkey devil tree stump bares its teeth at contractors and home owners alike. To take the edge off the menace, there's a smiling half-moon affixed to an adjacent tree. But who knows what hidden meaning that image may hold?

Totem Troupe

It's only a small row of trees near the Allegheny National Forest, but these sentinels outside the Skiddle Inn have their own peculiar way about them. The half-fashioned mushrooms, people, furniture, and other icons stand there as a mute reminder that art doesn't have to make sense. It just has to be.

Roadside Oddities

When people say, "It's the journey that counts, not the destination," they sum up what driving across Pennsylvania is all about. Pennsylvanians love road travel. In fact, it was Charles E. Duryea in Pennsylvania, not Henry Ford in Detroit, who made modern motoring possible. Duryea invented the three-cylinder engine, which Ford himself said did more to usher in the modern auto age than any other invention.

Whenever large numbers of people are mobile, there will always be someone at the side of the road providing something for them to look at. Sometimes roadside attractions are there to lure tourist dollars. Sometimes they are there to make you wonder. And sometimes they are there for no good reason at all, made by people who don't seem to realize how strange their works are.

Whether you're looking for unusual roadside attractions, bizarre place-names, or things that make you scratch your head and say, "What on earth was that?" the Quaker State has what you're looking for. Pull over up ahead—there's an oddity coming up now!

Invasion of the Giants

Giants invaded the roadsides of the United States about forty years ago, and some of them still survive to this day. Brightly painted fiberglass titans, like the provocative Miss Uniroyal, began as marketing tools but ended up in the hearts and minds of the weird-loving public.

The influx of mass-produced giant sculptures began in 1962, when Bob Prewitt of Prewitt Fiberglass built a twenty-foot-tall Paul Bunyan for the PB Café on Route 66 in Flagstaff, Arizona. Prewitt was a cowboy whose love was rodeos, so he sold his business to a boat builder named Steve Dashew, who renamed it International Fiberglass and began to ramp up marketing efforts. By mixing and matching standard molds for limbs, torsos, and heads, International Fiberglass could turn fabricated body parts into anyone—country bumpkins, musclemen, sexy ladies. Some of these statues naturally found their way into the Commonwealth of Pennsylvania. But more interesting are the one-of-a-kind pieces lovingly fashioned for someone's personal reasons. Whether it's the freaky mother–daughter team at Frackville's Granny's Restaurant or Amos of the late lamented Zinn's Diner in Lancaster County, Pennsylvania has its fair share of unique giant statues.

Yumpin' yimminy! Here come some of them now.

Famous Amos

For more than forty years, a fifteen-foot-tall Amish man with disproportionately huge hands stood guard over the front door to Zinn's Modern Diner in Denver, Lancaster County. Christian and Margaret Zinn put up this giant red-shirted man in characteristic Lancaster County dress to catch the eye of the Amish-crazed tourists. After a few years, the Zinns got more ambitious and installed a talking Amos. Visitors would press a button, and tapes of atrocious jokes in an exaggerated Pennsylvania Dutch accent would play back through a speaker, located in Amos's beard. For thirty-four years, this behemoth

cracked his jokes to millions of visitors. Then in 2003, the diner was sold and Amos disappeared. For almost a year, nobody knew where he was, until it came out that the Heritage Center of Lancaster County had acquired him. Amos was too big for the tiny town square in Lancaster, where the Heritage Center is headquartered, so he's currently on loan to the Hershey Farm Restaurant and Inn. He'll be there until 2008 and perhaps longer. Amos is now speechless (he's still wired for sound, but the Amish joke tapes are missing) and sports a new paint job, including a purple shirt.

Holy Cow!

There's no escaping the origin of the steaks at Centre County's Boalsburg Steak House. At least they don't actually taste as though they come from a ten-foot-high fiberglass cow.

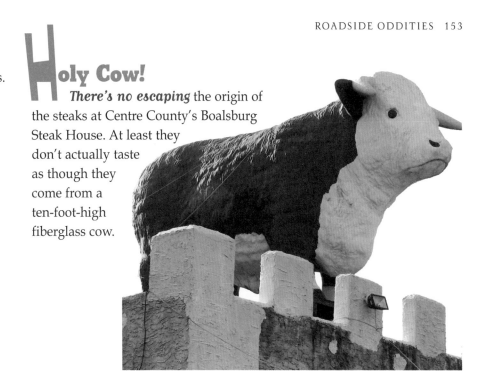

Roadside America's Dutch Couple

Amos isn't the only oversized Pennsylvania Dutch statue in the commonwealth. As you zip along I-78 in Shartlesville minding your own business, you'll see a man and a woman in the middle of a parking lot, leaning over as if to pat people's heads—or grab them by the throat. As you zoom by, you vaguely see the signs for an attraction called Roadside America . . . and then you're past it. Unless you get off at the next exit and drive back to see what it's all about.

Scary Amish

Dear Weird PA:

We took this picture of a strange Amish couple on a recent trip to Roadside America in Pennsylvania. By the way, that's one of the weirdest places I've seen since my uncle Frank's basement.–*Maggie*

Dauphin's Statue of Liberty

If you happen to be driving along Route 322 from Harrisburg toward State College, you'll pass close to the Susquehanna River at a stretch called Dauphin Narrows. And if you think you're seeing a brilliant white replica of the Statue of Liberty proudly holding high her torch out there in the river, you're not dreaming. Distance plays havoc with the sense of scale in this area. Although Dauphin's Lady Liberty looks tiny, she's actually twenty-five feet tall and quite sturdy. She's also the second replica of the Statue of Liberty to stand in the fast-moving waters.

A local lawyer and activist-artist named Gene Stilp put together the first statue with some friends for a bit of a lark to celebrate the original Statue of Liberty's centennial in 1986. When the ersatz replica was finished, they displayed it on the closest thing they could find to the plinth on Liberty Island—an old railway bridge piling in the middle of the river. There it stood for years, bringing smiles from motorists, until wind and weather finally carried it off in the 1990s. People missed it so much that Stilp and his team built a more durable replacement, made out of wood, metal, and fiberglass, and moved it onto a piling by helicopter and lashed it securely with cables.

This patriotic example of folk art is always a fleeting pleasure, however, since it's almost impossible to see from the nearest town, which is Dauphin. The best you can manage is a brief glimpse as you drive on Route 322, unless you're good enough at kayaking to navigate the treacherous waters in that stretch of the river.

Pennsylvania Takes a Little Liberty

A few years ago I was invited to join some friends to go camping in Perry County. As we journeyed to our destination, to my surprise I saw a Statue of Liberty right smack in the middle of the Susquehanna River.

To get there, you must take Interstate 81 to Harrisburg, cross the river, then turn north and head up river towards Duncannon. Keep your eyes on the river after you pass the world-famous Rockville Railroad Bridge. Shortly after you pass Rockville Bridge, you'll see in the middle of the river the Pennsylvania Lady Liberty.—*amx*

Pied Piper of Schellsburg

Zooming along Route 30 west of Bedford, you could almost miss the siren song of the Pied Piper. He's set back in the driveway of a boutique called Piper's Place Country Originals. But the eighteen-foot-tall character has a more storied history than the gift shop that bears his name. Originally, he had lured children on long car journeys to an attraction called Storyland, a playground of plaster buildings and statues modeled after fictional places and characters, like Humpty Dumpty and Mother Goose. Like many folksy Lincoln Highway attractions, the place closed after years of dwindling interest. But tucked away in the woods, behind very clear NO TRESPASSING signs, the storybook characters and castles remain, weathering away in neglect. The gift shop that is there now draws a different kind of customer from the road-weary families of yesteryear, but it retains the services of Storyland's patient shill, who quietly plays the pipes as the customers come and go.

Close Encounter with a Giant Granny

The storms of summer come in waves across eastern Pennsylvania, dumping millions of gallons of water with the flash and crack of a horror-movie thunderstorm. It seems too perfect a setting to be real. As the *Weird Pennsylvania* team drove down I-81 one dark day, waves of apocalyptic rain buffeted the car. Even at full speed, the wipers left only two or three inches of clear windshield before the water closed in again, obscuring our view.

Then a brief break in the downpour. The silence and light made the first word we read by the roadside seem even more comforting. It was Granny's, a motel and diner about half an hour down the road at exit 124B in Frackville. It sounded pleasant and warm and homey—everything that the drive hadn't been. And as a second wave of rain came and lashed the car, the name beckoned even more irresistibly. So as the Frackville exit approached, it was inevitable that Granny would be getting a visit.

The rain eased as we turned onto Route 61 and took the hairpin turn to the restaurant. But clouds loomed, heavy and pendulous, on the horizon. As we pulled into the parking lot, we saw a giant woman by the door, holding a pie while her deformed child clutched her. The woman's head, mostly hidden by a pioneer bonnet, stood at roof level, her wide staring eyes gazing out toward the storm clouds. But her daughter's head was stranger by far. It seemed too large for her body and featured the razor-shaped sideburns and angular face of a full-grown man. Dangling from her hand was a doll with no head. All three figures were made of painted fiberglass. We had clearly stumbled upon more giant citizens of weird Pennsylvania.

Once inside Granny's Restaurant, the strangeness of the statues melted away in the pleasant clutter of a comfortable little roadside hostel. The motel desk clerk and waitress told us that the giant pie-woman statue was originally built for the Pot-O-Gold Diner down the road in Hamburg, but when the place closed, the statue was brought to Granny's. It's hard to say whether the statue attracts attention and custom from Route 61 or scares people off. But on that particular stormy night, I noticed that members of our

Philly's Hidden Zoo

According to the Philadelphia City Archives, Joseph Thomas Varello was the architect of this folk art garden at Stephen B. Fotterall Square, a grassy patch of empty space at the corner of Eleventh and York streets. But the architect and his intentions have faded out of the harsh glare of research, and only the works remain. And what works they are . . . a classic hidden treasure that's been tucked away just out of sight of the nearby SEPTA train line since 1967, too far away from North Broad Street or Fifth Street to happen upon by accident. The animals are very bright and funky and out of character with their surroundings, like a cross between the creations of two other Pennsylvania greats: Isaiah Zagar's walls wrapped around Cyril Griglak's animal sculptures. A few of the more ambitious pieces are now missing pieces of themselves, but all the mosaic-tiled structures are as bright as the day they first found themselves on a square of grass in a little urban neighborhood, miles away from the typical tourist traps, wondering like everybody else who saw them what on earth they were doing there.

team lingered just a little longer over coffee than usual, as if steeling themselves—not just against the driving storm, but against the trek across the parking lot under the gaze of the pie woman's man-faced daughter.

Mütter Museum

The Mütter Museum in Philadelphia is a strong contender for the coveted title of Most Bizarre Museum on the Planet. The museum is housed in a two-tiered gallery, lined with the dark wood cabinets and wavy glass panes of a venerable learning institution. It is the public display area of the College of Physicians of Philadelphia, a school founded in 1787 to promote such noble notions as bioethics and the fact that medicine is both an art and a science. The Mütter Museum is also a medical freak show of deformed bones, diseased organ specimens, instructional wax models of various pathologies, and things in jars that will give sensitive people nightmares.

During *Weird Pennsylvania*'s visits to the Mütter, we've seen nursing students grow dizzy at cross-sections of human heads, teenage boys giggling at wax models of eyes afflicted with a variety of problems and disorders (including one eye with a huge splinter through the cornea), and rather creepy-looking people intently examining skulls of

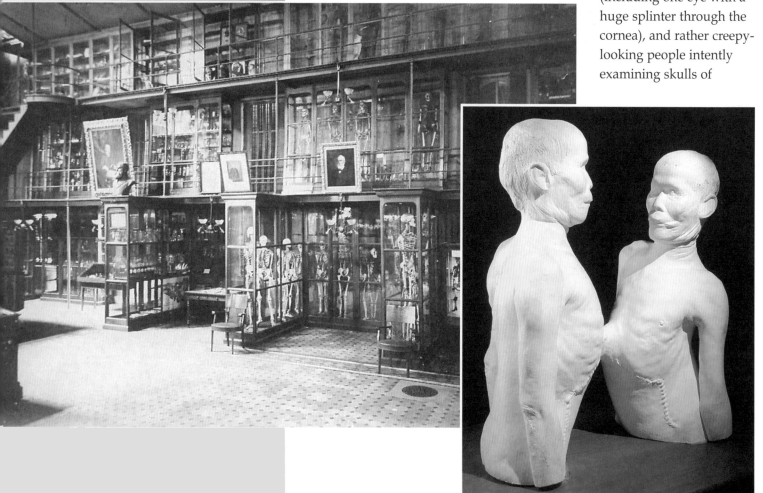

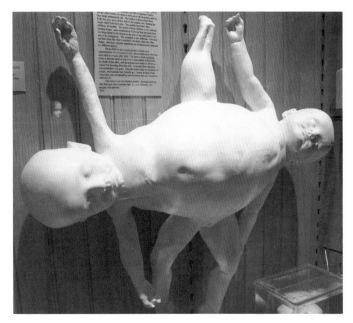

unfortunates who died from syphilis. All these responses are normal, and anyone who doesn't experience at least some of them during a visit is probably not looking carefully enough. (Incidentally, not looking carefully at some of these exhibits may be a good idea.)

On the more benign side is a collection of healthy-looking skulls, each accompanied by a brief biography of its owner. The exhibit was organized to debunk the myth that you can determine personality or intelligence by the shape of the cranium, a pseudoscience called phrenology. There are also medical instruments dating back hundreds of years that will make you glad you live in the present.

Less benign are the model of a hydrocephalic, a body cast of conjoined twins, a model of a face with a facial tumor, and two diseased skulls. At the top of the stairs are a wax model and a dark brown cadaver encased in a transparent sarcophagus. The wax model is that of a woman with a huge horn growing from her forehead. The cadaver, which dates from the early 1800s, was exhumed during road construction. They call this one the Soap Lady. Like many people of the time, the woman had been buried in a sackcloth sprinkled with lye. Under the ground, her body fat reacted with the lye to form a soaplike substance that preserved her body in a creepy sort of mummification.

Next to her openmouthed body is her X-ray portrait, which is a lot easier on the eyes.

Down the stairs from the mezzanine gallery, things get nastier. One exhibit, which looks like a long leather sack stuffed with straw, is actually a preserved colon. This horrifically distended stretch of guts lacked the power of peristalsis—the squeezing motion that nudges everything you eat steadily on its way. The poor fellow who once housed this organ was so backed up that he died as a result of pressure on his other organs. What you can hope to learn from this is limited, except perhaps to eat plenty of vegetables and other dietary fiber.

There are also some celebrities on display. Standing under a spotlight, glowing white, is a plaster cast of Chang and Eng, the nineteenth-century conjoined twins from Thailand (then called Siam), whose fame gave the world the term Siamese twins. And for history buffs, there's a tumor removed in secret from the jaw of President Grover Cleveland while he was in office, as well as the thorax of Lincoln's assassin, John Wilkes Booth, removed during Booth's autopsy.

The Mütter Museum, however, does have a serious teaching role, and if you're lucky, you may latch on to a group of medical or nursing students as they're given a guided tour. The rest of us must be led by our own curiosity, as long as we remember the cardinal rule: Wait at least an hour after a meal before jumping into these waters. You'll thank us for that bit of advice when you reach the specimen jars.

Talk About Horny!

I wanted to thank you for including the Mütter Museum in your book *Weird U.S.* A two-page spread with color images is pretty impressive. But there are several factual errors—for instance, what you describe as a skull with horns growing out of its head is actually a wax model of Madame Dimanche, a French washerwoman from the late eighteenth century with a horny growth protruding from the skin of her forehead. The horn is comprised of the same cells that make up our hair and fingernails. It seems incredible that she let the thing grow so large without doing anything about it, but then you look at the wax models showing the other dermatological conditions walking the streets, and it's not so shocking.—*Margaret Lyman, Interim Director, Mütter Museum of the College of Physicians of Philadelphia*

A Wild and Wacky Place

The Mütter Museum is one wild place that will either fascinate you or have you heading for the toilets. There is a giant 27-foot colon and a guy whose skeleton started to develop "outside" his body. That must have felt nice. And just in case you're hungry, there is a 2,000-item collection of foreign objects that people stupidly or accidentally have swallowed.—*Brian R.*

Laughed Outta Mütter

I've heard rumors of a secret "damaged human genitalia exhibit" at the Mütter that you have to ask a curator about. I went up to the only person I could find at the museum, a 300-lb. security guard and asked him. He took a double take and laughed. I felt like an ass, but it was hilarious. I guess the rumors aren't true, which is unfortunate since we went specifically to see the secret exhibit.—*Jay Sansone*

Teeth by the Bucket

People waiting for low-cost tooth care at the Temple University School of Dentistry don't have to rely on year-old copies of *Reader's Digest* to pass the time. Until the trainee drillmeister is ready to work on their gnashers, they can take an elevator ride to the third floor to scope out the museum of dentistry.

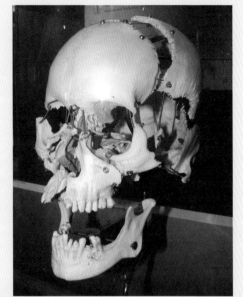

The Dental Museum of Temple University contains glass cabinets full of equipment, dentures, stainless-steel crowns, and historic documents. These items trace the history of dentistry in America from colonial times. You'll learn about the Amalgam Wars (there have been three, all centered around the most effective low-cost substitute for gold for filling cavities). You get to look at a Victorian-era dental office and give profound thanks that modern dentistry doesn't use a foot-operated treadle to operate its drills. In addition to X-ray machines, probes, and dental prosthetics, the museum displays equipment you wouldn't associate with dentistry, such as a coke-burning furnace for baking porcelain teeth and an electromagnetic hammer for tamping down gold into cavities.

All the while, you hear a very bizarre sound through concealed loudspeakers. The squeaking and rattling noise can't help but remind you of a hygienist scraping plaque from your gum line and, consequently, sets your teeth on edge. But it turns out that this is actually the sound of that treadle revving up the Victorian dental drill. Thankfully, it's not followed by the whine of a drill against a cavity.

There are other dental museums in America, to be sure, but can they boast a yards-long necklace made of human molars and a wooden pail full of extracted teeth? We think not. That's where the Temple University dental museum really stands out.

These exhibits commemorate a renegade alumnus of the Philadelphia Dental College (the forerunner of the Temple School of Dentistry), one Edgar R. Parker. Beginning in the early part of the twentieth century and until his death in 1952, Parker operated under the name of Painless Parker. One part dentist and six parts P. T. Barnum, Parker earned several fortunes from his chain of thirty dental offices across the West Coast. Parker dressed like Colonel Sanders of KFC fame, except, of course, for the human tooth jewelry he wore around his neck. Apart from advertising, frowned upon by others in his profession, his gimmicks included marathon tooth-pulling sessions (he once extracted 357 in one day), the handing out of whiskey to dull the pain of extraction, and the offer of free dentures (if the ones in the bucket of dentures he carried happened to fit).

It's hard to say whether visiting the museum is a good way to pass the time before dental care. The squeaking of the treadle will certainly not appeal to dentophobes. But if the subject matter appeals, this newly revamped attraction is free to the public during dental office hours at the Temple School of Dentistry, located at the corner of Broad Street and Allegheny in Philadelphia.

Remembering Wen

Like most things in Philadelphia from the 1700s, the Pennsylvania Hospital has a Benjamin Franklin connection. The hospital was actually the brainchild of Franklin's friend Dr. Thomas Bond, but in those days it took Franklin's approval to get major projects off the ground, so he cosponsored the place. Because of this, Ben's face appears throughout the hospital. One typical, though insidious-looking, portrait is in the library: a painted bust of the great man in his old age sitting at a desk. The hospital archivist, Stacey Peeples, told us that the wrinkle-framed eyes of this bust scare many younger hospital visitors. In fact, she confided, they scare her sometimes as well.

Fair enough, but it's odd to wig out over this founding father when there are four really creepy items in the library, not counting what may be hidden between the covers of the 8,700 books and 4,500 journals on the shelves. Front and center as you enter the room is the most famous bizarre item—a brain-sized thing, pickled in alcohol inside a tubular glass jar. Ignoring our own best advice ("Never look too closely at an artifact in a medical library"), we headed straight for the jar. From a distance, the object inside, floating in a yellow liquid, looked like a brain, except that it was smooth.

A sign on the jar's stand revealed its secret: It was actually a two-hundred-year-old tumor removed from the head of a Dauphin County resident named James Hayes. This tumor, referred to as a wen, had been growing on the man's left cheek for twenty years, until Christmas Day, 1805, when Dr. Philip Syng Physick removed it in the hospital's amphitheater in front of an audience of eighty medical students and doctors.

The other three creepy items are housed in three wooden trunks along the wall. They are teaching aids imported from England in the 1760s, and like most medical teaching aids, they are not to be taken lightly. They are life-sized plaster casts of the torso of a woman who had died during childbirth. Why are there three? Because one was made before the autopsy, and the other two were made during the procedure. We did mention something about not being faint of heart or stomach, didn't we?

This house of medical horrors is not generally open to the public, though the grounds of the Pennsylvania Hospital at 800 Spruce Street are open for self-guided walking tours. The library is open by appointment with the hospital's archivist. And the contents of the trunks are revealed only upon request. But one spooky item is always in full view: the bust of Benjamin Franklin, whose ever watchful painted eyes gaze at visitors from his desktop perch, quietly sizing them up from across the room.

She Had a Lotta Nerve!

When they said that Harriet Cole was a bundle of nerves, they weren't kidding. Of course, it was only after she had died and willed her body to Philadelphia's Hahnemann Medical College that they started to refer to Harriet that way. She had been a cleaning woman at the school until her death in 1888 and was probably never referred to at all by any of the famously aloof members of the medical profession. But after the school's most eminent anatomy specialist, Professor Rufus Benjamin Weaver, AM, MD, ScD, got his hands on her, she became an object of great attention and has remained so for more than a century.

Dr. Weaver decided to make her the subject of his most ambitious anatomical project, planning to extract her entire nervous system intact and mount it for display and educational purposes. Anatomical experts and physicians from all over the world told him it was impossible. But Weaver was a strong-minded Pennsylvanian and wasn't about to let others tell him what he could or couldn't do with his cadavers. So for five months, he toiled daily in the Hahnemann dissecting rooms, discarding flesh, muscles, tendons, and bones and leaving only the nerves, which he wrapped in gauze for protection. He then coated the strands of nerve fiber in white lead to preserve and strengthen them and finally shellacked and mounted them in roughly human shape with hundreds of pins.

It's in this form that you can now see Harriet Cole. She stands like a sentinel in front of the security gate to the library of Hahnemann University.

There, on the first floor, just inside the main entrance, her two blue plaster eyes stare out from a translucent amber skull. Everything else is a map of the human nervous system, intact, and made up of the real thing: a delicate filament of real nerves, coated in paint.

It's hard to appreciate just how big a feat this was. Under the grandiose title of "Dissected and Mounted Human Cerebro-Spinal Nervous System," Harriet's preserved nervous system met with great acclaim as a learning tool and a marvel of dissection. In 1893, at the Columbian Exposition in Chicago, the exhibit was awarded a gold medal and a blue ribbon, both of which are in the same glass display case as the preserved nerves. *Life* magazine and *Time* published accolades about the stunning nervous system of the former cleaning lady.

If you're in the mood to scope this out for yourself, visit the Hahnemann University Hospital, which is part of Drexel University in Philadelphia, a few blocks north of the city hall. The library is at the main entrance, at 245 N. Fifteenth Street, near Vine Street.

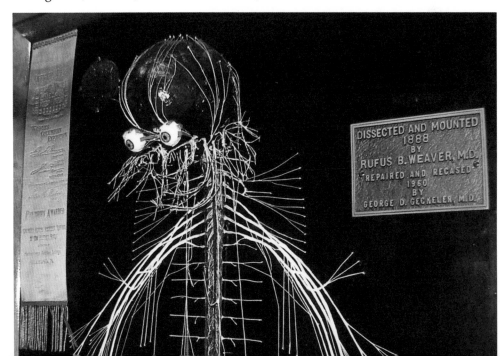

More Museums

It's hard to outweird the Mütter, so most museums won't even try. Having said that, there is no shortage of inspired collected strangeness in the state. Most of it won't raise your gorge as often as the Mütter collection, but it can raise an eyebrow. Ready for more strange collections in the Keystone State? Look no further than here.

Mercer Museum

Of all things a nice historic town in Bucks County could adopt as a cultural icon, the very last one that springs to mind would be a huge concrete building built by a lawyer. And yet this is exactly what the Mercer Museum is. This six-story reinforced-concrete castle dominates Doylestown's historic district, with a haphazard arrangement of arched and square windows, with towers and gabled roofs, all made of a material so crude that you can see the impression of the planks and burlap that made up the molds into which the concrete slurry had been poured.

Yet somehow the Mercer Museum has a kind of grandeur. And appearances aside, it's amazing to think that this structure is the work of a gifted amateur. Henry Mercer was a successful lawyer without formal training in architecture, but between 1913 and 1916 he designed and built this enormous structure with help from eight laborers and a horse named Lucy. Mercer and his team worked six days a week to complete the job. Now it's become so revered that it appears as a line drawing on the town's street signs and houses Bucks County's historical society.

As odd as the outside of this building is, nothing compares with the puzzling contents of its museum, which was also a brainchild of the busy Henry Mercer. At the turn of the twentieth century, he noticed that industrialization was wiping out trades that had once been part of every town or village, along with their tools. The small looms that once made rough cloth for everyday use were no longer needed. The wares of local blacksmiths, who at one time had created tools for farmers and fishermen, were being passed over. Except for the Amish models, horse-drawn coaches were disappearing too. Even the wooden statues outside cigar stores were vanishing.

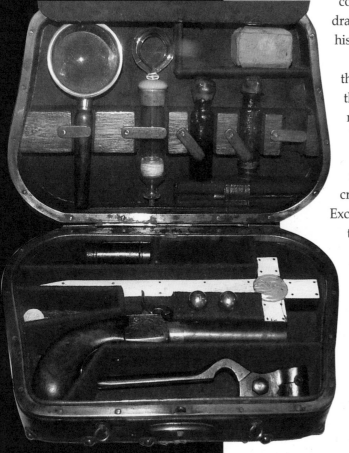

A Vampire Killing Kit *from the collection, containing a handgun, silver bullets, an ivory crucifix, powdered flowers of garlic, a wooden stake, and a serum: essential items "considered necessary for the protection of persons who travel into certain little known countries of Eastern Europe where the populace is plagued with a particular manifestation of evil known as Vampires."*

Part of America's past was slipping away, and to Mercer, this meant two things: It would be relatively easy and cheap to buy up these artifacts, and it was essential to preserve them.

And that's exactly what he did in the concrete castle. Walking into the Mercer Museum is an odd experience. There's a huge hall six

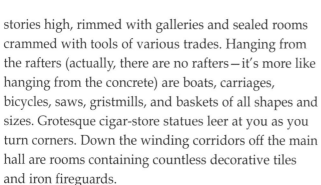

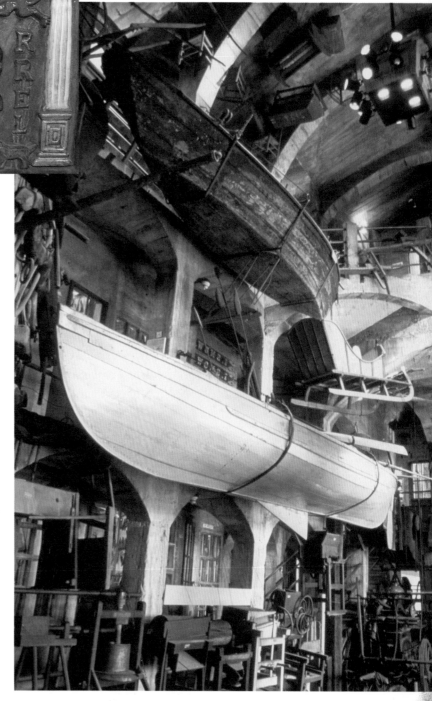

stories high, rimmed with galleries and sealed rooms crammed with tools of various trades. Hanging from the rafters (actually, there are no rafters—it's more like hanging from the concrete) are boats, carriages, bicycles, saws, gristmills, and baskets of all shapes and sizes. Grotesque cigar-store statues leer at you as you turn corners. Down the winding corridors off the main hall are rooms containing countless decorative tiles and iron fireguards.

You won't have to look hard to find weird images here. The fireguards show devils steering families into arguments and skeletons beating people. There's a Victorian vampire-killing kit, featuring among other things, a handgun with silver bullets, a combination stake and crucifix, and vials for holy water. (Too bad the authenticity of this kit is in doubt: Analysis of the glue, ink, and paper in the case shows some suspicious anomalies.) Upstairs, in a mezzanine above the sixth floor, is a gallows with an open trapdoor, as well as a noose, handcuffs, and cudgels behind glass. And this is a place they take kids on school trips!

The Mercer Museum ranks high on the charts of weird places that have been assimilated into the community. But even though Doylestown does embrace Mercer's concrete castle, there's no denying it's a strange place.

Roadside America

We gotta say it: Roadside America in Shartlesville turned out to be the most pleasant surprise we found. The surprise was all the better because it's hidden inside an uninspired-looking building with a touristy gift store. Only the strange fiberglass Amish giants in the parking lot hinted at anything odd—and they had no connection whatsoever with the exhibit inside. As you walk into the warehouse-size enclosure, $5 ticket stub in hand, you're overwhelmed by a vision that straddles the cozy world of Ozzie and Harriet America and the compulsions of an obsessive artist. No matter which camp appeals to you, you're likely to get a good hour's entertainment out of the visit.

Roadside America is a model railroad builder's basement on an insanely large scale—a miniature town filling a huge hangar. This small yet vast model town is filled with mountains and bridges, tiny people, railroads, working fountains, farms, churches, and everything else that typified life in the first half of the twentieth century. It's something that avoids the kitsch by its authentic

depictions of a time and place where old trades and the farming way of life were disappearing even as the model maker was documenting them.

The model is the brainchild of one man, the late Laurence Gieringer of Reading, who spent sixty years working on it with some help from his brother Paul. The story goes that as a child, Laurence looked out of his bedroom window at Neversink Mountain and, with a young child's lack of perspective vision, believed it was about the size of his window. When he began modeling, he scaled things to about the same relative size—three eighths of an inch to the foot, according to Roadside America's literature. Gieringer kept on working in private until 1935, when he displayed his village to entertain the town's children at Christmas. It was a great success, but he didn't need any encouragement to carry on his work.

Gieringer was a man of great religious faith and a commitment to constant activity. Something about its creator's personality shows in the great detail and joyfulness of the Roadside America town. Even though it was built in the shadow of two world wars, with a pall of economic depression hanging over it, the town seems busy and bustling, the tiny people secure in their world. As the work progressed, it became too large to put up and take down. Eventually, in 1953, it took up permanent residence in Shartlesville, where it has been open to the paying public ever since.

Every hour, night falls on the town, and the lights twinkle in the model's windows. On the wall nearest the entrance, a hokey but strangely touching slide-show presentation begins, depicting shamelessly sentimental images of America that culminate in the image of Lady Liberty holding her torch aloft to light the world while a scratchy Kate Smith record sings "God Bless America." Like the last scenes of Frank Capra's *It's a Wonderful Life*,

it's a moment you want to laugh at but secretly has you blinking back tears.

If you need to crank up the machismo after this experience, you can always scope out the off-topic display cases around the walls, showing Native American artifacts dug up in the area. There's one in particular that must have an interesting but untold story behind it: It's an arrowhead embedded in the side of what appears to be a human backbone.

It's hard to imagine a world in which Roadside America really belongs. It's not a modern whiz-bang attraction or an intellectually stimulating cultural experience. Nobody working with balance sheets and focus groups would ever build such a place now, and it's hard to understand how it has stayed open over the past fifty years. But it's here and during our visits had quite a bit of foot traffic. We hope that, unlike the scenes it depicts, Roadside America is here to stay.

Lincoln Flag

The Lincoln Flag is kept in a marvelous building called The Columns, located at 608 Broad Street in Milford. This building is also the home of the Pike County Historical Society.

As you walk up the wooden steps and enter through the wide doors, you will feel as if you are stepping back in time. What a magnificent home this must have been. Off to the right, a wide room opens up, and there it is— the Lincoln Flag. This flag was placed under President Lincoln's head after he had been shot. Plainly visible are the bloodstains from the wounded President. Not one of us spoke as we silently examined this most treasured standard.

It seems that after the President was mortally shot by John Wilkes Booth on April 14, 1865, the flag, which had been draped over the balustrade at Ford's Theatre, was placed under his head by Thomas Gourlay, a part-time stage manager at the theater. After the President was moved to the Petersen House, across the street, the flag was taken by Gourlay and eventually was given to his daughter. It was passed down through the family before it was finally given to the Pike County Historical Society in 1954.

Extensive research has confirmed again and again that this is indeed the flag upon which the dying Abraham Lincoln rested his head. It is amazing to see, to almost touch. It is a true American treasure and is right in our own backyard.

The Lincoln Flag can be seen at The Columns on Wednesday through Sunday from 1 p.m. till 4 p.m. For more information, call 570-296-8126, and donations are requested.
–*Dr. Seymour O'Life*

Shoe Museum

Of all the museums that you would expect to have foot traffic in, the Shoe Museum in Philadelphia ought to top the list. But this free display of footwear at Temple University's School of Podiatric Medicine is open only by appointment. The visiting hours and group sizes may be limited, but the collection itself is nine hundred strong and growing, with some two hundred and fifty exhibits at any given time. They range from Chinese footwear for women with three-inch bound feet to a bidet-size bespoke shoe for a woman with gigantism. There's a set of 1960s gold vinyl boots once owned by Ella Fitzgerald, some Egyptian funerary slippers, button-sided Victorian boots, wooden sabots from Europe, and a large collection of ethnic footwear on loan from the Mütter Museum. There are a fair number of celebrity donations here as well, including shoes from former First Ladies Mamie Eisenhower and Nancy Reagan; sports memorabilia, such as Reggie Jackson's five home-run World Series shoes; Andre Agassi's pink-and-black Nikes from his 1990 tennis victory; and sneakers once owned by local hero "Dr. J" Erving.

A short hop from the Philadelphia Convention Center and the city's Chinatown, the shoe museum was opened to celebrate the U.S. bicentennial in 1976 and was clearly meant to last. The collection is housed on the sixth floor of the Temple University School of Podiatric Medicine's Center for the History of Foot Care and Footwear, at the corner of Eighth and Race streets in Philadelphia.

These ancient Egyptian burial sandals are part of a collection on loan from the Mütter Museum and were presumably pried from the feet of a mummy by some antiquarian tomb raider.

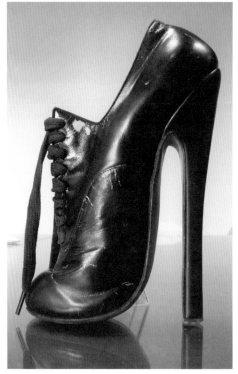

These training shoes for stilt-walkers and ballerinas have brought short women a few inches closer to the ceiling since the 1800s and rewarded them with corns, bunions, and the attentions of foot fetishists the world over.

To make this boot, a wolf had to die to provide the fur, and an Inuit woman had to chew the leather to make the sole. When her jaw got tired, she is said to have used a screwdriver!

These Middle Eastern sabots provide proof positive that shoemakers of the world have throughout time believed that the foot ends in a point.

Huh?

Some things you see by the roadside just defy description. In such cases, we raise an eyebrow, shrug a shoulder, and say, "Huh?" Then we pass the findings on to you, the reader.

Semichapel

One day while passing through PA, I stopped at a rest stop and couldn't help but notice this weird chapel thingy tractor-trailer. Maybe this is normal to Christian PA residents, but I thought I would send it to you all anyway. I call it PA religion on the run. –*Emily Madera*

Inverted Bus

As you drive along Route 322 in northwestern Pennsylvania through Cranberry, there's a graphic reminder to be careful at the busy junction. The upside-down school bus outside the 4 Your Car Connection dealership seems to be a grim reminder of a recent accident, until you see that it's supported on a platform and displays the public-service announcement SCHOOL'S IN SESSION. DRIVE SAFELY. Point taken.

Hay-Baler Mailbox

Out in the rural routes in Oil Country, who knows what vehicle will deliver your mail? One year, it'll be a four-by-four; the next, a truck; and the next, whatever makes sense to the mail carrier. So the creative folks out there learn to accommodate the changing needs of their swift couriers by recycling farm equipment into adjustable-height mailbox stands. This hay baler can be cranked to bring the boxes up a foot or two, or down, depending on what the mail carrier happens to be driving that year. Remember: The post office's promise is to deliver through snow, sleet, rain, and gloom of night. The completion of their appointed rounds will be that much swifter if they can avoid backache from stretching to reach the mailboxes.

You Want Crude with That?

Getting a Big Mac at the Bradford branch of McDonald's is unlike any other fast-food experience. The burgers, fries, sesame buns, and drinks are identical to every other McDonald's, of course, but is there another drive-through with a working oil well in the parking lot? There it is, on the left, as you drive up to the menu and loudspeaker, its bird-beak armature dipping up and down, bringing up about thirty gallons of crude a day, as it has been since the 1870s.

Of course, Texas and the Middle East crow about their oil yields, but northeastern Pennsylvania is the home of the "microbreweries" of the petrochemical industry. These little wells yield a crude oil that's rich in lubricating chemicals, ideal for making Vaseline and other petroleum-jelly products, and it's also great as an engine oil. (Why else do you think they call those high-grade engine lubes Pennzoil and Quaker State?)

The Bradford McDonald's well was the first one drilled by a prominent local company, Cline Oil, and one of the many small wells that you see in front yards, woods, and roadsides throughout McKean and Venango counties. But if you do order a Big Mac at the drive-through there, refrain from wisecracks about crude in their fries or about secret sauce. They've heard it all before, and they're not paid enough to hear it again.

The Strange Statue of William Penn

It's hard to know how to handle this topic delicately, but so many people have remarked on this curiosity that we have to include it here. It concerns the massive statue of William Penn on top of Philadelphia's city hall. No other statue atop a public building can match this thirty-seven-foot-high bronze for sheer size. And so the question leaps to the mind of anyone who looks at it while driving down from Fairmount Park and the Art Gallery: Did they realize how it would look from this angle? The official story is that Penn's statue is holding a copy of the treaty he had signed with the Lenni Lenape tribe, and it faces the place where the treaty was signed. However, the statue is holding the treaty at waist level, and to anyone driving or strolling down Franklin Parkway, it looks for all the world as though he's preparing to urinate off the top of the building.

Now, this could be purely coincidental, but then again, Philadelphia has a history of high-profile puckish humor that dates back to Benjamin Franklin. The city's art galleries house several famous examples of Dada art, including a thematically linked Marcel Duchamp creation: a porcelain urinal turned on its side and entitled *Fountain.* So the "Is that what I think it is?" moment you get at the sight of Penn atop the city hall may have been intentional. But one thing's for sure: The statue's sculptor, Alexander Milne Calder, didn't intend it. He never wanted his statue to be stuck on top of a tower.

In the interests of research, *Weird Pennsylvania* took a stroll beside the city hall to see where the statue appears to be aiming. The result raised more questions than answers. From an unscientific analysis of direction, distance, and angle, the intended target would appear to be the historic Masonic temple and Methodist Episcopal building. There's a punch line in there somewhere. Figure it out for yourself.

Hug a Nurse

We all agree that nurses deserve our friendly support, but surely there's a better place to remind us of this than in a large sign on the side of a gravestone engraver's shop? Is the Tri-City Monument Company trying to hint at dire consequences for *not* celebrating nurses? One thing's for sure—after driving by this three-generation-strong family stonemason's firm in Venango County, we thanked the first nurse we could find.

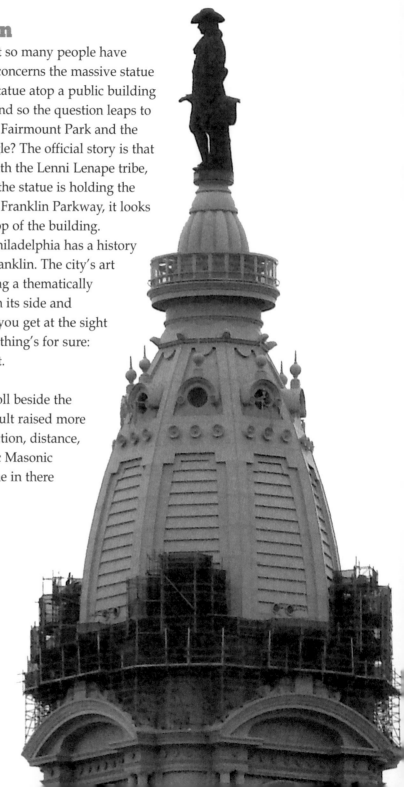

Roadside Space Capsule

We were on our way to visit a couple of friends in PA last year and came across a weird sculpture. On the side of the road, alongside a gas station, was a replica NASA Apollo space capsule, complete with a fully suited-up astronaut. Recently, I went back up there, and the capsule was moved. It now sits in the backyard of the newly renovated gas station, minus the astronaut! The owner of the station told me that a friend of his father's had been a career air force man and that, as a creative and proud American, he built this monument to the American space program. He gave it to the station owner's father years ago, and it has been there for a while.

So what happened to the astronaut? He's in storage for the winter, getting some cosmetic surgery. He should be back in his capsule, greeting all of the motorists stopping for gas soon. To see the space capsule for yourself, just take route 611 to Martins Creek and stop at the only gas station in town.–*Gary Z. (Mr. Road Kill)*

Smiling Stump of Peter's Mountain

Peter's Mountain, between Harrisburg and Halifax, used to have a great landmark that's now no more. The shack on top of the mountain has a black roof, but at one time, it was painted with a big yellow smiley face. It was something everyone used to point out as a landmark to their passengers during the drive up Route 225. Because it was so prominent, some wise guys painted graffiti on it. For a while, it had a bullet hole painted in the middle of its forehead. It's not surprising that the owners painted it black in the end.

Well, if you look closely by the roadside, you can still find a little memorial smiley face on Peter's Mountain. It's carved into a tree stump by the roadside, which you can see as you go up the mountain from the south. Better yet, people decorate it with hats. You'll see a witch hat on Halloween, a Santa hat at Christmas, and all sorts of other headgear. It's not like the shack roof, but it's still nice to see a smile as you drive.–*Jay Church*

Milord, the Carriage Awaits!

Driving south from Mount Pocono along Route 33, it's hard to avoid a sign for a beer outlet by the roadside. But it's harder to figure out why there's a battered horse carriage on top of the sign. So the *Weird Pennsylvania* research team took the next exit, wended its way through a tortuous series of right turns, and eventually navigated a huge bumpy gravel parking lot to the beer outlet. The man behind the counter had been expecting us (he'd seen us pull over and photograph the sign) and told us the story behind the carriage. The outlet used to deal in antiques, and the carriage caught the eye and made a point at the same time. It still catches the eye today, of course, and the fact that it no longer makes sense doesn't matter to him. "People still keep coming," he said. "In fact, some of them just climb down from the shoulder and jump the fence." This isn't legal or smart, of course, but the sight of a roadside carriage affects some people that way.

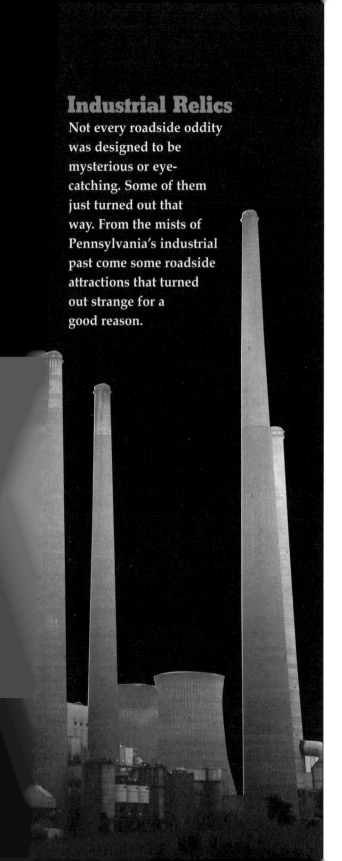

Industrial Relics

Not every roadside oddity was designed to be mysterious or eye-catching. Some of them just turned out that way. From the mists of Pennsylvania's industrial past come some roadside attractions that turned out strange for a good reason.

America's Tallest Smokestack

Whenever The History Channel runs their series on engineering marvels, I sit before the screen transfixed. There must be something exclusive to the male psyche that draws us toward such things. You're not likely to hear women waxing poetic on such topics as tall buildings, long bridges, or breakthroughs in engineering. But guys on the other hand? We try to one-up each other as we trade information about such things. That part of it may have something to do with a need to "compensate." What I am pointing to is a grand celebration of maleness in the form of a giant cylinder. I'm talking about the tallest smokestack to ever sprout from American soil. Sigmund Freud would have a field day with that.

Discovering that this monster loomed large in Homer City, I couldn't resist the urge to see it up close. I didn't have precise directions, but I figured if this puppy were as tall as it's billed, it would find me.

Nothing prepares you for a smokestack like this, particularly if you're accustomed to the common dinky ones that seldom top two hundred feet. How tall is this one, you ask? A grand 1,216 feet. If you placed it next to the Empire State Building, it would only miss the top by thirty-four feet! If you stood it beside the Washington Monument, it would be double the height, plus a hundred feet on top of that.

As I followed an access road to the power plant, I located a pull-off that was fifty yards from the smokestack's base. Seeing it from this vantage point cannot be expressed properly in print; "mind boggling" is the best I can do. Flanking it were three other mighty stacks, each in excess of eight hundred feet, and beside them were three cooling towers, each standing four hundred feet.

The reason for such colossal heights is quite simple: the Homer City Power Station generates electricity by burning coal. Regulations require that the burnt coal effluent be released high up in the atmosphere to give it time to dissipate before it falls back to Earth. The end result? Obscenely tall smokestacks.

This smokestack is not only the tallest one in America, it's very nearly the tallest one in the world. At the moment, only one—in Sudbury, Canada—betters it, and then only by a mere thirty feet.
*—Jeff Bah*r

Sparks Shot Tower

Anyone for a smokestack with a roof on top? This 142-foot-high brick column in South Philly only looks like a smokestack. It's actually a relic of the postrevolutionary war military industrial complex. Built in 1808, the Sparks Shot Tower was used to make lead shot for almost a century, supplying soldiers in the war of 1812 and the Civil War. It's a fascinating piece of industrial archaeology and a fine example of brickwork too, though most people see it only in passing as they zoom along I-95.

The tower is no longer in operation, but back in its working life, it contained a reservoir of molten lead under that roof. The molten metal dripped through a mesh and formed into spheres as it fell. After a long cooling fall, the shot dropped into water and solidified. The Sparks Shot Tower looms above Carpenter Street in South Philly and marks the spot of a building that's now used as a city recreation center.

Topless Pyramids

Weird Pennsylvania followed a lead to this mysterious-looking topless pyramid at the intersection of Route 26 and SR 1029 just outside Rothrock State Forest in Huntingdon County. Pumped up on the mythology of the Rosicrucians and Masons, our tipster was convinced the place was an abandoned temple of some kind. Each of the pyramid's four sides contains a six- to eight-foot-tall doorway, and the building itself is frequented by many nighttime revelers.

Too bad our tipster didn't know about the iron foundries of the Industrial Revolution. This is actually the Monroe Furnace, built in 1847, and it once had a wooden hut on top, from which iron ore was dropped into a massively hot fire below. When the pure iron was ready, it poured through a funnel into molds. But even though the furnace's origins are in science and industry rather than cultish religion, this imposing structure can still inspire slack-jawed wonder in visitors.

The South Puts One Over on Shamokin

Here is a photo of the Civil War monument in Shamokin, which was erected in 1898. The caption says it is dedicated to "the soldiers and sailors of the rebellion." Word is that the statue was commissioned, then given to a Southern sympathizer to carve. He carved in the heading as a tribute to the Confederate "Rebellion." Then he received payment and skipped town before the locals discovered what the wording really meant. *–Chris Lutz, Manassas, Virginia*

Devil in the Details

Gargoyles are ten a penny. We can see demon faces almost everywhere we look in almost any city in any Western country. But when it comes to grotesque representations on buildings, we have to give the Philadelphia Museum of Art top marks. Tucked to the right of a pseudo-Greek temple at the top of the steps that Stallone climbed in *Rocky* is a collection of painted Greek gods. Which god this particular horn-headed monstrosity might be is a mystery. We checked the index of *Bulfinch's Mythology* for a reference to Darth Maul, but he wasn't listed.

Pennsbury Hill

Visitors to William Penn's home at Pennsbury Manor have this imposing hill to admire as they gaze away from the river toward the horizon. Of course, the strange pipes rising out of the ground at regular intervals are a modern addition, and in fact, so is the hill itself. This marvel of topography consists of a thin layer of topsoil over a massive pile of garbage trucked to the site from elsewhere in the state and other states as well. Penn would have been so proud.

What's in a Name?

Pennsylvania has an unparalleled knack for naming places. Its own name accurately describes the state's lush woodlands, and its nicknames are equally germane. As the central of the thirteen original colonies, it was the Keystone State. It's also been the Quaker State, after William Penn's religious group, and the Coal State, Oil State, and the Steel State, after its industries.

But that doesn't mean that all the place-names in the state are prosaic and accurate. Among the 3,400-plus town names in the commonwealth, there are some real doozies. There's the perennial snicker-producing town of Intercourse in Lancaster County, which merely shows that seventeenth-century German immigrants knew more nuances of the English language than current Americans. (It just means "interaction," people. Get over it.) There's a Venus in Venango County and a Mars just west of it in Butler County. No word yet as to whether famed author John Gray visited before he proclaimed which place the women came from. There are other odd pairings too, like the legalese street names Null and Void outside Punxsutawney.

And then there are the phrase towns. Even when you know the origins of King of Prussia and Bird-in-Hand, the names still raise eyebrows. And it's not just because they're named after roadside taverns (in a Quaker state, no less!). There was always heavy commercial traffic between the farmlands of Lancaster County and the towns to the east, so word spread about the virtues of staying at the Bird-in-Hand. It was only a matter of time before the whole community took on the name.

And when a wily innkeeper in the town of Reeseville stuck a picture of Frederick the Great in front of his bar to attract German soldiers, the fame of the King of Prussia Inn spread. By the time the United States Postal Service established a post office there, the town's original name was all but forgotten.

But even odd names like these pale next to some others that the commonwealth has to offer. Couldn't someone have done a better job naming the towns of Burning Well, Drain Lick, Dry Tavern, Normalville, Gargol, or Yellow Spring?

We know that Jim Thorpe was named after a celebrity, but what about Glen Campbell?

Do people from Buck feel ten times better than people from Dime? Couldn't the town of Forty Fort have come up with a better adjective for its stronghold? And why are there Gates of Hell near Downingtown and York, but no paved path in that direction from Good Intent?

Do the good people of Avis and Nolo know that they live in the Latin words meaning "bird" and "I don't want"?

Does Shy Beaver lead to Blue Ball?

Why couldn't the townspeople of Energy, Force, and Endeavor have lent a little optimism to the folks over in Ono and Panic?

And were the good citizens of Susquehanna and Crawford counties hungry for dessert when they named the towns Choconut and Custards?

We can only guess the answers to these questions as we move quietly on, scratching our heads, to other stops in weird Pennsylvania.

Roads Less Traveled

Snaking through our commonwealth are legendary byways that have earned an honored place in the annals of the weird. These roads are surrounded by a special aura that sets them apart from all others. Some look perfectly normal when you first turn onto them, then become shadowy places where anything, it seems, could happen. And if we are to believe the tales that surround these places, weirdness—almost beyond belief—has happened there. There are roads that seem to defy the laws of gravity; there are wooded byways that time forgot. And there are ancient bridges, the sites of events so tragic that the rickety spans are forever cursed. Pennsylvania offers some of the most hair-raising late-night traveling adventures anywhere, so strap yourself in. It's going to be a bumpy ride.

Tales of the Blue Myst

There's something about headlights shining on an unlit road at night that stimulates the imagination. Roads, especially dirt roads with no streetlights, reveal shadows that could contain any kind of mystery—a wild animal, a ghost, a malevolent cult, anything strange and threatening. Of course, if you happen to be driving along such a road with a group of friends, the tales get all the wilder. And that's exactly what has happened with Blue Myst Road in Pittsburgh's North Park. To some, the mystery is more important than the mist, and they do spell it Blue Myst Road. (Its proper name is Irwin Road, but you can see how that doesn't lend itself to ghostly stories.)

The legends that surround this stretch of road are as varied as the imaginations of western Pennsylvanians. Like the Trojan War or Mount Olympus to the Greeks, it has become a convenient receptacle for any tale, ranging from obvious campfire yarns and recycled urban legends to material

with more heft and style. But always, the stories come back to a rolling mist that appears at night on a dirt road near the lake in North Park. After the mist rolls in, the tales diverge in the woods.

The classic local legend about Blue Myst Road is that the Ku Klux Klan used to hold rallies there at night and would lynch people on a gnarled tree by the side of the road. It's a good scary tale, but it lacks the ring of truth. Given the strong, centuries-long abolitionist tradition in the commonwealth, it seems unlikely that a group like the Klan would have established a stronghold here. Besides, the tree that's most often associated with this tale seems to be singularly unsuited to the task, with no strong, low-hanging limbs over which to throw a rope.

There are several houses on the road, one of them now a ruin, with only the foundation intact. In the ferment of storytelling, legends have sprouted up about the houses

too. One, they say, was occupied by a witch, and another, called the Midget Farm, by a little person. All the usual Midgetville stories apply to this house, including the one in which groups of angry and armed little people would attack your car.

As far as we can tell, these tales are mostly just good ways to scare your car mates. A fed-up resident of one of the houses did fire rock salt cartridges at nighttime trespassers, though. This type of attack is loud, scary, and will cause expensive damage to the paintwork of a car, but it causes no serious personal injury. It just stings, grazes, and teaches a lesson. The lesson in question is "stay away." Nevertheless, people do drive and hike down the road at night, and drivers claim that if you park your car and honk your horn three times, the engine won't start up again. When you consider that people live off the road, it's antisocial to honk your horn at night, anyway.

All of these stories are pretty much standard fare. But one is a little more unusual. There is a cemetery near the road with two tombstones that lean toward each other. People say that the occupants of the graves were thwarted lovers and that the stones are trying to kiss to consummate the love between them. In some tales, the stones actually do meet once a month on the night of the full moon. In other variations the stones do not meet, because if they did it would bring about the end of the world.

These tales are all well and good, but to most people who visit North Park, Blue Myst Road is just a great hiking avenue. It's marked CLOSED at both ends, though it's car accessible for a few hundred twisting yards before barricades block it off. Past the barriers, it degenerates quickly into a winding gravel path by the creek. On a quiet spring day, you can see deer and wild turkey around the road, with only the murmuring of the stream to disturb them. A dark and moonless night, however, might be another story altogether.

Blue Light Special

We've seen some unusual lights up at Blue Myst. They were large and blue, hovering in the distance and then fading away. It couldn't have been a flashlight because it faded out in a very distinctive way, like a firefly or a klieg light.—*AOakley*

Kiss the Stones

The cemetery near Blue Myst Road is old, with worn-out and very thin gravestones. You can't read the names on them. My friend took some of us there, and we saw two gravestones leaning toward each other, which were supposed to be the stones of two former lovers. They weren't touching, but the way the ground was subsiding, it looked like it was only a matter of time before they did. They are set apart by a few inches, and people say that they touch whenever it's a full moon. The cemetery was too creepy for us to go back, though. —*Anonymous*

Three Roads Diverge . . .

I have walked Blue Myst Road at night and come across three paths leading off the road, with one rusty mailbox. My companions told me that one of these paths leads to the Midget Farm and the Witch House, but nobody was able to confirm that. We saw car headlights coming our way from the driveway, so we got out of there as fast as we could.—*Mysterian*

Tales of Mist and Imagination

There's an old tale of the North Hills I once read called "The Legend of Blue Myst Road." The area was always surrounded by horror stories, some about a rabid dog roaming around, some about cults and mutilated animals being discovered, and so forth. But this didn't put off teenagers going to the quiet road to park. One young couple went there, and for a joke, the boy honked the horn three times before they began to make out. As if in answer to the horn, a clanging bell began to ring out, and the boyfriend panicked and tried to start the car. The engine was dead. The clanging continued and, thoroughly rattled, the boy popped the hood of the car to see what the problem was. When he slammed the hood down, a white hunting dog leaped on it and began dashing itself against the windshield, terrifying the girl in the car. It dashed itself unconscious, or dead, on the hood. All was silent for a while, and the girl got out of the car, too frightened to stay alone. Then the car began clanging, and she turned and saw a dark mark on its roof. She looked up to see her boyfriend hanging from the limb of a nearby tree, his blood dripping onto the car roof. I know, it sounds too good to be true, but it's a great way to get in the mood on the drive up there.—*Eddie*

Gravity Roads

A little knowledge of physics and a little personal observation will tell you the obvious: Unless something holds them up, objects tend to accelerate downward. Gravity is a force of nature that even babies understand instinctively. And yet there are places in the world in which this most fundamental law seems to be broken regularly. These weird sites go by many names: gravity hills, gravity roads, mystery spots, or spook hills. But they all work in pretty much the same way: If you put your car in neutral, slowly but surely it begins to move uphill on these roads instead of down. This phenomenon has been observed all over the world. There are gravity hills documented in Scotland, Portugal, Barbados, Australia, and Korea.

True to form, Pennsylvania offers several of these pixilated roads. Their attraction is plain. You can pour water onto the roads, or roll a ball or bottle downhill, and see it stop and begin to roll uphill. You can (if you're careful and obey traffic regulations) sit with your car in neutral and experience the phenomenon for yourself. It feels disorienting, but quite pleasantly so. Of course, skeptics dismiss the whole thing as an optical illusion. A road that appears to go uphill may in fact be pointing down, which would account for the weird feeling of disorientation that some visitors report. That may indeed be the explanation—but unless you've been to one of these places yourself, armed with surveying equipment for good measure, how can you be sure?

Gravity Hill, New Paris

Gravity Hill in New Paris is the only one in Pennsylvania to get the stamp of approval from the local tourist board. The Bedford County Visitor's Bureau gives out a leaflet with directions to the place and even sells souvenir T-shirts and hats. Heck, they even registered the Web domain www.gravityhill.com, so you know they mean business. This is just as well, because to get to this place, you have to traverse some winding roads and follow very particular directions. The visitor's guide is written (some might say overwritten) in bureaucratic breezy.

As you strain your ears to hear the laws of physics being shattered, put your car in neutral (after checking behind you for oncoming traffic, of course) and take your foot off the brake. Your car will roll uphill. Some people like to take water or various other non-flammable, bio-degradable liquids and pour them onto the road. The liquids will flow uphill.

The first time we tried to check out Gravity Hill, we just looked for New Paris on the map and chanced it. Not a good approach. The next time, we took the guide and found the spot, which is a stretch of road between two pairs of spray-painted letters, GH. We'd probably have missed it again, except for the spring-break revelers rolling basketballs, baseballs, and empty soft drink cans up (or was it down?) the hill.

For the benefit of those who miss the open hours of the Bedford County Visitor's Bureau, here are the directions to the mystery spot. It's a bumpy ride to get there, but it's worth a trip.

Gravity Hill
Defy Gravity

Before you come to the town of New Paris on Route 96, you'll come upon a small metal bridge. Turn left just before this bridge onto Bethel Hollow Road or S.R. 4016. Drive for six tenths of a mile and bear left at the Y in the road. After another one and one-half miles, you'll come to an intersection that has a STOP sign. Bear right onto this road and drive two tenths of a mile and look for the letters GH spray-painted on the road. Go past the first GH about one tenth of a mile and stop before you get to the second spray-painted GH.

Defying Gravity

Bedford is a tiny little Central Pennsylvania hick town, but they have quite a few things for seekers of the strange. First of all, there's a Gravity Hill there, and you won't even get a ticket for trying it out. You face up the hill, but when you put your car in neutral, you roll up the hill instead of down it! It's kind of a simple law of physics really—the road is tilted, but since you're on the side of a mountain it makes you roll the other way. . . . Cool nonetheless!—*Natalie Pappas*

Is North Hills Better?

In North Park, north of Pittsburgh, there's a golf course with a nearby Gravity Hill. It's just a short hop from Blue Myst Road, so you can take them both in on a single trip. And for my money, the Gravity Hill's more interesting. —*Morgan F.*

The Devil and the Gravity Hill

Bucks County's Gravity Hill, though not sanctioned by the local government, is one of Pennsylvania's legendary places. On maps, this gravity hill is on Buckingham Mountain, near the Mount Gilead African Methodist Episcopal Church. There, with a blatant disregard for the laws of nature and physics, things are said to roll uphill—cars, water, you name it. And dark legends say black magic and other evils are behind these amazing powers.

The church and graveyard at the hill are said to be the stomping grounds of local Satanists. Satanic or not, the road itself, which is on the other side of the hill from Mount Gilead Church, has all the regular features of a gravity hill. But don't try to use it to get away from those dark forces in the cemetery—you can't be sure which way your car will go!

Hoof It up the Hill

Buckingham Mountain isn't the only gravity hill with sinister tales attached to it. Just off Route 219 in Brandy Camp, Elk County, is a gravity hill that's supposed to be haunted by spectral quadrupeds. Before you perform your uphill-in-neutral stunt, roll down the window and keep an ear open. They say you'll be able to hear a horse galloping off in the distance. As your car rolls uphill, you can distinctly hear hooves clopping against the asphalt. Either that or you have a couple of Monty Python fans with coconut shells in the backseat!

Bridges Too Far Out

Bridges seem to breed legends. In times past, some European cities would hang criminals and traitors from bridges as a warning to those entering the city. It's no wonder many gruesome and supernatural stories center around dark spans over even darker waters. There's an old Scots belief, for example, that witches cannot cross bridges at night.

In Pennsylvania, bridge tales are almost as abundant as the covered bridges that span the creeks of our fair state. Some of these tales concern mysterious deaths and hauntings. Knecht's Bridge, in Springfield Township, Bucks County, is surrounded by undoubtedly spurious tales of death during its construction. They say that serial accidents killed several members of a family involved in building the bridge. One broke his neck, and another was impaled on a plank of hemlock wood. Another relative died mysteriously after the bridge was finished, and still another hanged himself from it. The lack of historic evidence for these tales in no way stops people from telling them.

But our favorite stories try to explain away the mysterious sounds you hear as you cross the bridges by foot. The "crybaby bridge" is a staple of local folklore all across the United States. As you cross these bridges, usually old wooden, covered bridges, you hear a strange sound that you can't quite place. Is it a low moan or a muted shriek? Is it the lapping of the water being amplified by the bridge's structure or is it the wind in the trees reverberating off the water? Whatever causes the sound, it has given birth to numerous legends across the commonwealth.

One bridge spans Tulpehocken Creek, just north of Reading. As the local legend goes, a desperate single mother threw her children over the side of the red-painted Wertz's Mill Bridge. Since then, it's been possible to hear murmuring children's voices when crossing the bridge on foot. Similar stories surround other rural creek bridges in Berks, Lancaster, and Bucks counties.

Unfortunately, the popularity of bridge tales leads to structural damage. Covered bridges have become favorite haunts of destructive underage drinkers and arsonists. In August 2004, two teenagers set fire to Knecht's Bridge, burning a yard-wide hole and damaging the supporting trusses. Fortunately, smoke alarms saved the structure from being completely destroyed, and the responsible parties were caught and sentenced. But not every bridge escapes destruction. Mood's Covered Bridge in East Rockhill was burned down to the trestle earlier the same summer (and the six men responsible were quickly charged). So don't be surprised if your nighttime bridge trips are interrupted by agents of the law.

The Legends of Van Sant Bridge

Van Sant is an old covered bridge in Solebury Township north of New Hope. Erected in 1875, when it bore the more authentic Dutch spelling Vansandt, the bridge has given shelter to many a passing horseman and pedestrian during our state's cold, wet winters. And the odd sounds that echo around the woodwork have given rise to many different stories. Often, these tales don't fit comfortably together. Here are two typical examples, courtesy of our ever-alert-for-the-weird correspondents:

"A woman with a baby was attacked and murdered there many years ago, and the killer drowned the baby afterward. When he was caught, they hanged him from the inside of the bridge. Now they say the woman walks back and forth on the bridge, bemoaning the loss of her child."

"A woman became pregnant with twins. She had no husband and no support for herself or her children. At that time, this was a serious social problem that drove her to despair. Soon after giving birth, she carried both of her children out onto the bridge and jumped with them off the side. They all died. My friends who have been out to the bridge told me that when they walked out near the center of the bridge, they heard the cries of what sounded like two screaming infant children from below, at or near the water."

Clearly, there's not much overlap between the two tales, except for the death of mother and offspring! Because the bridge is thoroughly walled in, any jump would be limited to a ten-foot drop to the bank, which would be fatal only if the jumper dove headfirst. Whether there's some truth to any of the stories is hard to say. It has certainly been hard to turn up any source material from newspapers, death records, and the like. On the other hand, when you walk over the bridge and listen for strange sounds, you get some spine-tingling evidence from your ears. Sure, that low, moaning noise may owe more to physics than the paranormal. But if you're hankering for a thrill on a pleasant hike around small-town eastern Pennsylvania, check it out.

A woman became pregnant with twins. She had no husband and no support for herself or her children. At that time, this was a serious social problem that drove her to despair.

The Pale Lady of the Bridge

Approaching the Van Sant Bridge, there is very thick forest that adds to the darkness. On the other side, there is nothing but large, patchy fields, sites from the Revolutionary War. A group of us parked and got out, and two of us immediately felt that we should not be there. Looking back at the bridge, we both saw a figure standing in front of it, as if guarding it. My friend had a high-end digital camera with a preview screen and quickly snapped a picture. When we looked on the preview screen, right where we had seen the figure was an orb of light. When we looked up, the figure was on the other side, then it disappeared.

The rest of our party gathered their equipment and headed onto the bridge. We were too scared to go. They took a minidisk recorder, a video cam, and temperature readings. The temperature dropped 25 degrees as soon as they entered the bridge.

Back at the house, we watched the video. All of a sudden, a white-gray figure in a billowing dress appeared on the left side of the bridge. She walked back and forth with her hands and her head down. Very faintly, you could hear a moan, as if someone were crying. Then, all of a sudden, a white orb floated up to her, she stopped walking, and they both faded out of the picture. Her child, perhaps? —Bill

Hanged Men Still Hanging Around Van Sant Bridge

My friend (who has ESP) said that back in the 1800s, there were actually about five or six men hung from the bridge for a crime they committed there. She said their spirits were very angry for the hangings because apparently they were innocent, so now they haunt this bridge. It's a very creepy feeling you get when you go there. I didn't get out of the truck because she told me that one of the ghosts (or whatever you'd call them) was right next to the truck. We could hear rustling in the trees. My friend wanted to leave because she felt that they were annoyed at us for even being there. —Melanie DiSalvo

Street Bridge Named Desiree

In Brandywine District, near the Pennsylvania/
Delaware border, there was a haunted bridge. It's been torn
down now, but it used to stand around Smithbridge. Everyone
who knew the story called it Desiree's Bridge, because her
name was written on the bridge and kept reappearing no
matter how much roadwork was done. The story goes that a
girl killed herself there because her boyfriend upset her so
much, and consumed with guilt, he painted her name on the
bridge and hanged himself there. Now even her name has
gone, along with the rest of the bridge.—*Smiddy*

Glen Iron Ghost Bridge

Glen Iron in Union County doesn't have a
covered bridge anymore. It used to, back in the days
when miners would cross the river from their houses
to work. Now, like the iron mines, the bridge is a
thing of the past. At least, that's how it appears to be.
But if you hang around town long enough and talk
to the right locals, you'll learn that on quiet nights, at
the hour just before dawn, when the miners would
go to work, you can hear the trudge of weary
footsteps on wood heading toward the mines.

The Turnpike Less Traveled

For more than sixty years, the Pennsylvania Turnpike between Harrisburg and Pittsburgh has been one of the most traveled stretches of road in the state. Yet twelve miles of it belong in the category of "roads less traveled." Here's a little history to explain this strange turn of events.

When the turnpike opened in 1940, it cut a straight path through the mountains of the Laurel Highlands and the Alleghenies. Unlike the builders of the state's previous super road, the Lincoln Highway, the turnpike engineers didn't work around mountains. If a mountain got in their way, these guys cut right through it. In some cases, they commandeered tunnels left by defunct railway companies. These were narrower than regular highway tunnels, but they had the advantage of being ready-made.

By the time the turnpike opened, a total of seven tunnels had been burrowed through the mountains. This gave the turnpike its affectionate nickname the Tunnel Highway. But by 1968, the nickname was less than affectionate. The highway had become so popular that the narrower tunnels were not nearly large enough to meet the demand, and traffic would back up for miles. Something had to be done.

The solution the state engineers reached was simple: Cut a big slice out of the hillside near the problem areas and reroute the turnpike through it. The process would add a couple of miles to the total length of the pike but make up for it by bypassing two of the most troublesome old railway tunnels: the two thirds of a mile stretch at Ray's Hill and the mile-plus tube through Sideling Hill.

And that should have been the end of that. Except that it

By the time the turnpike opened, a total of seven tunnels had been burrowed through the mountains. This gave the turnpike its affectionate nickname the Tunnel Highway.

never occurred to anyone to do something about the twelve-mile stretch of abandoned freeway and the tunnels left by the rerouting.

Where bureaucracy leaves a vacuum, people move in. For at least thirty-five years, hikers have been enjoying this weed-infested stretch of road and daring each other to go through the tunnels. In the early days of this century, the Turnpike Commission sold the property to an environmental group, and rumors spread that it would become a bicycle trail. But when I went to check out the highway, a different story awaited me.

I was spending some time in Breezewood, in Bedford County, a place that accurately markets itself as the Town of Motels but which sits in the middle of some beautiful hiking country. Some people told me how to hop onto the old stretch of road, and it seemed like a great way to spend the afternoon. So I drove out, parked my car, and climbed up an embankment on the outskirts of town. I followed a matted-down path through the scrub and found the deserted road. Huge weeds poked out of the cracked asphalt, and large concrete barriers, spray-painted with words of welcome, partially blocked the way.

As I snapped a couple of photographs, I thought I heard vehicles in the distance. Now, I'd just spent a couple of months researching ghost tales, so my imagination was working overtime, and at first I didn't quite trust what I'd heard. But there they were: Squinting down the road, I saw what looked like an army convoy belting down the long-abandoned highway. Two—no, make that three—green trucks were bringing a cargo of armed soldiers in my direction.

With my camera in my hand and Guantánamo Bay on my mind, I felt very nervous as they came closer and even more nervous when they stopped. A large soldier leaned out of the vehicle and stared at me without saying a word. He didn't have to. I was all too willing to open the conversation, if only to keep him from remembering he had a weapon in his hands.

"Is this the bike trail?" I squeaked, about three octaves above my usual pitch. I was imagining life in a cage on a military base, held indefinitely without trial for spying on military operations.

"Just go back to your car and drive away," said the soldier behind the wheel.

I don't know what level of education this camo-clad Socrates had reached, but his advice seemed extremely sound, so I hightailed it out of there pronto.

Back in my room in the motel capital of Bedford County, I summoned up a search engine on my computer and randomly tapped out words like "Breezewood," "military," and "abandoned Pennsylvania Turnpike." It turns out that the Southern Alleghenies Conservancy, which now owns the road, allows the military to use it for troop-training exercises on certain weekends. When training is in progress, hiking is forbidden. So check the Conservancy's Web site before heading out to hike the trail.

This started me thinking, however. It may have been my imagination, but on reflection, the soldier who told me to move on did have a weird look on his face. It was as if he were trying to keep the edges of his mouth from turning upward. And as the posttraumatic stress faded, I remembered that as I slid down the embankment on my backside, I had heard a sound that was almost drowned out by the roaring of the truck engines. Could it have been . . . laughter?

Turnpike Tunnel Tour

After learning that two shrines to motorized transport (the abandoned turnpike tunnels) had somehow defied the progress bulldozer, I went for a hike. Ah, but what a hike it was! There, right before my eyes, were the tunnels. A little overgrown, maybe, but none the worse for wear. Ray's Hill, the shorter and seemingly less scary of the two, beckoned me inside. While its structural integrity was never in question, its length proved longer than expected, as did its darkness. Sideling Hill offers everything Ray's Hill does, in a far longer tube. If you're looking for even greater thrills, this one is your baby! Probably the weirdest thing about this place is the unsettled feeling it brings. Walking it, I felt as if I were the lead character in an old sci-fi movie, *The Last Man on Earth,* perhaps. Nothing could be seen for miles except the crumbling old roadway, standing in defiance of the apparent evil forces that had removed from it all automobiles and structures. It's time to hit the bricks, highwaymen, wouldn't you say? Begin at Breezewood, head east on Route 30, and then look for an overpass.—*Jeff Bahr*

Ease on from the Parking Lot

The overpass at Breezewood is the hard way to get onto the abandoned stretch of turnpike. The Southern Alleghenies Conservancy recommends you walk through the parking lot at the Ramada Inn. There's a gate there that goes directly into the old Pike. The other end of the Pike is in Fulton County near Houstonton. You take North Hess Road west through Hiram and take a left at Pump Station Road. You pass under an overpass, and there's direct access to the trail on your right.
—*Alan Walker*

All Mixed Up

When the *Weird Pennsylvania* research team decided to track down the birthplace of Tom Mix, we found it was remote, poorly signposted, and mis-addressed in virtually every resource we could find. Most sites that actually mention the place fail to describe where it is, listing instead the nearest town, Driftwood, which is miles away. Even the official Pennsylvania Historical Marker doesn't give the correct address. So Tom Mix Lane, a dirt track off another dirt track, Mix Run Road, remains quiet most of the time.

Before Clint Eastwood, before John Wayne, even before Roy Rogers, there was Tom Mix, the definitive celluloid cowboy. Between 1910 and 1935, he starred in, wrote, and directed more than three hundred action-packed movies. His daring acrobatics and stunt work made him the Jackie Chan of the silent-movie world. He became so fabulously rich in his twenty-five-year movie career that when he died in a car crash, in 1940, he was carrying more than $7,500 in cash and traveler's checks. In those days, that was a big wad to take on a road trip.

But although Tom Mix started his showbiz career in Oklahoma, made his fortune in Hollywood, and died in Arizona, his humble origins were in Pennsylvania—and humble they remain. The tiny homestead where Edwin and Elizabeth Mix's little boy was born has been reduced to three holes in the ground: the house's root cellar, a well, and a latrine. The site has been cleared up, and next to it is a great little shack museum with a minimal entrance fee and folksy notices next to all of the exhibits explaining the joys of living in seclusion in the woods. The marker that describes the uses of the Sears-Roebuck catalog in the outhouse is particularly evocative.

But it's the Pennsylvania Historical Marker that makes this site special. The appearance of an elegant blue-and-gold object on a dirt track in the woods, six miles from the

nearest town and next to a silent-movie star's childhood latrine, is a sublime sight. If you want to share the vision, take 555 out of Driftwood in Cameron County, heading for the Elk County border. There's a plywood sign for Mix country at the outskirts of town. Take an unmarked right at Castle Garden across the river onto Mix Run Road and keep going after the asphalt turns to gravel and then dirt. Sooner or later, you'll come to Tom Mix Lane and cross an unmarked railroad crossing to his birthplace.

On a weird side note: The circumstances of Tom Mix's death were much odder than those of his birth. While zooming around Arizona in his roadster, he came upon roadwork that forced him to slam on the brakes. His suitcase slid from the back of the car into the back of his head, breaking his neck. But the museum that houses the notorious Suitcase of Death isn't here: It's the Tom Mix Museum in Dewey, Oklahoma.

Sorry Stretch of the Lincoln Highway

Traveling south down Old Lincoln Highway through Trevose in Bucks County, you may recall that this was the nation's first highway, a road that led from Times Square in New York City to San Francisco. Tooling down the old road takes more time than going along Route 1, which runs parallel to it along this stretch, but it offers a rare sense of history. However slow your stop-start driving seems by twenty-first-century standards, you're traveling a route that Model-T Fords once took across the country. Then, just as you enter Philadelphia County, you find yourself unexpectedly in the parking lot of the Lincoln Motel. The Old Lincoln Highway has ended, some 3,000 miles shy of San Francisco. You could turn onto Route 1 at this point, but apart from a weed-infested trail into Benjamin Rush State Park, there's no other road. The old highway has vanished.

Or has it? On closer inspection, that park trail seems mighty wide. And the stone walls on either side of it turn out to be the edge of an impressive arched stone bridge across the creek. That trail is in fact an abandoned stretch of the Lincoln Highway, now barely visible for the runoff soil and thick covering of thorny vegetation.

Anyone hiking through this dense undergrowth would do well to bring a machete. Snags tear threads out of jeans; thorns pierce even dense cloth and stick into skin. Except for the occasional patch of stone road surface, the only sign that this was once a motor highway is the presence of power lines and utility poles along the trail.

Less than ninety years ago, this trail was part of a great scheme to build a road across the continent. In 1912, Carl Fisher, who built the Indianapolis Motor Speedway and started the Indy 500, dreamed up the plan for a paved road between New York and San Francisco. At the time, most roads between towns in the United States were rough dirt tracks that meandered aimlessly

RAYS HILL 1958 FT. **SIDELING HILL** 2195 FT. BREEZEWOOD **TUSCARORA** 2123 FT. **UP and DOWN OVER THE BLUE RIDGE MOUNTAINS**

SCRUB RIDGE 1455 FT.

SALUVIA HARRISONVILLE McCONNELLSBURG FORT LOUDON ST. THOMAS

JUNIATA CROSSING

BEDFORD EVERETT CHAMBERSBURG

56 MILES OF SCENIC BEAUTY ON THE LINCOLN HIGHWAY IN PENNSYLVANIA

around the nation. Fisher's road was originally called the Coast-to-Coast Rock Highway until he adopted the name Lincoln Highway to bring a patriotic fervor to his scheme (and to attract some of the money Congress was planning to spend on a memorial to President Lincoln). Using local labor to pave existing roads, his company built America's first transcontinental highway, which roughly follows the path of today's numbered routes 1, 30, 530, 40, and 50. It had less than thirty years in the sun before the turnpike system created more direct routes for long-distance drivers. In some places, stretches of the old road still exist, billed as Lincoln Highway or Old Lincoln Highway. But in cases like that of this hiking trail, the highway has ceased to be a road at all.

Make no mistake about it: This trek into Benjamin Rush State Park is too much work to be a fun hike. But it's awesome to think that within a few decades, nature can reclaim a roadway so completely. Catch it soon, before the thorns take it over completely.

In 1912, Carl Fisher, who built the Indianapolis Motor Speedway and started the Indy 500, dreamed up the plan for a paved road between New York and San Francisco.

Some roads don't just have tales of danger attached to them; some have a very real history of danger. In 2001, State Farm Insurance identified two stretches of Philadelphia's Roosevelt Boulevard as the second and third most dangerous intersections in the country, so be especially careful where Red Lion Road and Grant Avenue meet Route 1, okay? And keep your eyes peeled on these more storied roads of danger too.

If Moosic Be the Food of Love . . .

He sideswiped nineteen neat parked cars,
Clipped off thirteen telephone poles,
Hit two houses, bruised eight trees,
And Blue-Crossed seven people.
It was then he lost his head,
Not to mention an arm or two before he stopped.
And he slid for four hundred yards
Along the hill that leads into Scranton, Pennsylvania.
–Harry Chapin

South of the University of Scranton, across two railway lines and the Scranton Expressway, runs a hilly road called Moosic Street. It's the eastern portion of Route 307, off Interstate 380. As hillside roads in Pennsylvania go, it's not that steep and not that winding. The Morgan Highway on the other side of town is much steeper. But anybody who ignores the REDUCED GEAR ZONE signs at the top of the hill is liable to get into an accident, especially if his brakes fail.

That's exactly what happened in the mid-1960s when a runaway truck slammed along the right side of the street. In a blocks-long trail of destruction from Meadow Avenue

down, the truck ran out of control until it rammed into a house on the corner of South Webster Avenue. The accident took the life of the driver, and yet to this day, the story actually raises a smile among out-of-towners, who recognize it from a witty little song by Harry Chapin that was loosely based on the incident. Even the song's title makes you smile: "Thirty Thousand Pounds of Bananas."

As Chapin tells the story, the fruit truck was driven by an inexperienced driver who failed to observe the signs advising him to shift down a gear. The truck careened across the road, crashing into a house, spilling its load of fruit, and dismembering and killing the driver. It's a testament to Chapin's song-writing skills that he makes an amusing song out of all this. (And it's a testament to his sense of decorum that he never performed the popular song at his gigs in northeastern Pennsylvania.)

To this day, the exit off I-380 for PA 307 is clearly marked TRUCKS OVER 10-1/2 TONS PROHIBITED. So if you have a truckload of fruit or any other slippery goods, observe the signs. The last thing you want is for some songwriter to make light of your untimely death, isn't it?

Narrow Escape

As you travel north up Route 6 in Bradford County, you'll pass by Standing Stone and Macedonia and head toward Wysox. The stretch of road up there was once accurately known as the Wysox Narrows. Many reckless drivers broke their last speed limit on that road. For years, you could see car wrecks stuck on the rocks below. Some said they were too hard to haul up, but I think the locals left them there as a warning. My dad used to stop the car there so we could count the wrecks when I was a kid. That may seem gruesome to you, but hey, it was better for us to count 'em than join 'em. And it was a great father-son bonding moment.–*Keith R.*

Along Ghost Mountain Road

There is a place called Ghost Mountain in Bucks Co., past Palisades H.S. It's a dirt road, and once you turn onto it, there's this house in which you can see an elderly lady upstairs knitting. But the great thing is you can see right through her! Across the road, there is a wine cellar that goes into the side of the hill. My friends say they see a huge dark shadow standing right there when they open it. Then you come to a place on the road that has a gate around it. If you shake the gates, there is a ghost with what appears to be lanterns that will come down over the hill to see who you are. Last but not least, there is the covered bridge. Go over the bridge, turn your car off, beep the horn three times, turn your headlights on, and you are supposed to see a man hanging there. I've only seen it once.–*Jenilee*

Constitution Drive, Allentown

My friends were telling me about this creepy road called Constitution Drive. You are driving down a dark and unkempt road, you're surrounded by woods, and the river is right next to you. You come across a house with a barbed-wire fence and a sign that says BEWARE: DOGS WILL BITE. I heard the house is where a group of albinos live and practice Satanic rituals. I was just there recently, and two of my friends and I saw a white shadowy figure with two other white shadows with four red eyes at knee level. I have never been so scared in my life. I DO NOT suggest you drive on this road without your lights on. Also, do not walk too far from your car—there is a story of an albino man who will steal your car and drive it into the river.–*Marc*

Snake Road

In the '60s, Snake Road near Scranton was a place to go parking with your boyfriend or girlfriend. Well, one night, four friends of mine didn't have dates and went up Snake Road to spot the parkers with their headlights, just to fool around. As they proceeded to go around a bend, a huge light came out of a small clearing. And then the lights and the radio in the car went out and the car stopped dead. The next thing that happened was all four of them had a tingling/numbing sensation in the back of their necks. After the light got in front of them, they noticed it wasn't touching the road. It looked like it was floating.

Then the car started, the lights and radio came back on, and the tingling/numbing stopped. The light disappeared around the bend. My friends said, "What was that all about?" They didn't know what to do and decided to follow it. The light kept them at a distance. If they slowed down, it would slow down. If my friends sped up, it would speed up. They followed it all around the mountain until it pulled into a quarry. As the car started to go past the quarry, the same thing happened as before. The car went dead, the radio and the lights went out, and the tingling/numbing sensation came back for a few seconds. When the car started, they looked at one another and decided to floor it until they got off the mountain.

Too Many Kicks on Route 666

Here is wisdom. Let he who has understanding calculate the number of the Beast; for his number is that of a man; and his number is 666. —Revelation 3:18

States all over the Union lay claim to a spooky road frequented by the devil himself. But much rarer are roads that carry the number of the beast, 666. Several states had a Route 666 at some point, but they tend to be renumbered for either practical or superstitious reasons. One of the more famous Routes 666 cut through New Mexico, Colorado, and Utah. It was assigned the number in 1926 because it was the sixth spur off the famous Route 66. However, after years of lobbying from Christian groups, in 2003 it became Route 491. (New Jersey's Route 666 was renamed for a more prosaic reason: economy. People kept stealing the signs.)

But Pennsylvania's Route 666 still remains, cutting a swath through Allegheny National Forest. It begins off Route 62 in East Hickory, Forest County, and winds thirty-four miles through the forest until it intersects with Route 6 in Sheffield, Warren County. And it's a devil of a road to drive through. Like many of northern Pennsylvania's forest-and-mountain routes, it's a two-lane road that winds darkly through dense forestation, with occasional stretches of potholes that jar your suspension and your nerves in equal measure. Don't open up your throttle on Triple Six.

There are some populated areas of this road, but they're hardly densely populated. Endeavor, which is the largest, boasts the oldest continually operating lumber mill in the area, perhaps in the state. It's been managing the hardwood population of Allegheny National Forest since 1834. The town itself has a Presbyterian church, built by a local man in memory of his two dead daughters and dedicated in 1897. Its spire is warped and twisted in a legend-inspiring way, but nobody seems willing to share the reason for its distortion. Once past the mill and town, you're into long stretches of dark woods with hardly a creature in sight—at least any creatures of this world.

Route 666 has a name as well as a beastly number. It's officially called the David Zeisberger Highway, named for a Moravian missionary who lived among the Native Americans while other European settlers were driving them out of their lands. Whether or not you believe that Zeisberger's brand of Christianity had a beneficial influence on the tribes or that it destroyed their way of life, it's appropriate that a godly man's name should balance out the Hadean influences of the route's number.

But just to be on the safe side, if you go driving there, make it a Sunday afternoon drive rather than a full-moon Halloween trip. And if you go there at night, drive carefully, with your high beams on—and a Saint Christopher on your dashboard for good measure.

Ghosts are so common, they barely even qualify as weird anymore. Popular fiction is riddled with images of dead souls restlessly wandering the earth.

You need only to flip on the television in the days before Christmas to see how much these pale specters permeate our thoughts. When the tale of four spirits scaring the stuffing out of an old miser is considered sentimental family fare, you know that ghosts have gone mainstream.

Quaker State Ghosts

But what are ghosts anyway, and why have they become so much a part of world culture? Most people who seriously study such phenomena believe ghosts are the unsettled spirits of people who are no longer in the world of the living but are unable to let go of their earthly haunts because of some trauma surrounding their death or life. Often they don't appear directly but, rather, manifest themselves somehow on the physical plane, maybe by causing something to move or by making a noise. And just as in the fictional Philadelphia ghost yarn *The Sixth Sense*, when they're around, they may suck the heat out of their surroundings and cause a sudden sinister chill to descend.

Of course, talk of ghosts brings out some extreme reactions. There are serious people who have such compassion for the dead-but-not-departed that they seek them out to help resolve the conflicts that keep them halfway between the worlds of the living and the dead. Many people are either spooked by them or skeptical about them, even derisive. And then there are the thrill seekers, looking for a good scare in places they hear are haunted.

Weird Pennsylvania doesn't fit into any of these camps. If anything, we are ghost agnostics—not prepared to dismiss the possibility outright, but unwilling to embrace it wholeheartedly. As we've walked the battlefields of Gettysburg or through the dank and crumbling corridors of Eastern State Penitentiary, something beyond reason does seem to be in the air. Peering in through the windows of the General Wayne Inn makes the skin on the back of your scalp crawl even before you know its haunted history. The weird feelings you get in these places do make one wonder.

The stories that appear in this chapter are the ones that are enough to suggest there is more to this ghost business than childhood fears about things that go bump in the night. You will no doubt have your own opinions about such matters, so read on and draw your own conclusions.

Many states tell tales of roadside ghosts appearing to late-night drivers on dark, quiet roads. These stories follow a similar pattern: Some unfortunate soul met an untimely death at a dangerous corner and now appears long enough to shock the unwary driver into taking his lead foot off the accelerator so he can survive to drive another day. Or else there are the ghosts who hitchhiked along these quiet roads and came to a bad end and now waft along the roadsides, thumbing rides. Usually it's a woman, and in many stories, the lass from the other side goes by the name of Mary. Chicago lays claim to Resurrection Mary, but Pennsylvania has its own legend—Bristol's Midnight Mary. She and the White Lady of the Buckhorn in Altoona are the Keystone State's most storied roadside specters.

Midnight Mary, the Lady of the Lake

Not far from the much haunted town of New Hope is the town of Bristol, near the Bordentown Road and Tullytown Lake. This is the territory of a lovely young teenager in a pink dress who sometimes walks along the roadside and occasionally hitches a ride; she has also been known to walk on the waters of the lake.

Her name is Midnight Mary. The story goes that she was a popular and beautiful young girl when she attended her high school prom. She accepted a ride home from a young buck with one too many beers inside him. The young man lost control of the car; it sped into Tullytown Lake, and both occupants were killed. The boy's body was dredged from the deep, but the girl's was never found. Now, some say, her spirit walks the night—a flower cut down in her prime, her rosy future replaced by frustrated longing for the life she never had.

Right—that's enough purple prose and overblown themes from B-list fiction. The fact is that many people do claim to have seen a girl in a pink dress on Bordentown Road. A trucker once called the police to report picking up a hitchhiker answering her description, only to find his passenger seat empty except for a large puddle. A mother walking her child in a stroller along the shore of the lake claimed she saw a pink-clad figure moving across the waters of the lake, almost as if she were dancing. Witnesses to these apparitions come from people of all ages, from matrons to teenagers, and many of the details are remarkably similar.

But when you look for hard evidence, there is none to be found. The nearby cemetery at St. James Episcopal Church on Cedar Street contains the grave of a Gertrude Spring, who died in 1935 and who is believed to be the girl behind the Mary legend. Nobody can say for sure why Gertrude is associated with the ghost or why the ghost goes by the name of Mary, though it must be said that Midnight Gertrude is a far less appealing name for a vision of loveliness on the water. Our own twilight strolls along the lake never turned up any ghostly visions, but there is something in the air about the place that has a special quality. So if you happen to give a ride to a bright young thing in a pink prom dress, in the vicinity of Bristol, Pennsylvania, be sure you have plenty of towels on board.

Lucy Hitches Through Norristown

Not far from Norristown on Route 202, a teenaged girl named Lucy hitched a fateful ride one night. She died shortly afterwards, when the driver swerved at an inopportune moment into the path of oncoming traffic. Like Midnight Mary, she is sometimes seen thumbing a ride by the roadside. If a driver picks her up, she will sit in the passenger seat without uttering a word. When the driver asks her a question or turns to look at her, she will disappear.—*Johann Saldeban*

Riding with Resurrection Mary in Schnecksville

My name is Julie, and I live in Schnecksville. I just wanted to let you know that we have our own Resurrection Mary here in PA. In Trexlertown, along Rt. 222 South, there is a cemetery by the name of Resurrection. It is said that there is a phantom girl who strolls along that cemetery hitching rides. The story is documented. I don't know how true it is, being that I've never encountered the spirit myself, but I thought you would be interested in knowing.—*Julie Waricher*

White Lady of the Buckhorn

Altoona has its own spectral hitchhiker up the Wopsononock Mountain, though she's most often called the White Lady of the Buckhorn (a nearby mountain that's much easier to pronounce). There was once a resort on the mountain accessible only by a treacherous stretch of road known as the Devil's Elbow, where a pair of newlyweds met their deaths on their way to their honeymoon. Since then, a woman in white has been seen in the area, earnestly searching for something by candlelight. Naturally, the stories suggest that it's her missing husband she's looking for; his body, they say, was never recovered. Some report that she only stops cars driven by young men and that, after seeing that the driver is a stranger, suddenly disappears. Other tales have her hitching a ride toward the summit but disappearing near the Devil's Elbow. The resort is now gone, and there is nothing but television and radio equipment on top of the mountain. But technicians sometimes report spotting her, and a few years back, one of them offered her a ride. She got into the back seat, and the driver tried to start a conversation. She did not respond, and when he glanced in the rearview mirror, he could not see her. He turned his head to look, and she was sitting there in plain sight, saying nothing. The driver quickly faced the road again—he knew it was about to get treacherous—and thought his eyes were playing tricks on him. After passing the Devil's Elbow, he looked back again, and she had disappeared.

Tate House Terror

In Newtown, Bucks County, stands a prestigious Quaker boarding school
named after George Fox, the founder of the Quakers. George School is built on
land once owned by a Revolutionary War surgeon named James Tate, and the
original Tate House is part of the campus,
housing the teachers' quarters. After the
war, James Tate became a researcher in
anatomy. He began by dissecting farm
animals in his basement and closely
examining their internal anatomy.
Eventually he graduated to human
anatomy—specifically, the body of a
recently buried Hessian mercenary.

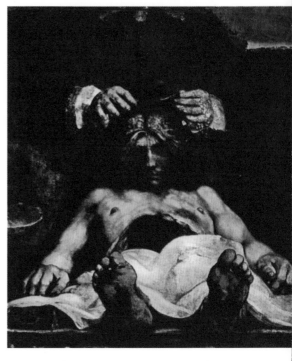

In the late 1700s, this kind of medical
research was out of the ordinary, but that
didn't stop the relentless Tate from carving
up and studying the body. When he was
done, he disposed of the evidence as any
man of science would—he buried it in his
basement. But at this point, the
paranormal entered the pragmatic world
of Tate's studies. As he carried his candle
through the basement, it would extinguish
as he passed over the Hessian's makeshift grave. Ever the scientist, Tate repeated
this experiment and noticed that the candle remained lit when he walked around
the grave. So he made the necessary adjustment in his path.

At this point, he began to hear heavy footsteps in the basement from upstairs.
When he would descend to the basement, candle in hand, he would find nothing,
but if he walked over the grave, the candle would go out. That's the extent of the
haunting: the sound of heavy footsteps and the occasional strange bit of physics.
As far as we know, nobody has ever seen the ghost of the Hessian. But to this day,
boilers in the basement frequently experience snuffed pilot lights. Freshly painted
walls in the house become cracked and scored with odd scratch marks. All in all,
the ghostly response is fairly muted, considering the fact that the German
mercenary was grave-robbed in a foreign land, dismembered, and dumped in a
hole in somebody's cellar.

Schubert Farmhouse

On the outskirts of Allentown in Lehigh County, there's a remote 18th-century farmhouse built by a soldier named George Schubert. The farmhouse rose from the ashes of a cottage he had built there earlier, but the bad luck that led to its creation did not abate when the new building was erected. A smallpox epidemic killed many of George's children, and the owner after the Schuberts apparently hanged himself in the barn. Perhaps their spirits are responsible for some of the weird events that I've been hearing about for the past thirty years—perhaps not.

They say that the residents of the farmhouse experience rattling sounds in the night—sometimes sounding like animal claws on wood, sometimes like window casements being shaken. A red-eyed apparition with an extravagant mustache has been seen at times, as have white figures that shimmer as though in a heat haze and a black-clad man. Even the barn displays some odd phenomena, such as the sound of shoveling in the stalls and the smell of strong tobacco. There's even a story of a man in a blue and white uniform hanging from the rafters. Although these tales are enough to scare the bejabbers out of me, apparently they don't bother the residents at all. They're clearly made of sterner stuff than most of us, and since they aren't afraid of their own shadows, they make the stories all the more believable.–*Morgan Frew*

The Black-veiled Ghost of Byberry Road

Somerton, outside of Philadelphia, is the site of the abandoned Byberry Mental Hospital, but that's not the only place where weird goings-on are reported in this neck of the woods. According to two sources—www.hauntedhouses.com and the book *America's Haunted Houses* by ghost hunter Hans Holzer—an old house that stands on the winding Byberry Road rattles strangely in the night. It was built almost three hundred years ago, and at least one resident has been there for centuries. Footsteps made by inhuman feet are a constant soundtrack in the wee hours. Doors open and close by themselves, even when there is no draft. And on one occasion, one of the nonghostly residents of the house surprised a woman with long black hair or a veil standing in his room. She vanished almost immediately. Holzer's investigation of the property, however, led him to believe that the ghost was male—a Quaker foot soldier from the Revolutionary War.

Phantom Priest of St. Nicholas Church in Millvale

In the town of Millvale, stands a stone church built at the turn of the last century. St. Nicholas Church is perched on a bluff overlooking the Allegheny River, an imposing sight to behold and a tribute to the faith of the Eastern European Catholics who built it.

The design of its interior is no less stunning than that of its exterior. The impressive frescoes were painted by the renowned Croatian exile Maximilian Vanka, a professor of painting in Zagreb who emigrated to the United States in the 1930s. They feature a mixture of social and religious imagery: Near depictions of the stations of the cross are what Vanka saw as modern-day demons—capitalists, stockbrokers, and invading soldiers. The frescoes are a true product of their time, when an impoverished Europe was being ravaged by war, spawning art like Picasso's *Guernica,* which depicts its horrors.

While Vanka was painting in St. Nicholas, his friend Louis Adamic wrote about some of Vanka's experiences in his autobiography *My America,* which was excerpted in the April 1938 issue of *Harper's* magazine. The experiences include nightly visitations from a ghost priest.

On Vanka's fourth night at work, painting above the altar, the dogs outside the rectory began a feverish bout of yelping and barking. Shortly

afterward, Vanka glanced at the altar beneath him, which was fully illuminated, and saw a figure, a man in black, moving this way and that, raising his arms and making gestures in the air.

Vanka assumed that it was Father Zagar, who had

commissioned the mural, practicing his religious duties in the still of the night. But during one of Vanka's nightly chats with Zagar at the rectory, he got a strange response when he brought up the encounter. Zagar looked at him for a long time, then finally said, "That was not me." This abruptly ended their conversation.

Four nights later Vanka felt a strange chill creep over him, and again he looked down to see the phantom priest dressed in black, with his arms outstretched, as silent as the grave but with his lips moving and his arms gesturing in a very animated fashion. Vanka continued to paint, but when slow footsteps and murmuring broke the silence, he looked down again. The figure was moving slowly down the aisle toward him. Vanka worked on until the apparition walked right up to the scaffold and quietly extinguished the lights. With only a dim lantern to guide him, Vanka beat a hasty retreat to the rectory and woke up Father Zagar.

This time, Vanka demanded an explanation. In Adamic's account, the priest gave a doozy:

> People began to whisper of the ghost in this church fifteen years ago. . . . I have never had any experience with it, but there are others, many others, who say they have. Years before I came here, there were fights among the Croatians about this ghost, spirit, whatever it is. I have always been skeptical about such things, but . . . there are times when I feel that maybe there are some phenomena we might not understand.

Zagar went on to explain that he had been hiding in the church and watching Vanka at work since the painter had first mentioned the mysterious priest.

That evening, he had succumbed to sleep and been unable to watch over the artist, and sure enough, the apparition had shown itself. So the following night, Zagar decided to keep Vanka company while he worked.

Things were quite convivial until a series of loud echoing knocks filled the church, followed by the baying of the dogs outside. Vanka was chilled to the bone as he saw the man in black standing at the fourth pew, much more clearly visible this time than ever before. His face was tinged with blue, very old and bony, and wearing an expression of utter misery. The specter vanished before Father Zagar could catch a glimpse, but he felt the presence very clearly. During the remaining months of Vanka's assignment, he continued to hear and see the ghostly priest, his visits accompanied by sudden drops in temperature, filling Vanka with terror. Father Zagar continued to pray for the relief of the poor phantom's spirit. When the work was finally finished, Vanka moved to the other side of the state, where he lived out the rest of his days.

When talking with his friend Adamic about his experience, Vanka described the phantom as being "perfectly mild, pensive-like, sitting in the pew or moving up and down the aisle; yet he filled me with indescribable horror, with something higher and stronger than fear." When Adamic's memoir was published, the ghost stole Vanka's thunder too—for decades, the tale of the phantom priest was more famous than the masterpiece Vanka had painted while being haunted by him. Thankfully, the artist's work has enjoyed renewed interest, with permanent exhibitions at the Doylestown Michener Museum, and of course, the magnificent frescoes at St. Nicholas still exist. But if you visit the church, don't mention the phantom priest. In private moments, the living priests may admit to having seen him, but they have tired of the relentless publicity that Adamic's *Harper's* article had stirred up nearly seventy years ago.

The Haunted "Big House"

If ghosts come back to the places they had suffered in during life, the ghosts of convicts must surely return to their places of confinement. Is it any surprise, then, that jails breed some of the best ghost stories?

Solitary Confinement
History and Hauntings of Eastern State Penitentiary

Philadelphia's Eastern State Penitentiary was built in 1829 to further the Quakers' idea of prisoner isolation as a form of punishment. Prisoners were confined in windowless rooms with running water and toilets. They would come into contact with no living persons, save for an occasional guard or a minister who would pray with them and offer spiritual advice. Penitence was essential in the punishment of the lawbreaker, hence the word "penitentiary."

If solitary confinement failed to produce the necessary penitence, more extreme confinement was used, beginning with the straitjacket and the "mad chair," a stool with chains and leather straps. The Water Bath was another punishment that was adapted from treatments at mental hospitals. It involved dunking a prisoner in ice-cold water and then hoisting him up in chains to spend the night attached to the wall. During the winter months, the water would freeze onto the inmate's skin. The most feared punishment was the Iron Gag, a device placed over the inmate's tongue and locked to his hands, which were crossed and tied behind his neck. Any movement of the hands would tear at the gag and cause intense pain.

Anyone who spent any time at Eastern State was certain that something supernatural was taking place. After the penitentiary closed in the 1970s and the last prisoners were removed, the guards told of sounds of footsteps in the corridors, pacing feet in the cells, eerie wails that drifted from the darkest corners of the complex, and dark shadows that resembled people flitting past. It seemed that the abandoned halls, corridors, and chambers were not so empty after all! Those who left the penitentiary on that final day were convinced that a strange presence had taken over the building. Most of them breathed a sigh of relief to be gone.

In the mid-1970s, the empty prison became a National Historic

Landmark, operated by the Pennsylvania Prison Society of Philadelphia, which still conducts tours there. Over the years, volunteers and visitors alike have had some pretty strange experiences. A locksmith named Gary Johnson was performing some routine restoration work one day when he had this odd encounter.

"I had this feeling that I was being watched," he recalled, "but I turned and I'm looking down the block and there's nobody there. A couple of seconds later and I get the same feeling. I'm really being watched! I turn around and I look down the block and shoooom. . . . This black shadow just leaped across the block!" Johnson still refers to the prison as a "giant haunted house."

Angel Riugra, who has also worked in the prison, agrees. "You feel kinda jittery walking around because you feel something there, but when you turn around, you don't see anything. It's kinda weird, it's spooky!"

One of the most commonly reported specters is encountered among the older cellblocks. The phantom is always described as being a dark, humanlike figure who stands very still and quiet until the visitor gets too close to him. Then he darts away. The sightings never last for long, but each person who has seen the apparition says that it gives off a feeling of anger and malevolence.

Another of the penitentiary's most frequently seen spirits is a ghost that stands high above the prison walls in a guard tower. It has been assumed that this is the spirit of a former guard who is still at his post after all these years. One has to wonder why a guard, who was free to leave this place at the end of the day, would choose to remain. But perhaps he has no choice—we can only speculate about what dark deeds this lonesome man may have been witness to, or perhaps taken part in, during his years at the prison. Maybe he is now compelled to spend eternity watching over the walls that confined so many who were not free to leave.

Is Eastern State Penitentiary haunted? In the end, that must be up to the reader to decide. Certainly it is a place with a long history of violence, bloodshed, and terror. If the events of the past really do create the hauntings of the present, Eastern State Penitentiary could be a very haunted site indeed.—*Troy Taylor*

Haunted Hotels

If ghosts do indeed haunt the places where they once lived, then it's hardly surprising that so many hotels and inns seem to be haunted.

Screamfest at Hollidaysburg's U.S. Hotel

Ghost hunters are a breed apart. They're a little obsessive, to be frank. They congregate at places that have a reputation for supernatural occurrences and wait to see what's going on. They're not psychic; they don't see visions or hear voices that nobody else can pick up. If anything, they overcompensate for their New Age counterparts by being as scientific as possible. They tote cameras, video equipment, digital audio recorders, electromagnetic sensors, ultrasensitive thermometers, and other equipment and gather as much data as they can in an attempt to "prove" that ghosts are at work. Unfortunately, all they usually come up with are orbs—little blobs of light that to the skeptical eye could be mere flaws or reflections in the lens. That said, ghost hunters are generally not given to exaggeration or histrionics.

That's why the events at the U.S. Hotel in Hollidaysburg a few years back are so surprising. This Blair County hotel was built in 1835 and has a checkered past that includes hooch brewing, an upstairs bordello, and underground tunnels for hiding either runaway slaves or illicit goods. But the supernatural story that appeared in the October 2001 issue of *Fate* magazine takes the cake. Patty Wilson's report reads more like a splatter movie than a typical ghost hunter's report.

The place had fallen into decay by the mid-1990s, so the new owners began extensive remodeling. As the work progressed, noises were heard during the night—laughter and footsteps—and one of the contractors, who was staying at the hotel, apparently awoke to see a woman dressed in a white gown hovering footless above the floor.

These stories attracted six members of a ghost-hunting group called the Paranormal Research Foundation, including the author of the *Fate* article. They spent a night at the place in a routine ghost hunt, exploring and taking pictures wherever they could. Then suddenly, one of the group experienced a panic attack and fled from an upstairs room. Two of the others ran up to investigate. Keen to find some evidence, they attempted to take photographs, and the flash of one camera illuminated a fleeting vision that horrified the witnesses. Patty Wilson, one of the pair that saw the apparition, described it on her Web site, www.ghostsrus.com, this way:

> I saw a pretty woman with long auburn hair lying on a bed in that room. . . . She was writhing in pain and holding her head. As suddenly as I caught this glimpse, she was gone in the darkness after the flash. I had this sudden intense fear and a sense of terrible pain and the word "Run!" kept screaming in my head.

With the vision gone, there was nothing left to do, so they left the scene. Unsettled by the experience, the group pushed on for a while, exploring the rooms as thoroughly as they could. But agitation got the better of them when one of their members, a man named Al, said in an unequivocal tone, "Everybody out of here now!" In the *Fate* article, he explained the reason for his barked order: He had seen a shadow step into the light, carrying an ax or some other kind of weapon, and just knew that this was the man who had killed the woman they had seen in agony upstairs. The scrap of information they had heard about a footless female ghost in the building came crashing down on him, and he felt as though he had witnessed a grisly murder reenacted in spirit form. The evening ended with these systematic explorers in a state of jittery agitation.

When you look at the story on Wilson's Web site, you're struck by how ordinary the photographic evidence of that trip is. There are a few orbs here and there in some otherwise mundane pictures of rooms. There's nothing unusual at all. In fact, Wilson is quick to explain that the atmosphere on the first floor of the hotel is very warm and welcoming. The key to feeling comfortable, it seems, lies in never spending a night on the second floor.

The Handy Apparition of Tannersville

Up in the Poconos, in the town of Tannersville, there's an old stagecoach house now called the Tannersville Inn. It's a cool place to chill and get some eat and drink. Three years ago, I drove up there for my birthday lunch. I am fairly sensitive to temperature drops and presences, so when I went into the back bathroom, I knew immediately that I wasn't alone. My skin felt funny—supersensitive, as if I could actually feel each cell, alive and tingly. Feeling the presence, I began talking. I started with my name and told her she was safe to show herself to me if she'd like. Looking back, I feel silly, but during that moment, it all felt as if those were the words that needed to be said. As I stood next to the sink drying my hands on my pants and facing the door, it happened. A hand, about shoulder height, began to appear. It was like a soft grayish white, and it was waving slowly, like a bird fluttering its wing feathers. It was so pretty and delicate. Just as I began to see more of her arm, my cousin came through the door, and she disappeared as my cousin burst right through her. I was so disappointed. –*Crazee Chrissy in Clinton*

Hessian Mercenaries Haunt the General Wayne Inn

William Penn stayed there in the early 1700s. In 1777, so did George Washington and General "Mad Anthony" Wayne. Edgar Allan Poe drank there—copiously by all accounts. But the General Wayne Inn in Merion, Montgomery County, has had more mysterious residents in its time. And one of them has a novel way of attracting attention.

The inn's owner during the 1970s and 1980s, Bart Johnson, loved to tell stories about his three-hundred-year-old hostelry. One favorite began with an after-hours get-together with two of his friends in the bar. As they sipped coffee, a loud bang at the other side of the room brought their conversation to a sudden halt. They saw a cannonball rolling toward them on the floor. There was no hole in the ceiling and nobody in the room who could have dropped or thrown it. When Johnson attempted to pick up the ball, it vanished before his eyes.

This was just one of the bizarre physical manifestations at the place. Napkins placed on tables at closing time would be found lying unfolded on the floor in the morning. In the parking lot, lights and car radios would turn on automatically. And on one occasion, the cash register and wine racks flooded, even though there was no water leak anywhere in the building.

Clearly, something bizarre was afoot at the General Wayne. Stories had been circulating for years about soldiers dressed in old-fashioned uniforms in the bar. At least one frightened custodian had left because of these apparitions, but their presence wasn't always threatening. Once, after hosting a large party, Bart Johnson received compliments for hiring an actor in authentic historical dress to mingle with the guests and add atmosphere to the place. But he hadn't hired any such actor.

Eventually Johnson brought in psychics Jean and Bill Quinn to hold a séance. During the session, Jean spoke with several presences (though the other guests heard nothing) and found that one of the apparitions was a Hessian mercenary called Wilhelm, who had been ambushed and killed nearby by colonials during the Revolutionary War. The following day, his body was discovered and brought back to the inn for burial. But the commanding officer of the Revolutionaries took a shine to

EARLY TAVERN

Opened in 1704, this tavern was known in Colonial times as the William Penn Inn, the Tunis Ordinary and Streeper's Tavern. Familiar to Franklin and Washington, the inn was renamed, shortly after the Revolution, in honor of Gen. Wayne, who had lodged here.

PENNSYLVANIA HISTORICAL AND MUSEUM COMMISSION

the dead mercenary's uniform and had him stripped before burial. Now, the story goes, Wilhelm is unable to rest because of the embarrassment or anger connected with his burial.

Several other presences spoke to Jean, including a lost little boy looking for his mother, two serving girls from the 1800s who had been accused of stealing rugs from a guest, and eight other Hessian soldiers, one of whom had been killed and buried in the basement.

Whether you believe the psychics or not, the General Wayne Inn is party to far more weird goings-on than a regular bar. All in all, it's no surprise that Edgar Allan Poe liked it so much. He left his own mark on the place: He once carved his initials into an upper-story window with a diamond ring.

In the late 1990s, after Bart Johnson's time, the General Wayne went through many incarnations—from southwestern bar and grill to a sports bar—and finally closed its doors in 2002. Now only the ghosts remain, though they may soon have company. Plans are afoot to reopen the building as Chabad Center for Jewish Life. According to an article in the May 10, 2004, issue of the *Philadelphia Inquirer*, Rabbi Shraga Sherman believes that "whatever negativity transpired in this building, the positivity and holiness that we're going to bring in will marginalize it and push it out the door."

We hope so, Rabbi. We certainly hope so.

Burning Ghost Bride of City Tavern

During the colonial period, Philadelphia's City Tavern was the in place to be. Everybody who was anybody went there. It's hardly surprising when you consider that Ben Franklin, George Washington, and Thomas Jefferson were among its clientele. It's still standing today at the corner of Second and Walnut streets—sort of. In fact, the current building is a facsimile of the original, which stood on the same spot until a fire destroyed it in the mid-1800s. That fire also gave the new tavern its most famous resident: the ghost of a young bride who died in the flames during her bridal party.

In the rebuilt City Tavern, meticulously reconstructed in 1975, many people hold bridal showers, wedding receptions, and other functions. Sometimes they have odd stories about the events. Many people tell of having weird problems with their cameras, some of which produce pictures that look like double exposures, with transparent female figures nobody remembers being at the party. Some people claim that they have seen a ghostly figure in white wandering the upper floors. One story that's often repeated concerns a young woman who dropped her camera when she felt a sudden sharp burning sensation in her hand. No candles or cigarettes were smoldering nearby.

Logan Inn, New Hope

It's no coincidence that New Hope's Ghost Tour attraction starts at the corner of Main and Ferry streets. That's the site of the Logan Inn, a haunted hotel that mixes old-school fireside spook stories with more credible tales. Amid the claims that Aaron Burr stayed there after shooting Alexander Hamilton—and is still staying there—comes a more chilling tale from just after the Second World War.

In 1946, during an annual street fair in the inn's parking lot, a palm reader named Parker Dehn and his customers heard the loud and uncontrollable screaming and weeping of a child. No child was found there or nearby, but the experience was so unsettling, Dehn closed up his tent and went for a drink. That was on the opening Thursday night of the fair, and on Friday, the same thing happened. After the fair closed down, the sobbing stopped. The next year Dehn set up in the same spot, and again the sobs and screaming were heard. By Saturday, crowds gathered around the tent to see if they could locate the source of the crying. But Dehn had had enough and left. Subsequent annual fairs avoided the spot.

The inn itself has plenty of stories associated with it, including windows that fling open in the small hours, and apparitions of ghosts and small children. The most storied guest room is Room 6, which the innkeeper claims is haunted by a former proprietor who had lost the inn because of debt.

An Evening in Logan Inn's Room 6

There is nothing more macho, more manly, than a good old-fashioned ghost hunt, especially in a place as well documented as the famous "Room 6" of the Logan Inn. So it was on that August night that my best friend Jeff and I drove south to ultimately be humbled by the thing that dwells in that old room. We had all the proper provisions two novice fellows would need (a notebook, camera gear, audio recorder, and other paraphernalia). Most notable was the thick textbook on parapsychology that contained the documented history of the room we had booked for the night. The same tome also listed the name of the woman who worked the front desk, a woman we would refer to as "The Proprietor."

It was The Proprietor that initially held the most mystery for us. Regal in demeanor and stature, she seemed every bit the lady. But every time we had seen her in the weeks leading up to our reservation, a new piece of finery hid her neck from sight. It was no different on this night, a scarf wrapped around her throat in the middle of August. When we arrived, she instantly knew us by name and ushered us to our fated room. I couldn't help but tell her our plans and the fact that she was written about in a credited book on the paranormal. The mountain of gear gave us away anyway. We were either there to catch ghosts or do something worse.

The room was very small, with no scent of lavender, as described in several books. Beyond the new paint and TV (in an old oak cabinet) you could see the history of the place just hidden under the skin of new amenity. But there was nothing odd or supernatural to be noticed. After we set up our gear, we went down to the porch to have dinner. We had laughed at the sign that swung in the summer night. It read "Fine Food, Lodging, and Spirits." So far we had two out of the three.

Upon our return to Room 6, The Proprietor was waiting with a smirk to tell us that the portrait outside our room was an image of the owner's grandparents from Bolivia and that it was the owner's mother who is said to haunt our quarters. We were gone maybe an hour, but now, square in the center of the far wall of the room, we discovered a wet handprint with elongated fingers that was definitely NOT there when we had left. Alarmed but skeptical, I began to orate our findings in my micro-recorder. As I was playing it back, my heart leapt with wonder and horror. At precisely the moment Jeff's hand touched the print on the wall, an inhuman, raspy sigh seemed to float off the tape. We had come looking for evidence, but we didn't really want to find it. We ran several tests to see if any other ambient noises could have made the noise on our tape, but even when pointed directly at the traffic, it didn't pick up anything remotely like what we'd heard. For the rest of the night, we did everything we could to avoid the room for as long as possible. There was now a tangible feeling that there was something else in there with us. We wandered the town, visited a spider-infested bridge, and procrastinated returning to our digs as long as we could. When we made our way back, The Proprietor was grinning even broader, wishing us a good night's sleep with a toss of her scarf. We finally went to bed at around 4:30. Wide-eyed, we stared into the darkness around us, trying to focus our thoughts on the continental breakfast waiting for us should we survive the night. Very manly, indeed.–*Ryan Doan*

It must be tempting for the people who market historical buildings to throw in a spicy ghost story or two to attract the crowds. It brings out the carnival barker in anybody who's trying to attract tourist dollars to some old building that lacks the mass appeal of Disneyland. Ghost tours of historic sites seem to be a big draw during the tourist season, and it's exactly the kind of thing that turns *Weird Pennsylvania* off. If it's too good a story, if it fits too perfectly or sounds too familiar, we think it's been tailored to an audience and can't be trusted. Then again, some stories can't be ignored. They come from sources that either seem too reliable or aren't tidy enough to be just another marketing message. It's these stories we include here.

Wayne's World

The Waynesborough estate in Paoli, Montgomery County, is best known as the family home of General "Mad Anthony" Wayne, the Revolutionary War hero. But even though the estate has now passed out of the Wayne family, one of his relatives apparently lingers on. Stories have been circulating for years about how during the Civil War era, one Hannah Wayne set her clothes on fire with a candle while climbing to the top floor. Rumor has it that people have been hearing screams and sounds of breaking glass from the attic area ever since, but to us, this smacked of something to attract tourists to this out-of-the-way historic building. We could find no Hannah Wayne on record who had died at Waynesborough or even lived there as an adult. But one piece of research gave credence to the legend. During a recent trip to Mad Anthony's estate, an older volunteer in the gift shop told us an authentic-sounding insider story that changed our minds. Apparently, the previous live-in caretakers at Waynesborough used to hear noises at night from the attic area — a rhythmic noise like the rocking of a chair. Whenever they got up to investigate, the sounds stopped. These caretakers were a levelheaded younger couple, not given to spook stories, but they soon quit the post. The current caretakers have heard nothing, but perhaps that's just because they sleep more soundly.

A Penny Saved Is a Penny Thrown

Back in the 1970s, people used to throw pennies on the grave of Ben Franklin at Christ Church Cemetery at 5th and Arch streets in Philadelphia. It was a tribute to his old saying "A penny saved is a penny earned" and a way to celebrate locally manufactured goods (the Mint in Philadelphia makes pennies). Several reports at the time hinted that the ghost of Ben used to throw them back! A few young women reported hearing weird "ping" sounds while waiting for the bus near the founding father's resting-place. In each case, the road was deserted except for the witness. A Philly online zine called *Digest e-zine* tells the story of a

nurse who saw pennies rolling around the pavement during one of the mystery penny throws. Oddly enough, the only people who experienced this were women. Well, they say that old Ben had an eye for the ladies.—*Bill Fields*

Ben Bowls Over the Ladies . . . and Dances!

I heard that Ben Franklin's ghost knocked over a cleaning woman in the Philosophical Society library in Philadelphia. This was back in the 1880s, and apparently he was making a dash for the bookshelves there. He founded the Philosophical Society, so there's some connection, I guess. Some other folks say that they've seen his statue from outside the Philosophical Society dancing along city streets. —*Debs*

Burr—De Rigueur

Aaron Burr was one of the most colorful men in U.S. political history. Brilliant, volatile, and thwarted by his own fatal flaws, he was destined to live on in stories long after his death. And in the weird world, it was inevitable he'd feature in a haunting tale or two. But it's odd that this bad boy of American politics should haunt the Keystone State. He is more strongly associated with two other states and a well-known district to the south. After all, he graduated at the top of his class from Princeton in New Jersey, became governor of New York, and moved on to the vice presidency in D.C.

But apparently, Burr moves around in death, as he did in life. New York City stakes a claim on his spirit: He is known there as a plate-throwing poltergeist in a Greenwich Village restaurant on West Third and Sullivan streets, a house in which he used to live. But Pennsylvania also claims him, with two sites in New Hope that boast of his ghost. One is the Logan Inn, which has enough of a ghostly pedigree without needing Burr. The other site is a bed-and-breakfast called the Aaron Burr House, which had sheltered Burr when he was on the run from his most famous exploit—the shooting and killing of American founding father Alexander Hamilton in an 1804 duel in Weehawken, New Jersey. This hotheaded act secured Hamilton's place on the $10 bill and destroyed Burr's political aspirations forever. He was soon on the run to avoid a hasty judgment in a murder trial.

Burr had family friends in New Hope, the Coryell family, who hid him in the foundations of an unbuilt house near the Delaware River until the heat died down enough for him to slip off to hide with his daughter in South Carolina. Now visitors standing at the top of the stairs to the basement of the Aaron Burr House speak of a cold wave washing over them and a strong sensation of being stared at. Doors jam, as if someone's holding them closed in the empty room on the other side, then make you stumble as they swing freely open. And at night, furtive creeping sounds are heard, like those of a killer on the lam venturing out cautiously to avoid capture from enemies.

Banging Around in Carpenters' Hall

Any well-versed East Coast tourist or student of American history can tell you a thing or two about Carpenters' Hall. It's on Chestnut Street in the Independence National Historic Park area of downtown Philadelphia. It was newly built when the First Continental Congress met there in 1774 to complain about British rule, a gripe that led to the birth of a nation. Part of Ben Franklin's library sits on shelves on the second floor. The steeple was built to house the Liberty Bell. And just to show that there are no hard feelings, Queen Elizabeth II visited the place in 1976 to celebrate two hundred years of British nonrule of its former colony.

What's less well known is that this three-story building is haunted by some of its former residents. The attic floor was divided into apartments during the early years and rented to members of the Carpenters' Company, the oldest trade guild in the United States, which built and still owns the hall. The apartments were small, with just enough room for a bed, chair, small chest, and a clothes rack, so they were rented to unmarried members of the guild.

According to research by Delaware County library director Elizabeth Hoffman, one of the tenants was implicated in a daring bank robbery in 1789, an exploit that led to his untimely death and presumed haunting of the building.

On September 1, 1789, two men on horseback arrived at the bank in the basement of Carpenters' Hall, entered with a key they carried, and made off with an astounding amount of money for the time—more than $160,000. The police from the Walnut Street station arrived too late to catch the bandits, but the fact that they had had a key led the cops to Pat Lyon, a locksmith who had just changed the bank's locks. He was arrested and put in jail. Two weeks later, when two men tried to open an account at a bank with a sum slightly over $160,000, Lyon was joined by his two accused accomplices. Both were members of the Carpenters' Company, and one of them, Tom Cunningham, lived in one of the upstairs rooms. Oddly enough, Cunningham was released from jail a few days later and returned to Carpenters' Hall with a case of yellow fever, which killed him within a week.

After Cunningham's death, the ghostly sounds began. Other residents heard heavy-booted feet stamping down the hallway and sometimes part of the way downstairs. Loud banging noises came from his old room. These noises continued for decades, after the company stopped renting out its attic. Sixty-odd years later, in 1857, when the

Carpenters' Company opened the building to the public, its caretakers continued to hear the mysterious sounds.

According to Elizabeth Hoffman's 1992 book *In Search of Ghosts,* in 1960 the Philadelphia police investigated loud noises in the attic that the new caretakers James and Hazelle O'Connor had reported hearing from their second-floor apartment. The lawmen found no evidence of activity. Indeed, the floors were coated with a thick layer of undisturbed dust. But the place smelled foul. When the caretakers tried to check the upstairs out later, the stench was so bad, it drove them downstairs. The following day, the smell was completely gone. A few nights later, the footsteps and banging returned—and so did the disgusting smell. This continued for years, but because the O'Connors were never physically harmed or scared by it, they learned to live with the disturbance.

In 1974, when Philadelphia celebrated the bicentennial of the first Continental Congress, Pennsylvania's Governor Milton Shapp hosted a meeting of the National Governors Conference in Carpenters' Hall. That night, the O'Connors heard loud shouting and scraping of chairs, but this time it was downstairs from their apartment. The day had been a busy one, but James O'Connor knew that the building was deserted and that the doors were locked. Yet the couple heard several voices raised in argument. Used to ghostly sounds, they ignored what they heard and found no physical evidence of disturbance the following morning. However, they did detect the smell of fresh tobacco smoke in the room. The O'Connors' conclusion was the obvious one: The hotheaded revolutionaries of 1774 had been reliving their turbulent times in a kind of ghostly playback.

Old School Ghouls

I am an alumnus of good ol' Penn State and now work there. The Schuylkill Campus, located 20 minutes outside of Pottsville on Route 61, was once an asylum. The administration building was where the insane were housed. (We joke that they still live there.) The campus computer lab was formerly the morgue. Among the list of ghosts haunting the place is a little girl in the attic of the classroom building, a lady in white in the computer lab, a group that you can hear talking in the library, and several in the farmhouses behind the dorms.

The huge University Park Campus of Penn State has a lot of great weird stories. In November of 1969, Betsy Aardsma was murdered in the Pattee Library. Though no one has ever reported seeing Betsy's ghost, strange voices, odd shadows, and ghostly figures fill a floor there that the staff calls Spooky Two.

The ghost of Mrs. Schwab haunts the Schwab Auditorium, where she walks around or sits up on the balcony to watch performances.

Frances Atherton, wife of former Penn State President George Atherton, sits at the window of the Old Botany Building, watching over the grave of her husband across the street.

The most famous ghost at University Park, though, is Old Coaly, the donkey that was Penn State's original mascot. His ghost is often seen at the top of Old Main's bell tower and in the hallways of the dorm where his stuffed body rests in a storage closet.
—*Nicolle L. Brandle*

The Ghosts of War

Theaters of war, it seems, generate more ghosts than any other place. It may be the sheer volume of the dead at the sites of great battles, or the horrors they had endured at the time of their passing. Who knows what the cause may be. But whatever the reason, whenever you find a place where blood had been shed in battle, a ghost story or two cannot be far behind.

The Many Ghosts of Fort Mifflin

Just south of Philadelphia stands a bastion of defense against naval attacks from the Delaware River. The great stone ramparts of Fort Mifflin protected the young nation's capital of Philadelphia against siege ships of the British Empire, which, ironically enough, had built the fort in the first place in 1772. But the British destroyed their own defensive handiwork in November 1777 with a pitiless barrage of cannonballs estimated at a thousand rounds every twenty minutes. Nearly three quarters of the defenders perished. The fort was rebuilt twenty years later and served as a garrison in the War of 1812 and as a prison during the Civil War. It's now a tourist attraction featuring guides in historical dress, but not all of the participants seem to be live actors.

The second-floor balcony of the barracks is said to be visited by the spirit of the lamplighter, the man who lit the oil lamps every evening. Though he's barely discernible in the twilight, people can see he's carrying a long pole with a flickering light on the end.

The casemates are the sites of many other apparitions. The most visible is the Faceless Man, and supposedly, he's the ghost of a war criminal imprisoned in the fort during the Civil War. William Howe was his name, and he was hanged at the fort for the murder of his superior and desertion of duty. When he appears these days, he's fairly easy to see, they say, except that his face is in shadow. The reason? Before hanging, deserters were said to have had their heads covered with black bags as a mark of their shame.

The Screaming Lady is the loudest of the ghosts at Fort Mifflin. She's never seen, but wails from the old officers quarters, where she appears to be living out an eternity of regret for disowning her daughter. She is said to be the soul of Elizabeth Pratt, an eighteenth-century neighbor of the fort whose daughter took up with an officer. Elizabeth renounced and threw out her daughter, who died shortly after from dysentery. Consumed with guilt, the story goes that Elizabeth took her own life. And there is another spectral sound heard at the fort. Near the blacksmith shop, the clash of hammer against anvil often sounds out, only to be silenced when people enter the empty but slightly echoing room.

Here is a detail of a photograph *taken at Ft. Mifflin in 1997 with what appears to be a ghost image. I am a wet plate photographer doing images on glass using the original process and equipment from the 1860s. This shot was a staged and posed image of the garrison troops of the fort at a Civil War reenactment. I was up on the parapet overlooking the soldiers, and there was no one out there but the troops in formation. At first when I developed the plate, I thought the small markings to the upper-right center were blemishes on the surface of the plate. But looking closer, it appears to be human and not exactly standing on the ground. What is it? I don't know.—Ray Morgenweck*

Great Ghosts of Gettysburg

Between July 1 and July 3, 1863, more blood was shed in a formerly little-known Adams County farm community than at any battle in history. The deaths on the battlefield at Gettysburg numbered 7,500, and probably a tenth of the wounded died later. With around 10,000 men down in a few horrific days, it's hardly surprising Gettysburg has its fair share of ghost stories. But oddly enough, one of the stories comes to us from the time of the battle itself.

Although the Confederates were ultimately defeated on July 3, 1863, the Union soldiers were actually in trouble at one point. The 20th Maine Division had arrived to reinforce the flagging troops, but they had no idea where to go. The story goes that a striking figure in an old-fashioned uniform appeared on a white horse and led them to Little Round Top, a strategic point that enabled them to rout a flank of Confederates and ultimately win the battle. The soldiers insisted that the glowing apparition they followed bore an uncanny resemblance to George Washington. There's no denying this story reeks of propaganda. It's only one step away from the old claim that "God is on our side." But nevertheless, the story has had a remarkably long life.

If you visit the National Military Park on a clear summer night, you will sometimes see fog creeping in and surrounding the field where so many people fell. Fog always brings an eerie sensation with it, and such ground mists are not unusual for this kind of topography. But what's inside the fog is a little more unusual. Lights flash on and off, appearing to advance along the same path that the Confederates had taken to Little Round Top. Sometimes shadows or transparent apparitions appear on horseback. Although it's hard to see anything in those conditions, these riders are often reported as being headless, though this may be due to overactive imaginations fired by too many readings of the Sleepy Hollow legend.

But far and away the most common ghostly phenomena at Gettysburg concern cameras. There were many photographs taken during the battle, but it seems nowadays an unusual number of cameras malfunction on the field. Visitors often experience a chill when this happens, maybe because of the weather, maybe from a sudden supernatural fear, or perhaps from the presence of something not of this world.

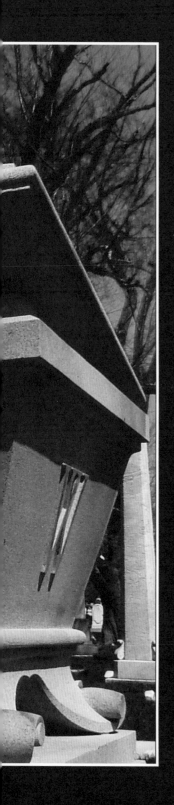

Cemetery Safari

"Show me your cemeteries, and I will tell you what kind of people you have."—Benjamin Franklin

BELOVED SCOTTY
1980 ——— 1995
GONE TO THAT GREAT BICYCLE
BASKET IN THE SKY, TO WAIT
FOR MOMMY & SISTER

CONOVER

You can call a burial ground whatever you like: final resting-place, necropolis, city of the dead, cold storage, bone orchard, slab city. By any name, cemeteries play a significant role in the life—and, of course, death—of any town or city. When Europeans first settled in Pennsylvania, they brought with them burial customs that may seem odd to us now. In seventeenth-century Europe, graves were usually dug in churchyards and marked, if marked at all, with simple stones. When the churchyard filled up, the bones of those long dead would be exhumed and placed in bone rooms, called ossuaries, in church crypts. Most grave markers were not permanent, because a grave was seldom the final resting-place of the departed, except among the wealthy.

Beginning in the early nineteenth century, when death claimed increasingly larger populations, graveyards were moved outside the cities. These leafy burial grounds, called rural garden cemeteries, were very much like public parks, where people would go for pleasant strolls even if they had no loved ones buried there. It was not long before the graveyard tourists were given plenty to look at: impressive mausoleums, statues, and beautifully carved headstones. In the two centuries since the modern cemetery was born, things have definitely taken a turn for the weirder.

Not-So-Final Rest

Though Pennsylvania boasts several beautiful garden cemeteries, none quite match the long history of Philadelphia's Laurel Hill Cemetery, established in the 1830s. Situated on the banks of the Schuylkill River, in the western part of the city, this massive necropolis is still a working cemetery and a walk along its winding paths takes you on a tour of all the different ways Americans have celebrated the deaths of friends and relatives.

However, Laurel Hill has not always been respectful of the dead and the bereaved. In fact, one of the most famous stories about the cemetery is anything but respectful. Like any business, a cemetery has to market itself, and Laurel Hill's founders thought that a good way to attract new customers was to have some famous occupants. To that end, they approached the family of a major player in the Revolutionary War, Charles Thomson, the designer of the Great Seal of the United States and secretary of the Continental Congress. At the time, he had been dead and buried in Montgomery County for fourteen years, and most of his family were content to keep it that way. Laurel Hill, though, wanted his illustrious bones for their cemetery. One nephew agreed to the idea (history is silent on what persuaded him), and on the strength of that, a group of men went with shovels to Montgomery County and came back with bones they said were Thomson's. The bones could easily have been someone else's, including Thomson's wife's, but they were good enough for Laurel Hill and were buried beneath a grand obelisk on the grounds. So should you go there to honor the hero, be aware that his spirit may still be there but not his mortal remains.

See the Spirit Rising

Victorian tastes in memorials have aged about as well as the pockmarked marble and fallen headstones that litter garden cemeteries throughout the world. What seemed profoundly symbolic and thought-provoking to the nineteenth-century eye appears just plain strange to the children of the new millennium. Just look to the tomb of young William Warner. This son of wealthy Philadelphia socialites died in 1889, well before his time. The grieving parents purchased a lot in the most celebrated rural garden cemetery of the time, the same Laurel Hill that had hijacked Thomson's bones, and to create a fitting memorial they commissioned the best-known local artist of the time, Alexander Milne Calder, sculptor of the Philadelphia City Hall's statuary. Calder was the first of the famous Calder family of sculptors.

With the best available sculptor, a large budget, and the perfect setting, the results are surely the grandest memorial a Victorian family could wish for. Out of a marble sarcophagus bearing the letter W (for either William or Warner), an angel releases the immortal soul of the dearly departed, which ascends toward heaven, undaunted by death, destined for eternal life. It's a perfect mixture of Victorian sentiment, exacting craftsmanship, and religious symbolism. And it's the kind of art that inspires the visitors of today to say, "Whaaaat?"

It is a weird-looking sculpture by any standards. Neither time nor the elements have been kind to it. The angel holding the sarcophagus open has lost both arms, and while the spirit of the boy may be immortal, his earthly image is missing its nose. Somehow weathered stone is too solid a material to represent the wisp of smoke that wreaths the soul, and in marble it looks more like Mr. Frosty ice cream.

But apart from these details, what counts is the idea of making a sculpture of a winged boy being carried out of a coffin on a wisp of carved marble. It shows just how far tastes have changed over the past 125 years. But one thing hasn't changed: People still like to visit the place and look at the statue. The reaction may be different, but it's as strong now as it ever was. And that's surely the mark of a great work of art.

Mother and Children Reunion

Of all the monuments in Laurel Hill Cemetery, the famous marble sculpture of a grieving mother holding

her infants is probably the most poignant. All three appear to be weeping. The pedestal contains the following heartfelt poetic inscription:

We live in deeds, not years
In thoughts not breaths
In feelings not in figures on a dial
We should count time in heart throbs
He most lives
Who thinks most
Feels the noblest
Acts the best

The woman's name was Helena Schaaff. She was born in Neustadt on the Rhine in 1823 and died thirty-four years later in Philadelphia. She married a man named

Henry Dmochowski-Saunders and clearly had children with him. But the inscription on the statue gives no other details aside from the statement HER CHILDREN REPOSE WITH HER.

For many years, the story circulated that the mother and her twins died in a boating accident on the Schuylkill and that her husband carved the memorial to them. He placed it strategically to face the stretch of the river where they had died, then retreated to his former home in Poland, never to be heard from again. But that's not really what had happened.

In fact, the real story behind the statue is every bit as poignant as the myth. Helena Schaaff was a celebrated concert pianist married to a famous sculptor. Among other works, her husband had carved two sculptures that are on display in the U.S. Capitol: the busts of his fellow countrymen Tadeusz Kosciuszko and Casimir Pulaski. The couple was happily married, and in the natural course of events, Helena became pregnant. Sadly, the child she bore in 1855 was stillborn. The couple tried to start a family again, and Helena became pregnant toward the end of the following year. In the summer of 1857, she went into labor, and in the end, both mother and child died.

According to Thomas H. Keels, the author of *Philadelphia Graveyards and Cemeteries,* the grieving widower spent eighteen months carving the memorial to his family. When the task was finished, overwhelmed with sad memories of the New World, he returned to Europe. There, in his homeland of Poland, he died a few years later, leading an uprising against the Russian army.

All that remains now to commemorate the untimely deaths of the four members of this family is this severely weathered statue at Laurel Hill. The grieving widower executed his labor of love with such care that the pathos shines through. It has taken on new radiance since 2004, when Philadelphia's Polish community cleaned up the statue and restored the faint inscriptions on the pedestal.

The Whole Wide World

Most memorials are built of solid rock. It may be gray, white, sandy, or red, perhaps marbled with different colors, but it's rock all the same, and it's that tradition that makes the memorial for Alexander Evan

Weeping Mother Close to the Edge

I heard a story about the mother and twins statue. Apparently, a woman was visiting Laurel Hill with her young son and was taking a photograph of the statue. She saw a figure moving quickly in the corner of her viewfinder, but when she put the camera down and looked around, there was nobody there. She turned to check on her son and saw him dangerously close to the edge of the precipice, in danger of tumbling down the hill. She quickly retrieved him. A case of a mother helping a mother from beyond the grave?–*RrSelavy*

Mother Gets Ahead

I know it's wrong, but I got a fit of the giggles visiting the statue of the mother and her babies. There's a lot of crumbled and worn memorials in Laurel Hill, and you see missing bits all the time. As I approached the mother and twins statue, I saw that the right side of her chair has a head under it. The thought that she had taken the head off another statue to prop up her chair struck me as hilarious. I really embarrassed my friends.–*Anna*

Conway Milgrim so special. Barely twenty-two when he died, the young father was interred at Laurel Hill Cemetery for years while his family pondered a suitable way to celebrate his short life. The result is a stunning work of brightly colored tiles inlaid on two curved upright slabs.

The mosaic depicts Europe and Africa on the right and America on the left, with lines indicating the migration of the family from northern Africa, Poland, and England to various points on the East Coast of the United States and farther inland. The grounds staff at the cemetery told us that the work took a long time to get right. Apparently, the family had to fire one company that just wasn't cutting it. The memorial appeared almost six years after young Milgrim died, and he had to be moved to a new plot that could accommodate the large memorial.

Bizarre Burials

Mad Anthony Wayne's Two Graves

Of all the heroes of the Revolutionary War, Major General Anthony Wayne tops the list for weirdest Pennsylvanian. Even if he hadn't ended up in two separate graves, this Chester County boy would still have earned his place in the ranks of the strange. During wartime, he led bayonet charges against the British army in the face of overwhelming odds and lived to tell the tale. During peacetime, while maintaining a plantation in Georgia, he rode his horse through the lobby of a luxury hotel while in his cups. He famously told his commander-in-chief, George Washington, that on his order, he would lay siege to hell. He probably would have. He had a quick temper and a fearless nature that earned him the nickname that has stuck with him for more than 240 years—Mad Anthony.

But apart from the dozen or so Wayne counties across the United States named after him, the most enduring symbol of General Wayne's stature is the fact that he has two graves—one in northwestern Pennsylvania, where he died, and the other in southeastern Pennsylvania, where he was born. These are not mere monuments: Both graves contain the actual remains of the great hero—or at least parts of him. And the story goes that his bones are scattered here and there along the road between the graves.

The story behind this postmortem distribution of the general is the weirdest part of the legend. It began thirteen years after his death, with his son Isaac Wayne traveling in a small horse-drawn cart along what is now U.S. Route 322 to retrieve his father's bones from the military base at Presque Isle near Lake Erie. Mad Anthony had died there and was buried beneath the blockhouse flagpole. His son's mission was to take the bones to the graveyard of his family's church—St. David's in Radnor—for reburial. Though Mad Anthony's deathbed wish was to be buried where the sudden illness had ended his life, his family wanted the hero back home.

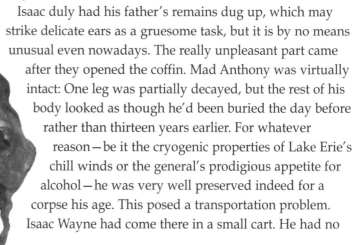

Isaac duly had his father's remains dug up, which may strike delicate ears as a gruesome task, but it is by no means unusual even nowadays. The really unpleasant part came after they opened the coffin. Mad Anthony was virtually intact: One leg was partially decayed, but the rest of his body looked as though he'd been buried the day before rather than thirteen years earlier. For whatever reason—be it the cryogenic properties of Lake Erie's chill winds or the general's prodigious appetite for alcohol—he was very well preserved indeed for a corpse his age. This posed a transportation problem. Isaac Wayne had come there in a small cart. He had no

room for a second person for the four-hundred-mile trek back to Chester County, especially one who would soon begin to decay in the open air.

The perfect solution, albeit a radical one, came in the form of Dr. James Wallace, who for a large fee agreed to separate Mad Anthony's bones from the rest of his remains. But butchering only goes so far, so Wallace ended up boiling the bones in a large cauldron to remove the last clingy bits of tendon and meat. The raw filet of Wayne, his organs, and his uniform were placed in the original grave, and before it was filled with earth again, several quarts of General Wayne stew were poured in as well. Isaac then placed the warm bones in a box and drove home with them. Along the rough road, the story goes, the box fell off the wagon several times, spilling some bones by the roadside. Rumor has it that every year on the general's birthday, New Year's Day, he rises from his grave at St. David's and rides across the state, looking this way and that for his missing parts.

So when the *Weird Pennsylvania* research team decided to visit the final resting-places of Mad Anthony Wayne, we had to split the duties: Pat Wetherby drove to Erie to visit the blockhouse, and Matt Lake tooled around the Main Line in search of the bones.

The Fleshpot

When you ask around Erie about Mad Anthony Wayne, you're more likely to hear, "Oh, I went to Anthony Wayne Middle School" or "That bar over there serves Mad Anthony's Ale" than get information about his burial place. Some people around town will direct you to the Erie County Historical Society, which proudly displays the iron kettle in which the Revolutionary War hero was boiled up.

In a masterstroke of odd taste, this big black cauldron features a cellophane fire beneath it and hollow plastic bones inside. This alone is worth traveling to Erie to see. But on the outskirts of town, behind the retired soldiers and sailors home, at Third and Ash, stands a restored blockhouse on the very same spot where Wayne died more than two hundred years ago. The Wayne Blockhouse is a Victorian-era re-creation of the original, and it's labeled as the general's death site. Nowhere does it say that part of the general's remains were left behind. But perhaps that's not surprising, given the gruesome circumstances of the reburial.

Bone Orchard

Most of Mad Anthony's bones rest in pieces in the churchyard of St. David's Episcopal Church in Radnor, nowhere near the Pennsylvania historical marker that celebrates the fact. The marker is on Church Road, where you'd expect to find a place of worship, but the church is on Valley Forge Road, where you wouldn't. To get there, take Valley Forge Road, off Route 30, south for a little less than two miles. In the churchyard, a large stone pillar marks the general's bones, erected by his comrades-in-arms, the State Society of the Cincinnati of Pennsylvania, on July 4, 1809. The inscription notes that the date was the thirty-fourth anniversary of the independence of the United States, "an event which constitutes the most appropriate eulogium of an American soldier and patriot."

Perhaps so, but one has to ask, Is there a more appropriate way to treat a soldier and patriot than to exhume him, cut him up, boil him, cart him four hundred miles, scattering bones along the way, and dump him under a stone pillar? Perhaps there is, and perhaps there isn't. But there's no denying it's the weirdest way.

Dead Corvette

The grave of George Swanson, a former beer distributor, looks like many others in Brush Creek Cemetery, near Irwin in Westmoreland County. At the head of a double plot measuring seven feet by sixteen feet, the marker mentions his service as a sergeant in World War II. It also features a touching message from his grandchildren to their beloved grandmother, George's first wife, who had died four years before George and is buried in the same plot. In addition, the name and birth date of his widow are also etched into the stone. Nothing weird so far.

But what's that above George's name on the stone? It looks like an etched outline of a sports car. And that's just what it is—George's white Corvette. It's on the gravestone because it, too, is buried there.

On his deathbed at the age of seventy-one, George told his second wife, Caroline, that he wanted his ashes buried on the driver's seat of his '84 Vette. The car was George's pride and joy. It sported the vanity license plate HI-PAL, George's greeting for people whose names he couldn't recall. He loved to drive the car and drive it fast, according to Caroline. With only 27,000 miles on the odometer, it might seem that the sporty Vette was meeting an early death, but that's what George wanted.

His wife promised she would do what she could, but she met stiff opposition at first. The cemetery officials had visions of rowdy vandals being attracted to the site, and they feared the service itself would create an unseemly carnival atmosphere. But after several weeks of negotiation, the management relented: George would go to glory behind the wheel of his Corvette.

The car, like George, was drained of all its fluids. And in late May 1994, with fifty mourners looking on, a crane lowered the mausoleum on wheels, with George Swanson in the driver's seat, into an extra-large hole in the ground. Cued up to play on the stereo was a cassette of Engelbert Humperdinck singing, "Please Release Me."

After the service, George's widow summed up the man's life and interment perfectly: "George always said he lived a fabulous life. He went out in a fabulous style."

This is what happens when nobody claims responsibility for a historic neighborhood graveyard. Yeadon Township's 380-acre Mount Moriah Cemetery was established in 1855 as a place "forever secure against disturbance from opening of streets or the growth of the city." Fine, but no one provided funds for its upkeep. The elaborate gatehouse is being destroyed by tree growth, the grave markers are sinking into the ground or are fallen over, and the grounds are littered with smelly trash. It's hardly surprising that in 2004, Mount Moriah made Preservation Pennsylvania's annual listing of endangered historic properties.

Dead and Dying Cemeteries

The whole point of cemeteries is to remember the dead, so it's particularly poignant to see abandoned graveyards, overgrown with weeds and brush, their ancient markers crumbling and forgotten. The upkeep of historic gravesites is a complicated matter, both in finding responsible parties and in ensuring that there are sufficient funds to do the job. Some cemeteries are tied up in legal battles that go on for years, with the graves left untended while the courts ponder their decisions.

Tucked away behind some very nice houses in Gladwyne, Montgomery County, is the overgrown ruin of the abandoned Mount Olive Cemetery (a.k.a. Har Ha Zetim), a one-hundred-and-fifty-year-old cemetery that's been abandoned since the late 1930s. After thirty years of litigation, the cemetery was turned over to the nearby Beth David Reform Congregation five years ago, but it remains largely untended.

What do you do with fallen gravestones? You could take a hint from an enterprising Somerset County taphophiliac (for non-weirdophiles, that's people devoted to morbid stuff, like cemetery art) and make a wall out of them. But if you do, you'll be committing a misdemeanor under Pennsylvania's Historic Burial Places Preservation Act of 1994, P.L. 141, No. 22, so we'd strongly advise against it.

Worthy Monuments

Herman the Diver

Everything about Herman Wolter's statue in Fernwood Cemetery outside Philly seems funny: his huge fin-de-siècle mustache and goatee, the fact that he's staring with great dignity at a giant water tower across the street, and, most of all, his unusual outfit. Wolter chose to be remembered as a figure straight from the pages of Jules Verne's *20,000 Leagues Under the Sea*—in a deep-sea diver's suit wrapped around with breathing tubes, his bulbous diver's helmet at his feet. Except for the fact that he died in 1901, details about this heroic-looking man are scarce. We don't even know whether he was a diver. Either way, hats—and helmets—off to Herman for wearing his aquatic gear with all the dignity of the Edwardian gentleman he was.

Going Down with the Ship
This is a little weird, even for Philadelphia. Talk about going down with the ship! It's located in Mt. Moriah Cemetery.–*Ian Schultzultz*

Mount Pleasant's Tree-Trunk Owl

How many cemeteries in Pennsylvania, or anywhere else on the planet, can boast of an owl sculpture eight feet tall, standing side by side with a smaller owl, a bear, and a wooden-faced effigy of a man driving a corn walker? After extensive research, we can name only one: Mount Pleasant Cemetery in Mariasville, in Venango County, near the border with Clarion County.

When we screeched to a halt on Route 38 at the sight of this huge sculpture, the man responsible for it and for the upkeep of the cemetery strolled out to greet us. Joe Russell is a retired refinery worker, a stonemason, a jack-of-all-trades, and a fount of information about the tiny abandoned cemetery. Like many cemeteries attached to towns in decline, it was abandoned in the late nineteenth century. When federal funds were made available in the 1990s to help honor Pennsylvania's dead, the undergrowth and the iron fence around the graveyard were bulldozed away, and Russell began to take proper care of the stones.

Not long after, a particularly large but rotted-out oak in the cemetery was cut down, and Russell saw interesting artistic possibilities in the stump that was left behind. With a little work, he thought, it could look like an owl. So he removed the stump, which was so large it had to be cut into three pieces, and dragged it on a sled to a field next to the cemetery.

Once reassembled, the three pieces became the owl sculpture that stands there today. Its companions came along in subsequent years, as the mood struck. But by 2003, rot had overtaken the big owl sculpture. Russell remained undeterred. He brought in dozens of bags of cement to reinforce the piece, gave it a new paint job, and provided the driving public with a more permanent monument to gawk at as they tool around in their cars. Like hundreds of folk artists around the state, he keeps busy with projects that combine creativity and structural engineering, and the state is the better for his efforts.

Mount Lawn Cemetery

Mount Lawn Cemetery is an African American cemetery on Hook Road in the busy Philadelphia suburb of Sharon Hill. It's a quiet and unshowy place, and unless you know what you're looking for, you might flash right by without even noticing it. There are few mausoleums or large grave markers, but Mount Lawn is the final resting-place of two famous musical stars from two different eras. Their grave markers were erected in the same year—1970—but their deaths were thirty-three years apart.

One name doesn't even look familiar. It's Thomasina Montgomery. Thomasina was better known during her singing days as Tammi Terrell.

Tammi had already been recording for six years when she was paired with Marvin Gaye in 1967 for a new Ashford and Simpson song, "Ain't No Mountain High Enough." It quickly became apparent that her voice was a perfect match for Marvin's, and Motown lost no time in turning them into a double act. But not long after, while on tour, Tammi collapsed performing at Hampton University in Virginia. She was diagnosed with a brain tumor, which would slowly kill her before three years had passed.

Motown continued to release albums featuring Tammi and Marvin duets. But as time went by and her decline set in, the songs were increasingly engineered—Gaye's voice was simply added to recordings Tammi had made. (In fact, it's widely rumored that Valerie Simpson is actually performing on some sessions promoted as Marvin and Tammi duets.) When Tammi died on March 16, 1970, she was buried in the family plot at Mount Lawn.

A scant six months later, a grave that had lain unmarked since 1937 finally got a gravestone, reportedly paid for by Janis Joplin. The timing is too coincidental; it's likely that Joplin heard about Mount Lawn Cemetery's other famous occupant in news reports of Tammi's death. Whatever the background, a simple but affecting stone now marks the final resting-place of the Empress of the Blues, Bessie Smith.

Smith was the most celebrated blues singer of the 1920s, selling 2 million records in 1924 alone. Though she made only a pittance from the sale of her records, she raked it in at the box office, becoming the most highly paid black entertainer in the country. She was also a hard-living woman who drank gin by the pint, smoked onstage, and got into brawls. One of her more celebrated song titles, "Gimme a Pigfoot and a Bottle of Beer," speaks volumes about her stage persona. Bessie was a mistress of vocal inflection, able to tease emotional power out of songs like "Downhearted Blues" and "Empty Bed Blues." Her grave marker is simple and touching: THE GREATEST BLUES SINGER IN THE WORLD WILL NEVER STOP SINGING. But a comment Janis Joplin made in an interview provides a more personal eulogy. "She showed me the air and taught me how to fill it," said Janis. "She's the reason I started singing, really."

MONTGOMERY

THOMASINA
1945 — 1970

THOMAS H.
1907 — 1980
JENNIE B.
1917 — 1983

Satan Lies in Francis Vale

We have seen the grave of Satan, the beloved of the Vigilantes. He shuffled off his mortal coil in 1979, and the Vigilantes buried him just off Upper Gulph Road in Radnor, Chester County. Nearby lie the mortal remains of Thor and Donar and other characters of equal mettle and presence: Corky, Sparky, and Fuff Boo. So how did the Prince of Darkness come to be in such company? Well, he was presumably a hound of hell, because all these creatures lie at rest in the cemetery attached to the Francisvale Home for Smaller Animals.

Like most pet cemeteries, Francisvale treads a fine line between pathos and silliness. It's hard to feel sad about creatures called Muffin or Chin-Chin if you've never known them. But it's also hard to mock the clear sorrow behind some of the epitaphs. The story of Leon, who died on May 5, 1970, can only be a sad one. Why else would his marker bear the words MY BELOVED ONLY CHILD? Likewise, nineteen-year old Suzy, whose overgrown flat stone reads YOU DID NOT GO ALONE FOR PART OF ME WENT WITH YOU. The effect of walking through this place is almost as poignant as walking in a human cemetery, except for the daft names and the yard-high statue of the fattest cat on the planet.

It's also hard to ignore the living in this hilly graveyard. Francisvale's primary mission is to rescue cats and dogs in need of care and to place them for adoption. The volunteers regularly walk retired racing greyhounds and limping golden retrievers around the yard until some lucky dog gets welcomed into a loving family. The animal refuge has been in operation since 1909, a few years after Dr. George McClellan and his wife found the first Francis, for whom the vale was named. One evening, they were taking a carriage ride when they noticed a shivering puppy in the snow by the road. They took him in, named him Francis, and then bought eleven hillside acres in Radnor, where they could take in other homeless animals.

The pet cemetery is almost an afterthought next to the important animal-rescue mission — virtually no mention is made of it at Francisvale's Web site (www.francisvale.org) except for a small picture of the final resting-place of Francis himself. It also doesn't mention the horse that's buried there or the grave of Satan. Incidentally, Satan was the pet of the Vigilante family, whose members gave him the sobriquet Duke of Bunting. That has a nicer ring to it than Prince of Darkness, don't you think?

Jayne Mansfield's Final Rest

Finding a big heart-shaped tombstone in a little boneyard like Fairview Cemetery in Pen Argyl shouldn't be too difficult—except that an inordinate number of graves there seem to have heart-shaped markers. After wandering around many graves checking out false leads, the *Weird Pennsylvania* research team finally found the final resting-place of movie queen Jayne Mansfield. Like Jayne's persona, the marker is large, over the top, and just a bit tacky.

In fact, Jayne was too big for just one memorial. This grave is one of three places that celebrate the life and untimely death of the buxom blonde who in her day had rivaled Marilyn Monroe. Naturally, there's a cenotaph in Hollywood, and there's also a death-site marker in Slidell, Louisiana, where Jayne's 1966 Buick Electra had plowed into a tractor-trailer obscured by a fog of insecticide spray. Rumors spread that Jayne was decapitated and that her head is buried in Hollywood Forever Memorial Park. Not true. Although she died of severe head wounds, all of Jayne lies buried just off South Main Street in Pen Argyl. It's almost a homecoming, for while she achieved fame as a Tinseltown sex symbol, Jayne was born a hundred miles or so south of Pen Argyl, in Bryn Mawr.

At first, we thought there was nothing weird about the giant heart at the grave, given that giant hearts are a common motif in this part of the afterworld. Then we saw the fresh flowers and teddy bears placed there, almost forty years after her death. The groundskeeper at the cemetery stopped his weed whacking and strolled over to us. "I could have saved you some wandering if you'd asked me where she was," he commented. "We get people coming to see her almost every day."

We felt somewhat awkward about this, as if we might be mistaken for fanatics, and we mumbled something about just passing through. The groundskeeper nodded, clearly skeptical. "One fellow was here last week with a huge bouquet of flowers," he said, and added with a note of disbelief in his voice, "He left her a card." Slowly he raised his hand and tapped his finger three times against his temple. Then he turned away and fired up the weed whacker again.

Yep, there's something weird about this grave all right. It's the fans.

America's Unknown Child

Walk through the imposing gatehouse of Philadelphia's Ivy Hill Cemetery on a summer afternoon and practically the first thing you will see is a blaze of colorful flowers at the left-hand fork in the road. These annual blooms grow so high, they almost cover the black granite gravestone behind them. You'll usually see more bright colors along the top of the stone in the form of teddy bears, plastic toys, and silver coins.

It seems as though everyone who stops at the monument and sits on the memorial bench nearby feels compelled to leave some tribute to the departed. And they do this because the poor soul beneath the stone died without anything. He didn't even have a name—at least none that we know. His grave marker calls him AMERICA'S UNKNOWN CHILD, but for forty years, he has been better known by the sordid circumstances of his death as the Boy in the Box.

In February 1957, this boy was found dead, clothed only in a threadbare blanket and stuffed into a large cardboard box. The box had been shoved into the undergrowth beside Susquehanna Street, in those days a weed-ridden semirural road and a popular dumping ground. The box might have stayed there unnoticed for weeks had it not been for a student, out for a walk, who became curious about the big cardboard container lying in the weeds.

The young man opened the box and found the body of a bruised and frail-looking boy no older than seven. His hair had been hacked clumsily off after his death in an effort to make him harder to recognize. Except for the box and blanket, there was no other evidence.

The postmortem examination of the boy revealed that he had died of blunt force trauma and was bruised in many places, though none of the bones had been broken. He had a scar in the groin area from hernia surgery and an intravenous-tube scar on his ankle, both of which indicated that he had received professional medical care. Over the next few months, the media and police cast the net wide: Photographs of the dead boy appeared in newspapers and on posters throughout the area. Doctors were asked about young male patients treated for hernias and given blood transfusions. But despite intensive investigation, no solid leads emerged. More than forty-five years later, the boy's identity and that of his killer are still a mystery.

Nevertheless, the investigation continues. The boy had been buried in potter's field, but in the late 1990s, his body was exhumed for DNA testing. The case was profiled on a segment of the television show *America's Most Wanted*. This turned up a number of leads, some of which didn't pan out, but some of which are still under investigation.

Around the same time, the Boy in the Box got his new name and burial ground, courtesy of Philadelphia's unsolved-crime club—the Vidocq Society. This exclusive club consists of more than eighty professional investigators and forensic experts and includes some of the original investigators of the crime. The plain stone from the boy's potter's field burial, with its simple inscription HEAVENLY FATHER, BLESS THIS UNKNOWN BOY, sits at the head of the plot where he now lies.

The Vidocq Society continues to work at solving the case. As its commissioner, William Fleisher, said, "We are validating this little boy's life. Our mission is to . . . put a name on that tombstone."

Paranormal People Plantations

Some graveyards are stranger than the memorials placed in them, subject to odd phenomena that science cannot explain or chooses not to recognize. So if science ignores them, their existence needs to be recorded elsewhere, and what better place than right here?

St. James Episcopal Cemetery

Bristol in Bucks County is an old town even by Pennsylvania standards. It was founded in 1681, a year before William Penn arrived in his new province. Bristol is home to Gertrude Spring, the girl most people believe to be Pennsylvania's famous hitchhiking ghost, Midnight Mary. But with all due deference to that spirit of local legend, she is just one intriguing feature of this cemetery.

There's an odd assortment of grave markers here, all of which have a real connection with some of Pennsylvania's most famous features. For years, Pittsburgh and Philadelphia were leading producers of steel castings. And sure enough, there are two grave markers that prominently feature the twenty-sixth element of the periodic table: Charles F. Norton's grave is marked by an iron gate-shaped nameplate about the size of a cat door, and Merritt P. Wright's stone appears to be propped up by a wrought-iron Art Deco armchair. This chair is said to be haunted. Some say a woman can be seen sitting here late at night, after the cemetery gates have closed. A coy thing, she's visible only for a short while after being spotted. Then she vanishes.

As if to commemorate the ancient rock piles that are scattered across the northeastern part of the state, George Allen or his family decided that his and his wife's plot should be marked by a giant marble cairn. There's no hint as to why the Allens chose this distinctive marker, but it certainly brings to mind the man-made mystery piles in the state.

But the oddest stone in the whole graveyard is a column resting at the foot of a tree. It looks like an albino log—very white, with a barklike grain carved into it and concentric annular rings along the cut end. There's even a notch that looks like an ax wound in a tree trunk. But it's definitely marble. It does not appear to be a broken remnant of someone's grave marker. It's just another piece of sculpture. Tree trunks were a popular Victorian symbol of youth cut down in its prime, but this horizontal log is something altogether different. Perhaps it's a memorial to the passing of the great woodlands that once extended across the state and gave it the second half of its name, from the Latin *Sylvania*.

Bristol's Witching Chair

St. James Episcopal Cemetery contains a black iron chair that's known locally as the Witching Chair. It stands by the grave of Merritt P. Wright (1850–1911) and his wife. Local legend has it that when you sit in the chair at midnight during the month of October, the arms of a witch will come out and hold you onto the chair. I can't say I've checked this legend out. There are plenty of no trespassing signs, and the graveyard's surrounded at close quarters by plenty of houses. In fact, I read in the local newspaper that one of the residents looking out of his window saw a woman sitting in the chair late one night. I think he was about to call the cops, when she disappeared right before his eyes.—*Griffin Landis*

They're Coming to Get You, Jim

I'm a 19-year-old college student who got scared on a ghost hunt at New Hope Cemetery in New Hope. Off to the side of a well-traveled road, this graveyard contains the dead from the 1800s and earlier. They're not buried in any sort of row or column fashion, just strewn about as the digger thought fit. It was dark when we got there, and my friend, an experienced Wiccan, and I attempted to light white candles. These attract spirits but also protect the living against them. We tried perhaps ten times and failed every time. There was no wind whatsoever, and we were using those long wooden matches that always work.

The cemetery has a main plot of about fifteen headstones, and down a large hill, there are other tombstones buried in thick woods, indicating that they have been there for much longer. Our Wiccan started descending toward this older plot, but was "held back" by an unseen force. So after snapping a few pictures, we all started on our trek to the car. My friend Jim was behind us, when all of a sudden he lurched back, as if jerked by his jacket. We spun around and asked, "You okay?" He returned with another question: "Did you guys feel that? Who did that?" But none of us were behind him. Then Jim started twitching, as if someone was pushing him, trying to start a fight with him. His face turned a nice shade of postmortem white, and he took off down the hill toward the parking lot. He's a big guy and afraid of nothing, but he ran a mile and a half back to the lot, nonstop. We found him trembling feverishly, crying, and pacing back and forth, deranged and hysterical. At the time, Jim was a nonbeliever in the supernatural. Our Wiccan guide believes that's why they went after him—to say, "Hello, we're here!"—*Bill*

Talking Guardians of Elizabethville

There's a cemetery in Elizabethville, Dauphin County, across from the Upper Dauphin High School. It is huge and surrounded by large trees. I remember many a day when I've watched a funeral because math class was so boring. Anyway, the cemetery has four statues, referred to as the Four Guardians. One statue, located up front, is an angel, one is the Virgin Mary, and the other two are young girls. The interesting thing about the Guardians is this: You can hear them talk! To hear them, take a tape recorder and let it record while you're there and just walk around a bit. After five minutes or so, hit stop, rewind, and play. You'll hear the last five minutes of their conversation. Sounds stupid, right? Try it. I have, and it works.—*Anonymous*

Telltale Ticking Tomb

I live in Delaware (Dela-weird) and have many stories of the weird. There is the "Ticking Tomb" near Landenberg, PA, where Poe got the idea for "The Tell-Tale Heart." Evidently, you would be able to hear a ticking like a heartbeat from a certain tomb in this cemetery. Locals tell that it was an underground stream that cut through the grave. The ticking is gone now, and debate circles about which tomb was the original ticker.–*Gary Morgan*

Tick, Tick, Tick . . . SCREAM!

A lot of weird stuff happens near the border between Pennsylvania and Delaware, out toward Hockessin. It's called the Ticking Grave, and it has sent tough guys screaming and asthmatic kids to the ER. I can't remember the exact location, but it's in an old graveyard that is very easy to get to. It wasn't abandoned, just old. On the left side there is a flat stone marker that sits on uneven ground. If you get down and put your ear to the tombstone, you can hear things. People rumored that whoever was buried there, sometime in the 1800s, still had a working watch, because the sound was like a ticking. Others said it was a heartbeat. The one time I had enough guts to listen, it sounded very much like an empty hallway. By that I mean echoing sounds and footsteps. I listened longer, and all of a sudden, a louder sort of "tick" came from right underneath the marker. Of course, I screamed, jumped up, and ran away, and so did all of my friends. After I calmed down, I concluded that there must be some sort of underground well or piping that made the noise. But who knows? I have seen some things on those back roads that have defied all of my logic and reasoning.–*Dupree*

Has Your Book Made Me Psycho?

I got this book for Christmas called *Weird U.S.* It's a really cool book, and I'm getting into that kind of stuff a lot now. Now here's my story. I live in Glenmoore, across from the Fairview Graveyard. One night, I told my brother we should go in the graveyard with the video camera and see if we can find anything. Then he said, "You're a freak," and "That book is turning you psycho." Then as a joke, I said, "I feel someone else's presence in the graveyard." So we were too scared to go in the graveyard; we just went outside to shoot some hoops. Then I saw this blue light at the very end of the graveyard. My brother said, "It's probably some house light in the distance or something." Five minutes later, I looked over, and the blue light was closer. We screamed and ran inside and came back out with a baseball bat and a golf club. Now the blue light was moving. I pointed my flashlight in that direction and saw the black figure of a woman. We could hear her screaming at someone, but no one else was around. We figured that the blue light was from a cell phone, a video camera, or even a walkie-talkie. We began to follow her, and when we reached the top of my street, after keeping a close eye on her, she was gone—like that. This strange occurrence led me to really believe I had some strange power. After all, I did say that I felt a presence in the graveyard. Tonight, I just might venture out into Fairview Graveyard, which I have concluded to be haunted.–*Greg Bonnem*

Abandoned Places

If *you've never* wandered around an abandoned place yourself, rent the first episode of the classic television drama *The Twilight Zone,* "Where Is Everybody?" A single actor, Earl Holliman, walks around an empty town with a mounting sense of panic. Where did everyone go? What happened here? After twenty minutes of rising tension, the audience finds out that it has all been an experiment into how much extreme isolation the human mind can tolerate. Forty years later, anyone who sees that episode experiences the same emptiness and desolation as the main character, walking the streets of that eerie deserted town.

There are hundreds of places in Pennsylvania where you can feel these sensations for yourself. From ghost towns in the mountains to the town-size structures that were the state's network of mental institutions, the Keystone State is full of cavernous, hollow-eyed structures. Watch out, though: Many deserted properties are patrolled by police or security companies eager to arrest trespassers and vandals. So if you wander through any abandoned places, remember to observe posted signs and keep off other people's property. And most of all, remember your way out.

Ghost Towns

When we think about ghost towns, the image that comes to mind is some western gold-boom settlement gone bust, with tumbleweeds, dust, and swinging saloon doors. But any town that goes through a boom-and-bust cycle could become a ghost town. Pennsylvania has been through plenty of those as the lumber, coal, oil, steel, and rail industries have grown and waned. Some such places have become bona fide tourist traps—like the remains of the 1860s oil town Pithole City, which you can see for two bucks when you visit Drake's Well Museum in Venango County. But many abandoned towns are deserted, except for the occasional visits by intrepid urban archaeologists. It's these towns that we turn to here. So put on your hiking boots, strap on your camera, and come explore the ancient ruins of Pennsylvania.

Frick's Lock

Like the canal system that put it on the map, Frick's Lock is history. It's a completely deserted Chester County village of about ten abandoned buildings, some dating from the 1700s, some from about fifty years ago. Although it's within striking distance of highly populated areas, it will never be developed or lived in again, because it's in the shadow of the Limerick power plant. When nuclear power looms on the horizon, even real estate developers steer clear. But this old village is an ideal destination for fans of stone buildings on the National Historic Register, especially for those who like to avoid tourist traps.

The stone buildings of Frick's Lock are now boarded up and overgrown, and the place looks appropriately mysterious. Some of the buildings are clearly from the Revolutionary War era, others are more modern, but all are in a state of disrepair: Roofs are collapsing, iron railings are rusting away, and shutters are dilapidated.

In its heyday, Frick's Lock was a thriving commercial boat town, a big economic factor in the early 1800s. Before airplanes, trucks, and railroads, canals were the best way to transport materials from mines and factories to the retail market. So when the

Schuylkill Navigation Company routed a sixty-mile-long canal through the area in the 1820s, Frick's Lock really took off. The eighteen acres of farmland became the village of Frick's Locks (originally plural because there were two locks there). The surrounding area had been a 120-acre farm owned by the Grumbacher-Engel family, into which John Frick had married in the 1780s. The canal ran about a hundred feet north of the farmhouse, circa 1757, and the lock is more than two hundred feet west of it.

In 1884, the Pennsylvania Railroad laid track on the south side of the village and constructed a station at the town, which by then had become the singular Frick's Lock. This helped the town survive when the canal company, unable to compete with the new-fangled railroad transport, ran into financial difficulty in 1890 and the lock was closed down. The canal was drained in the 1930s.

In a case of karmic retribution, the railroad industry suffered a similar fate with the advent of trucking and air traffic. The rail station closed, and the little village declined so much that nobody put up much opposition when the huge Limerick power station was built in its backyard. But there are plans afoot at the East Coventry Township Historical Commission of Chester County to restore the village. It will take time and funds, so there's still a chance to catch this quiet and unsullied ghost town while it has its cachet as a tourist-free zone. You can get there from Pennsylvania Route 724 near Parkerford.

The stone buildings of Frick's Lock are now boarded up and over-grown, and the place looks appropriately mysterious.

Fire Down Below!

As you drive north on Route 61 through Columbia County, the road suddenly narrows and swerves off to the right for a mile or so. You see empty shacks and abandoned cars by the roadside and a huge sign screaming WARNING–DANGER.

The sign is unequivocal in its message. The words UNDERGROUND MINE FIRE grab the attention, and the road notice continues with a dire warning of serious injury or death to any who venture there. What the sign doesn't tell you is that the mine fire has been burning for more than forty years and all but emptied the once prosperous town of Centralia.

Of the twelve hundred people who lived and worked here at its peak, fewer than a dozen remain. As they moved out, the houses and businesses that once lined the streets have been

demolished. The streets themselves split, crack, and buckle as the coal seam beneath them burns away and crumbles, and acrid steam vents through the cracks. Snow that covers the surrounding area in winter soon melts away on the warm ground of the ghost town.

The fire began in 1962, when a burning trash pit in the local dump spread to one of the mines that honeycomb the area. Underground mine fires are not that rare in hard-coal areas, and most people just wait for them to burn out. One burned underneath the nearby town of Carbondale from the early 1930s until 1965, when six deaths by asphyxiation pressed the federal Bureau of Mines into action. They dug out the Carbondale fire and poured wet slurry into the hole to prevent it from starting up again.

But Centralia proved a tougher nut to crack. Without

WARNING - DANGER

UNDERGROUND MINE FIRE

WALKING OR DRIVING IN THIS AREA COULD
RESULT IN SERIOUS INJURY OR DEATH

DANGEROUS GASES ARE PRESENT

GROUND IS PRONE TO SUDDEN COLLAPSE

Commonwealth of Pennsylvania
Department of Environmental Protection

any serious damage or injury to spur them to action, the residents were reluctant to take desperate measures. The gentle solutions they tried, such as sinking vent pipes into the ground, did not stanch the fire. Trees died from the roots up, and gas stations closed down as temperatures in their underground tanks rose as high as 172 degrees. And there were cases of carbon monoxide poisoning. Six families moved out when carbon monoxide monitors registered dangerous levels in their homes.

The Bureau of Mines began buying up homes in the highest risk areas and demolishing them, beginning with twenty-seven houses in the opening months of the 1980s. As federal firefighting measures stepped up, more people moved. Amazingly though, others stayed put, relying on carbon monoxide monitors and canaries to protect them. Many hung on even when the U.S. government offered to buy out their properties. They thought that like many fires, this one would peter out soon enough and that the government was just trying to land-grab. In 1991, the state actually bought these people's homes, but they continued to live there and pay their property taxes to avoid forcible eviction.

The subterranean Centralia fire burns on. When *Weird Pennsylvania* last visited what's left of the town, steam and smoke still rose through the soil and vented through the fissures that peel apart stretches of Route 61. Snow covered unplowed road and roadsides, except where the fire was burning down below. There, the ground was clear, warm to the touch. Three massive trucks, each as high as a three-story house, drove along the road, carrying their loads of anthracite from a nearby mine. The coal, the

driver told us, would go to an electricity-generating plant to keep air conditioners running the next summer.

Summer seemed a long way away on that road, as the nor'easterly gusts brought the windchill down into the single digits. Meanwhile, thirty feet below ground, the temperature has been clocked at close to a thousand degrees. And with thirty-seven thousand acres of coal below the ground, it could continue that way for centuries to come.

Centralia's Thousand Years of Hell

When I visited the town of Centralia, some of the roads were spewing fire and brimstone. Throughout the area, toxic fumes fill the air, and the smoke rises off the ground like a Hadean fog. It was as if the dark abyss itself was coming to Pennsylvania to claim its own. It's an amazing tragedy, one that does not seem like it will ever have a happy ending. Centralia is now Helltown, and it seems like Satan is here to stay. But on an even worse note—what if these seams of coal continue into other coal deposits in Pennsylvania? Experts told me that there are twenty-four million tons of coal in Centralia alone—enough to burn for a thousand years.—*Dr. Seymour O'Life, Ph.D.*

A Hard Place to Love

I used to drive through Centralia all the time to see my fiancé. There are only five houses left and a place to buy auto parts on the corner. If you happen to drive by, you can see the smoke rise up through the trees surrounding the town. The few people who still live there have a place on the corner with lawn chairs to sit in underneath a tree with a big sign in the shape of a red heart that says WE LOVE CENTRALIA.—*Nicolle L. Brandle*

Centralia Church Unscathed by Hell's Fires

Centralia is quite a sight to see. All the vegetation is dead, the ground is hot, and you can feel the heat radiating from the ground. One observation I made, however (though I haven't been there in a few years and things may have changed by now): While all the grass and trees and such are dead in the town, the grass around the church still grows and looks fine. I found this to be pretty curious.—*Will Capehart Jr.*

Big Scary Buildings

Sometimes, you don't need a whole deserted town to create a sense of mystery.
Sometimes, just a single building or complex of buildings is enough.
Take, for example, some of Pennsylvania's more imposing structures.

Mount Airy Lodge: The Last Resort

Thanks to relentless television ads, many people know beautiful Mount Airy Lodge as if "beautiful" were part of its name. The ads were a bit corny, but they successfully evoked images of old-timey postwar resort vacations and brought crowds from New Jersey and eastern Pennsylvania to the Poconos, the honeymoon capital of the East Coast. If you provided the marriage license, they'd provide the preacher, a beautiful mountain setting for your wedding, and honeymoon suites with heart-shaped bathtubs.

But the advertising campaign of the 1970s and '80s does nothing to prepare you for the Mount Airy Lodge of this century: a closed-down, boarded-up massive ruin left to leak, warp, and crumble in the mountain elements. The complex of huge resort buildings, secluded cabins for honeymooners, and the indoor and outdoor pools and man-made lakes entered a steady decline in the last decade of the twentieth century. The resort's majority owner, Emil Wagner, declined with it. The two were so closely associated that when the resort went bust in 1999, its seventy-seven-year-old owner took his own life.

Wagner's friend Bob Uguccioni summed up the symbiotic relationship between Wagner and his resort in various interviews following Wagner's suicide.

"He was married to Mount Airy," Uguccioni told reporters. "Mount Airy was his family, and he saw it was about to be taken away from him. I think the pressure of that was too much."

In his native Czechoslovakia, Wagner had been a hotel owner since he was seventeen. When his aunt and uncle Suzanne and John Martens sponsored him to immigrate to the United States, it was inevitable that he would work for

them at their place, the Mount Airy Lodge. Both he and the resort grew in stature. Wagner became a fifty-six percent owner, and the lodge turned into the largest employer in the region. In the early 1960s, Wagner brought planeloads of immigrants from Communist countries to work in the lodge, a social, political, and marketing coup that eventually earned him the Ellis Island Medal of Honor.

Wagner was something of a showman and marketing wizard, if not altogether an honest one. His mantra was "Use big words; exaggerate." If people called to ask about the conditions during winter, reservation clerks were encouraged to mention snow, even if it was fifty degrees outside. Instead of talking about gourmet food, the clerks were under instructions to use fancy terms like "epicurean delights." This grandiose bluster fit the image of a classic, statue-laden luxury resort to a T, and during the 1950s and 1960s, that's exactly what Mount Airy's visitors got. The lodge captured a huge following of guests from the tristate area, and almost all activities were included in the room rate: food, horseback riding, skiing, snowmobiling, and all kinds of other recreation. The only

extras were drinks, souvenirs, and greens fees.

By the 1970s, Mount Airy's enormous holdings still weren't enough, and the company acquired the neighboring properties, Stricklands Inn and the Pocono Gardens Inn. For the next ten years or so, the resort was able to cruise along on its reputation, but its finances were getting more and more parlous. Competition from Atlantic City's casinos as well as cheap travel to Caribbean island paradises began to siphon off a lot of the area's business. Wagner sank still more money into expansion, a move that proved to be a mistake. With cash problems growing, basic maintenance began to suffer. Plumbing was blocked, linens and furnishings were dirty, and employees joked that the "epicurean delights" at the lodge's kitchens now included powdered eggs and out-of-date dairy goods. In short, the place was becoming positively squalid.

By 1999, the company owed $46 million in unsecured debts to four hundred creditors, and it was clear that Wagner would lose control of the resort. It was a fate he could not face, and the once bigger-than-life entrepreneur grew so despondent that he shot himself. After his funeral, the resort filed for Chapter 11 bankruptcy. Mount Airy Lodge, Stricklands, and Pocono Gardens were sold at a sheriff's sale. Shortly after that, they closed down.

In March 2005, *Weird Pennsylvania* and several hundred others attended a massive auction of all the movable goods at the resort. The piles of heart-shaped tubs, still fringed with white caulk where they had been ripped out of their settings, went for around $300 apiece, with their fixtures thrown in. During the auction, reporters pointed their microphones at sad-looking individuals who had once played a major part in the resort. One VIP attendee hissed her disapproval at a lowball bid for the contents of singer Englebert Humperdinck's suite. "It cost $15,000 to make," she whispered in protest. And she should know—she was Marcella Ravell, the suite's designer.

Now that the place has been strip-mined for its immediate valuables, its future is up in the air. Some believe that Pennsylvania will allow slot-machine betting in the area and hope that the lodge will once again attract out-of-town visitors and their dollars. For now, the only viable part of the business is the golf course. As you drive your cart around the course during the summer in the shadow of the unused ski lift, it's hard to keep your eyes on the greens; they keep wandering to this colossal wreck of a resort. From a distance, in its own way, it's still a beautiful sight.

Maybe Not So Beautiful

In August of 1998, we spent part of our honeymoon at the not-so-beautiful Mount Airy Lodge. I say part of our honeymoon because after four days, we left because we were so upset. The love seat in our room looked as if it was about twenty years old and had not been cleaned in ten years. The bed was uncomfortable, and the sheets were not clean. The hot tub didn't work properly, and getting hot water was a feat in itself. The outdoor deck was filled with leaves and the wood was splitting.

I called the front desk to ask if they could send someone to clean it up and fix the things that were broken. Six hours after we called, at 9:30 p.m., on our first night together as man and wife, the knock at the door came. They kept knocking, yelling, "Housekeeping! We know you're in there. Open the door."

My wife scurried into the bathroom, and I answered the door. I explained that it was the first night of our honeymoon and it was a bad time, that's why we had the DO NOT DISTURB sign on the door. They threatened that if they didn't fix it now, they wouldn't ever be back. They were there for fifteen minutes, till I threw them out. I spoke with the hotel manager, and his attitude was basically "Tough." When I said I would file a complaint, he stated that they were already being sued by guests and had several complaints with the Better Business Bureau, so he didn't care what I did.—*Steve Cruz*

Hot Stuff

Although the Mount Airy Lodge is boarded up, some enterprising explorers have ripped down a couple of the plywood boards covering the doors to get inside. The rooms are the same as they were when the resort closed—dirty, smelly, and looking like the set of a cheesy 1970s porn movie. The fake brass trim and the red plastic hot tubs with their corner mirrors paint the picture pretty well. —*APstyling*

Well, It Was Beautiful

We stayed at Mount Airy Lodge one summer in the early 1990s, and it wasn't bad at all. The food was good and the place was enormous, with plenty to do. I'm kind of sad it's closed. We had a great time there.—*Alan Walker*

Eastern State Penitentiary

We've written elsewhere in this book about the ghostly apparitions at Eastern State Penitentiary, but it also qualifies as an authentic and intriguing Abandoned Property. It stands only a short walk away from Philadelphia's Museum of Art, and is a massive, blocks-long fortress. Its vaulted windows and arches look almost churchlike, but its towers and turrets reveal a darker purpose.

In its time, the Eastern State Penitentiary, an innovative prison from the early Victorian era, was the most expensive building ever erected in the U.S. For 140 years, it housed hardened criminals in harsh conditions, driving many of them into chronic illness and insanity. Hundreds of people still pass through those gates to this day, but nowadays, they pay for the privilege and tour the place for fun. For any lover of urban decay and horrific history, it's a worthwhile tour.

Architecturally, Eastern State is an imposing hub-and-spoke building with cellblocks radiating out from a central administrative hub, all wrapped in a high-walled fortress. But inside, it's a damp, decaying ruin with many roped-off areas that are dangerously crumbling. Some cells that housed famous inmates have been restored

somewhat (Al Capone's cell, for example, has a nice desk and bedside lamp, albeit with ugly peeling walls), but most of them are in a pitiful state. The penitentiary closed in the early 1970s because of its poorly maintained state. Since that time, even the tourist trade hasn't injected enough cash into the system to improve its condition.

The Eastern State Penitentiary was built over the space of ten years, beginning in the early 1820s. It was established on Quaker principles of repentance. Each cell was small but had the relative luxury of running water and a latrine, along with a single skylight window called the Eye of God. Prisoners were to meditate on the errors of their ways and eventually pass back into society humbled and changed.

But for all the good intentions of the prison fathers, the place became a hotbed of abuse almost immediately. The first prisoner, a burglar named Charles Williams, was admitted in 1829, more than five years before the building was completed. He was assigned a number, dressed in a prison uniform, disoriented by having a burlap bag stuck over his head, and escorted to his cell. Other inmates followed and were treated similarly. The bag treatment stayed in effect until 1903.

Since redemption was a personal business, prisoners

were kept in isolation, made to maintain complete silence, and given no reading material or other distractions. Some lost their minds quickly; others acted out and were swiftly punished for it. Repeat offenders were bound, strapped in chairs designed for restraining mental patients, and in some cases doused in water and left to freeze. The first investigations into prisoner abuse began two years before construction of the prison was finished. Subsequent investigations turned up tiny unventilated isolation cells and even pits dug beneath the cells, in which especially troublesome inmates were "buried," sometimes for weeks.

When British author Charles Dickens toured the United States in 1842, he made a point of visiting Eastern State Penitentiary. As a man who had experienced debtor's prison during his childhood, he was dedicated to prison reform. His visit to Eastern State convinced him that the place was a horror. While he was there, he was impressed by the mural artwork of one inmate, but when he was granted permission to talk to the prisoner, he got only blank stares in reply. The inmate's isolation had deeply affected his mind.

Over the next 130 years, the prison underwent massive changes. The solitary confinement method was abandoned, and new cellblocks were added, along with a wood shop and other educational programs. But over-crowding and neglect eventually took over, and in 1972 the place was closed down. Except, that is, to paying customers. This historic site is now open to the public from April through November. With no climate control and very little artificial light, it's often an uncomfortable place to be, but then again, it was designed that way.

Dwarf Cells at Eastern State Penn

In high school, my sociology teacher took us to Eastern State on a field trip. I stepped in there and got the eeriest feeling. It looked like all the prisoners had just left. Cell doors were left standing open, and remnants of beds and chairs were left in some of the cells. The cell doorways looked like they were made for dwarves; you had to bend over to get inside. The silence was deafening. I didn't even hear any birds. I definitely recommend seeing it, especially on their Halloween Tour!–*Jenn*

Some of the best places you've never been aren't on any street. No, they're underneath the ground. Like Alice, you begin your adventures in these underground wonderlands by finding a hole somewhere and dropping in. But instead of a clean journey, you sometimes have to wade through water, catch a glimpse from the window of a passing subway train, or peer through metal doors to a rubble-filled tunnel and wonder what lies beneath.

Subterranean SEPTA Blues at Spring Garden Station

With two employees of the Southeastern Pennsylvania Transit Agency swinging flashlights to illuminate the way, your *Weird Pennsylvania* reporter crunched along the darkened subway platform. Remnants of fluorescent light tubes splintered beneath our feet. Spray-paint cans and old blankets lay in piles by the thickly graffitied tile walls. The sounds of flowing water echoed off the hard surfaces all around—it was impossible to figure out where it came from. There would be no other sounds for the next twenty minutes, until a train, bypassing this bleak and abandoned station, rushed through the tunnel. We were off the map, with no other living things around except for rodents. We were on the platform of the Spring Garden Station on SEPTA's Broad/Ridge Spur.

Don't look for Spring Garden on a subway map. The Broad/Ridge Spur between Fairmount Station and 8th and Market Street Station appears to have only one stop: Chinatown. But as you travel on the line, you'll quickly pass something the subway maps don't tell you about: a dimly lit station so thickly covered with graffiti that it could pass for a street art gallery.

No trains have stopped here for more than fifteen years. But the Spring Garden Station was once a huge, bustling commuter station. It was solidly built in a functional but attractive 1930s style, with cream, white, and maroon tiles laid in bold angular patterns. It had floor-to-ceiling wooden turnstiles and a wood-paneled ticket office. Its rest rooms were finished with brass, and its platforms accommodated eight-car trains, four times

longer than the SEPTA cars that now ride this line.

By the 1980s, though, the station was in bad shape. Ridership had severely dropped off, and Spring Garden became a haven for drug dealing and other crime. SEPTA's obvious choice was to close the place down. Because of the pervasive threat of crime, the Transit Authority sealed its surface entrances with galvanized metal. There are only two ways to reach the old Spring Garden platform now: You either walk along the lines like the graffiti artists do (which is not recommended) or enlist the help of some SEPTA agents.

We had arrived, SEPTA agents at our side, via a

subway train. As the train drew up to the huge platform, only four fluorescent bulbs provided light. Other passengers looked up from their newspapers in confusion when the train stopped and a yellow-vested SEPToid used his key to open up just one of the doors. He stepped out, and our little group moved onto the dirty platform as the door slid shut. The conductor waved a cheerful farewell as he pulled out of the station, as if he were glad that it was us and not him who was left behind.

Luckily, the place was deserted except for trash, broken glass, and discarded Krylon cans. To get a good look around, we fired up a two-million-candlepower camping light. It revealed an unsightly mess. Barely a square foot of tile work had been spared the onslaught of spray paint. Rival street artists had obliterated each other's work in several thick layers of paint. On the ceilings, the untended plasterwork and paint was peeling.

At the other end of the platform was another stairwell, behind a still-secured iron gate. One of our SEPTA hosts undid the padlock to let us in to see the station's original tile work, unsullied by wayward Krylon paint. A note to spray painters: Though we're not particularly fond of 1930s geometric patterns, the tiles really do look better unpainted.

Strangely, the vandalism in this old station is only surface deep. The plumbing in the bathrooms is intact, and the gates and walls, while messed up, are still sturdy. And that gives hope to some enthusiasts that the station may reopen someday. As the urban-renewal pendulum swings, anything's possible.

Submerged Street

According to two correspondents who prefer to remain anonymous, there is a hidden street underneath Norristown with long-abandoned and seriously waterlogged houses. Solid information about the site is pretty vague, but our suburban spelunkers claimed that about a century ago, an existing street was seriously damaged by flooding. The houses remained intact and stable, but water made them uninhabitable. Instead of demolishing them, developers shored up the existing buildings and used them as a foundation for a new road set higher up to avoid the Schuylkill River flood plain.

The water table is higher now than it was even then, and the place is accessible only by wading waist deep through underground drains (not something we'd recommend). Most of the area is underneath road and rail tracks, and the dangers are clearly palpable. And any subterranean salvage operations that would make such a trip worthwhile took place decades ago.

"Back in the '70s, when I was a kid, I found some paintings, jewelry, cutlery, and wrecked clothing and furniture," one urban explorer told us. "What I brought up had water damage, but some of it was sellable. I even found a leg from a suit of armor."

Suffice it to say, somewhere beneath the streets of a Montgomery County town lie the waterlogged remnants of a former street. And that's a fact you can appreciate without swimming through dirty and dangerous drain water to see it.

Abandoned Asylums

The thrill of exploring abandoned places is never more intense than at a closed-down mental institution. Even if you're immune to the fear of being incarcerated among the insane (and deep down, who is immune to that?), the sheer scale of Victorian-era asylums is enough to inspire awe. And the speed at which they have fallen into ruin is enough to make anybody ponder the vanity of human wishes. Like the statue in Shelley's poem *Ozymandias*, these giant mental hospitals were meant to stand as a testament to the power of the human spirit, but they now lay, half fallen, in disrepute and disrepair. The words of the poem go through your mind as you tread around the fallen plaster from their graffiti-strewn walls: *Look on my works, ye mighty, and despair.*

Two hundred years ago, Pennsylvania revolutionized mental health care. It was a Philadelphia doctor and signer of the Declaration of Independence, Benjamin Rush, who first suggested that his colleagues treat mental disturbances as illnesses instead of signs of a degenerate soul or demonic possession. Another Philadelphia doctor built on Rush's groundwork in the late 1800s. Thomas Story Kirkbride managed a private hospital for the mentally ill just outside Philadelphia. Decades before Freud's theories were published in Europe, Kirkbride began a revolution in American mental health care.

His innovative plan was described to us by Andrew Hill, an expert on one of the buildings built along Kirkbride's theories, the Dixmont State Hospital. "The Kirkbride building had a distinctive V shape with wings," he told us. "This afforded the residents a better view of the rural surroundings, which was said to be more calming to the patients, who needed a serene setting for their recovery. The patients were kept busy with chores and had a regular program of exercise, the origins of occupational therapy."

But what began as experiments in humanitarian treatment quickly became overcrowded hellholes of abuse. In his book *Great and Desperate Cures,* Elliott S. Valenstein described the state of mental care in the United States by the middle of the twentieth century:

> Patients were beaten, choked and spat on by attendants. They were put in dark, damp, padded cells and often restrained in straitjackets at night for weeks at a time. . . . *LIFE* magazine's article "Bedlam 1946" vividly described the deplorable conditions . . . "little more than concentration camps. . . ."

By the 1980s, the horrors described in large mental hospitals, along with a swing away from in-patient programs and an emphasis on self-administered medication, brought about a major change in mental care. Most large mental institutions were closed down by 1984. Many were left abandoned and locked up, with records and equipment still in place. Naturally, wherever organizations leave a vacuum, the hordes swarm in. The first wave of damage is usually for profit, with thieves taking anything they can sell, nailed down or otherwise. After that, the vandals and thrill seekers move in. Nowadays, these places remain closed to the public and patrolled by security companies. When you consider the suffering these walls once contained, perhaps it is better to view them respectfully from a distance, cap in hand, and telephoto camera at the ready.

Philadelphia State Is Not a College

It's hard to miss the old Philadelphia State Hospital, better known by its original name of Byberry. There are ten enormous buildings in a distinctive Victorian style on the west side of Route 1, covered with graffiti. Even in a city with as many abandoned properties as Philly, this one stands out. And so do some of the tales of what goes on in the abandoned structure.

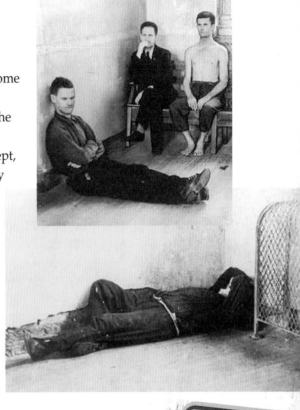

The ivy-covered brick buildings of this hospital for the insane went up in the early 1900s. There are more than ten massive buildings connected by tunnels through which the patients were transported. There are the cells where they slept, the cafeterias where they ate, and most terrifying of all, the morgue, where they made their final exit from the sad lives they lived. Walking in, you see piles of rubble from the slowly cracking ceilings and desiccated walls. The floor is covered with broken glass from doors and windows. When you look down the long dark hallways, every door is open or broken off and lying on the floor. Some rooms have windows that once let in light but are now boarded up forever.

Beneath the ground are tunnels linking the buildings, which people call the catacombs. Many homeless people live there, so you take a great risk entering these places.

If you do visit, be prepared with flashlights and extra batteries. Because once your lights go out, you, like so many others who have stayed at that hospital, will be left confused, frightened, and worst of all, in the dark.
—*Sarah G.*

Byberry's Spirit Boy and the Burnt Room

The second time I was at Byberry was the trip that freaked me out. We were on the third floor and there was a room that was burnt to a crisp. It had a huge steel door blocking the entrance. Every inch of the room was burnt. I didn't see anything, but I definitely felt something when I opened the door of this room. It was like this presence that didn't want us there. Not that night but the next, I had a really weird dream. I was lying in my bed, and (in the dream) I woke up. There was this little boy standing in my room. He looked like a normal nine- or ten-year-old in black pants, a red T-shirt, and dirty blond hair. I couldn't move or talk. He just looked at me and said, "I don't come into your house, don't come into mine." All I could do was nod, and he turned around and walked away. Then I woke up in a cold sweat. This may sound like a lie, but it happened and I haven't been able to explain it.–*Dennis*

Hanging On for Dear Life at Byberry

One Byberry story has stuck with me over the years. In one of the buildings, there is a hole through the floorboards. The story says that gangs would tie a new joiner to a rope and lower them into the hole. The next morning, if the new guy was still on the other side of the rope, he was welcomed into the gang. I've heard many guys were never pulled back out.–*Jill*

The Hell That Is Byberry

Allegedly, a Satanic cult took over Byberry and desecrated the hallways with their evil markings. You can still see the remains of animals sacrificed for their rituals. Dogs hang from ceilings, chickens with their heads cut off lie on the floor, and bloodstains serve as a testament to the horror of this cult. My neighborhood organized a meeting with the Philadelphia police to get rid of the devil worshippers. The big field right behind Byberry was filled with cop cars, and my neighbors were right behind them. I think that the raid must have worked, but who knows? The cult could have just moved deeper into the dark recesses of the forlorn buildings.–*Mark Werner*

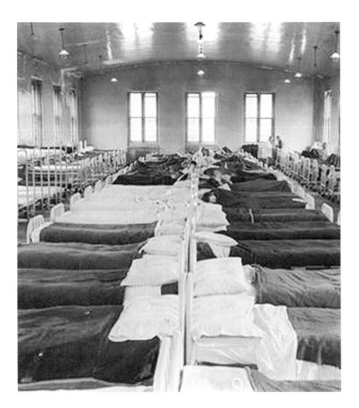

Strolling the Satanic Byberry Grounds

One Friday night, I planned to take a group of friends to the morgue at Byberry, since it was by far the creepiest place in the hospital. We started walking down the main road and that's when we saw it: There was a flame in the distance. It was hard to tell how big the fire was, so we proceeded to move closer. It was then that all four of us realized exactly what it was.

I had heard of Satanic rituals being performed on the property, but I never expected to see what I saw. There, on the ground in the middle of the road, was the upper half of a deer carcass. It was obvious that the deer had been dead for quite some time, since there was no visible blood on the ground around it. The flame that we saw was actually a small candle that had been deliberately placed on the neck of the rotting deer corpse. But that wasn't the worst of it. Covering the face of the deer was a mask. That's when we all started frantically looking around us to see if there was anybody watching us. As I was scanning the place in the dark, I saw in the shadow of one of the many ominous buildings the light from the end of a cigarette. Almost as quickly as I had noticed it, it was gone, put out by whoever was smoking it.–*Jeff*

Byberry Mental Asylum: Do NOT Go There at Night!

In the summer of 2001, several friends and I went to the abandoned Byberry mental hospital at around 11 p.m. Flashlights were necessary, as it was a moonless night. In hindsight, it was the flashlights that gave us away. About half an hour into our journey, three police cars pulled up in front of the building we were in. We came out on our own and were given a lecture on the dangers of the building by the police. We were fined $300 each for what amounted to criminal trespass.

I cannot stress enough that Byberry is a dangerous place. Floors are rotting badly in some places, and ceiling plaster and tiles can fall at any moment. Many homeless people have taken up temporary residence inside, and they, like the police, do not appreciate trespassers. I do not recommend making this trip to anyone.–*isabel5*

Pennhurst

Back in the mid-1960s, fledgling TV reporter Bill Baldini ran a five-episode exposé of Pennhurst State School and Hospital on Philadelphia's TV10. The documentary, called *Suffer the Children*, painted a picture of neglect and abuse in the Chester County institution that was hard for viewers to stomach. On the flickering monochrome

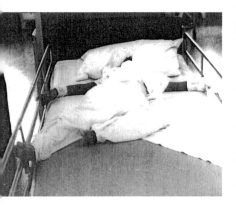

televisions of the time came images of hands and feet bound by straps to adult-size crib beds. Inmates of the institution were shown rocking, pacing, and twitching. Many were severely disabled, either mentally or physically. Others were quite lucid and coherent, but withdrawn into themselves because of over-stimulation in the loud and sometimes frightening place.

By the mid-1960s, Pennhurst had been open for fifty years. It housed 2,791 people, most of them children, about nine hundred more than the administration thought the buildings could comfortably accommodate. But as a state

school, they had to take what they were given. Only two hundred of the residents were in any kind of art, education, or recreation programs that would help to improve their condition, though many of the patients were high-functioning enough to improve with the right care.

Probably the most chilling scene in the entire footage showed one of the hospital's physicians describing how he dealt with a particularly vicious bully who had brutalized several of the other inmates. The doctor described how he had asked one of his colleagues which injection would cause the most discomfort to a patient without permanently injuring him. Then he proceeded to

administer that injection to the bully.

From that point on, it was inevitable that the hospital would close down, but it took two decades of legal action and growing financial crises before the place was finally shuttered. After it closed, it suffered fewer invasions than other Pennsylvania hospitals, due in part to the presence of a National Guard post and Veterans Hospital on part of the property. Today, it is decayed from years of neglect but is still relatively sound. There is some talk of opening a veterans' cemetery on the grounds. Perhaps the presence of respectful mourners will finally quiet the memories of the loud and scary scenes from that television documentary forty years ago.

Bullied, Not Bad

Lots of medical professionals I work with did a stint at Pennhurst early in their careers. Most of the people there weren't insane, but were mentally retarded, autistic, or suffering other serious physical impairments. Some residents apparently just had learning disabilities or emotional problems that made them seem more impaired.

My colleagues told me that the staff would have the high-functioning residents who acted out work in low-functioning wards as punishment. Many of those kids who acted out weren't bad kids; they were often victims of bullies. Some cases of death that were attributed to suicide or accident were probably extreme cases of bullying. But Pennhurst wasn't a bad organization in itself. It just suffered the problems that many institutions do, and so its residents suffered too.–*MelB*

The Pennhurst Family Photos

When I went to Pennhurst one night, it scared me halfway to death. When the wind blows across the buildings, it sounds like someone walking. There were dead animals there and what looked like blood on some of the equipment. Once is enough. I'm never going back. But there was this one room that was really interesting. It was strewn with papers and photographs, carpeted with them, wall to wall. I didn't read the papers, but the black-and-white photographs looked like something from a family album.–*Anonymous*

INDEX
Page numbers in **bold** refer to photos and illustrations.

WEiRD PENNSYLVANiA

By
Matt Lake

Executive Editors
Mark Sceurman and Mark Moran

ACKNOWLEDGMENTS

Special thanks are due to the following individuals for their
diligent research, editorial work, and photography:

Patrick Wetherby	Troy Taylor	James Pasternack
Andrew Hill	Nicholas Taraborrelli	Jeff Bahr
Joel Rickenbach	David Perillo	Donna Carpenter
Andre Prokoski	Holly Thomas	Julia Lake
Loren Coleman	Christopher Lake	Caroline Craig
	Carol Kulp	

This book would not have been possible without the dedication of a dozen or more complete
weirdos. First and foremost are the Marks, Messrs Sceurman and Moran, who pioneered the
Weird States movement, dragged me on board, and primed the pump with a wild assortment
of strange tales. I don't know what you were thinking, but whatever it was, don't stop now.

Serious applause goes to the excellent research, photography, and story telling of countless
Weird U.S. contributors, but a few individuals deserve a special shout-out. Thanks to Pat
Wetherby for wild rides through the forests, Emily Seese and Barbara Morgan for reining the
process in, Marjorie Palmer for making me sound better than I do in real life, and Richard
Berenson for shuffling a squillion random contributions into something resembling a book.

Publisher:	Barbara J. Morgan
Assoc. Managing Editor:	Emily Seese
Editor:	Marjorie Palmer
Production:	Della R. Mancuso
	Mancuso Associates, Inc.
	North Salem, N.Y.

PICTURE CREDITS

All photos and illustrations by Matt Lake except for
public domain art and as listed below:

SHOW US YOUR WEIRD!

The Commonwealth of Pennsylvania has many more stories of strangeness to be told. We know that. We've already heard some of them, but we need to know more before we can commit them to the pages of a book. Here's a great example: We didn't cover the mysterious Head of Shamokin in these pages even though it's one of the weirdest stories we've ever heard. The tale involves a headless murder victim found naked with six bullet holes in him in the early 1900s. His head was eventually discovered, with an extravagant mustache and no other distinguishing marks, and kept in the basement of a local funeral parlor, waiting to be identified. It wasn't until seventy years later, by which time viewing the Head had become a rite of passage for local teenagers, that a judge finally decreed the Head be given a decent burial. Why not include a story this juicy in a book of local weirdness? Because we know there are photographs out there somewhere—we just don't know where.

That's where you, our readers, come in. If you have any stories we should have included here, write to us. If you have any personal anecdotes, they could always become part of a new book on this subject. And if you happen to have any headshots of mustachioed murder victims from Shamokin, we'd like to see them.

You can e-mail us at: Editor@WeirdUS.com,
or write to us at:
Weird U.S., P.O. Box 1346, Bloomfield, NJ 07003.

www.weirdus.com